GW00771001

201497528

Military Detention
Colchester
From 1947

Military Detention Colchester From 1947

Voices from the Glasshouse

Carole McEntee-Taylor

Pen & Sword
MILITARY

First published in Great Britain by
PEN AND SWORD MILITARY
an imprint of
Pen and Sword Books Ltd
47 Church Street
Barnsley
South Yorkshire S70 2AS

Copyright © Carole McEntee-Taylor, 2014

ISBN 978 1 78340 059 1

The ri   **WEST SUSSEX** aylor to be identified
as the   **LIBRARY SERVICE** erted by her
in accordanc   with the Copyright, Designs and Patents Act 1988.

A CIP recor | 201497528 | is available from the British Library.

| Askews & Holts | 24-Mar-2015 |

All rights reserve   No part of this book may be reproduced or transmitted
in any form | 365.48 | means, electronic or mechanical including
photocopying   ording or by any information storage and retrieval
system,   ithout permission from the Publisher in writing.

Printed and bound in England by
CPI Group (UK) Ltd, Croydon, CR0 4YY

Typeset in Times New Roman by CHIC GRAPHICS

Pen & Sword Books Ltd incorporates the imprints of
Pen & Sword Books Ltd incorporates the imprints of Pen & Sword
Archaeology, Atlas, Aviation, Battleground, Discovery, Family
History, History, Maritime, Military, Naval, Politics, Railways, Select,
Social History, Transport, True Crime, and Claymore Press, Frontline
Books, Leo Cooper, Praetorian Press, Remember When,
Seaforth Publishing and Wharncliffe.

For a complete list of Pen and Sword titles please contact
Pen and Sword Books Limited
47 Church Street, Barnsley, South Yorkshire, S70 2AS, England
E-mail: enquiries@pen-and-sword.co.uk
Website: www.pen-and-sword.co.uk

Contents

Acknowledgements

There are so many people I need to thank that I am not too sure where to begin.

It's probably best I start with Lieutenant Colonel David Steele, ex-Commandant of MCTC, for giving me permission to write the book. Of equal importance are Dan Cowley and Les Pearse (MPSC Association) who between them are responsible for all the photos and the captions. Thank you both so much for all you help. Dan has also made several contributions to the text.

Many thanks to Lieutenant Colonel Jim Robinson for being a wonderful proof reader, Brian Chenier for being one of my 'readers' and ex-WO2 Craig Patterson for allowing his phone number to be circulated as a contact for those interested in submitting their memories. All three have also contributed to this book.

Last, but certainly not least, I would like to thank all those who took the time and trouble to share their memories, good and bad. Without their help *Military Detention Colchester from 1947: Voices from the Glasshouse* would not exist. There is a full list at the back of the book.

My biggest problem was deciding what to leave out as it was very tempting to be side-tracked by some of the stories about other detention facilities around the world. But this book was always intended to be about the MCTC so perhaps that is for another day.

Finally, as always, thanks to my lovely husband David for his encouragement and support and because this book was actually his idea!

Foreword

Military Detention Colchester from 1947: Voices from The Glasshouse tells the story of detention in the Military Corrective Training Centre in Colchester through the eyes of those who were there. But it is not just a series of eye-witness accounts. It is also a history of how the ethos of military detention has changed through the centuries.

There is very little written about military detention, which historically has been judged to be harsher than its civilian counterparts. However, the book clearly demonstrates that detention within the military has successfully evolved from its purely punitive role in the eighteenth and nineteenth centuries when flogging and branding was the norm, to a twenty-first century rehabilitation model which HM Inspectors of Prison have suggested could be used to improve options in civilian prisons.

This is a fascinating insight into the evolution of military detention. It is reassuring to know that the system has become an enlightened and forward thinking institution where detainees undoubtedly come out well-trained and better motivated, whether being discharged to 'civvy street' or soldiering on. I congratulate author Carole McEntee Taylor on her excellent book.

Mike Jackson

General Sir Mike Jackson GCB, CBE, DSO, DL
President ABF, The Soldiers' Charity

Introduction

'If my unit was like this
I'd want to stay in!'

The haunting sound of the lone piper echoed round the immaculately manicured lawns and fragrant borders. The timelessness of its lament was only punctuated by the continuous applause of the military and civilian staff and detainees lining the paths to pay their tribute to the outgoing Commandant, Lieutenant Colonel Steele. His vehicle of choice, a 1950s Land Rover, followed slowly behind the piper, resplendent in his red jacket, tartan kilt, thick, white socks, and regulation spats, as he headed towards the gate for the last time. After three years in charge he was leaving for his new post, but, like many Commandants before him, he had left his mark on a unique establishment.

His last view of what had essentially been his home for the past three years, was of the compact, understated brick buildings, the neatly cut grass with its tree-lined borders and the manicured flower beds. These now stood where once Nissen huts had stretched as far as the eye could see and barbed wire fences loudly proclaimed the centre's punitive purpose. Initially home to some Italian POWs in 1943, followed by upward of 6,000 Germans and Austrians from 1944 to late 1947, this once peaceful meadow in Berechurch Hall Road, Colchester, had gradually evolved to become the home of the military's only remaining detention centre: the Military Corrective Training Centre (MCTC) Colchester.

But it is not just the huts and the barbed wire that have been replaced. The whole ethos of military detention has also changed over the years.

In one sense the MCTC's transformed regime and culture is a reflection of the changing values of society that have occurred gradually over many years. But institutions do not evolve by themselves. Change is invariably a process that stems not only from society's changing values but also from the people who work within those institutions. Those who staff the MCTC have always been part of that evolutionary process. It is often the implementation of their innovative ideas, vision and initiatives drawn from their years of experience of working with detainees, which has been the real driving force for change. Thus, it is the staff and detainees who have passed through the gates of the MCTC who provide the living history that I have tried to capture in this book.

So who are the players on this unique stage and how have they and the MCTC evolved over the past sixty-five years?

First and foremost, the MCTC is not a prison. It is a military corrective training facility built on the foundations of military training, ethos, discipline and mutual respect (both between detainees and staff and amongst the detainees themselves). The relationship between the Military Provost Staff (MPS) and Detainees Under Sentence (DUS) relies, in part, on the MPS being exemplary soldiers and military instructors with current operational experience.

The MPS have a crucial role to play. They are carefully selected from across the three services to ensure there are excellent relationships between staff and detainees. These relationships are often built around shared experiences either on operations or from more general service life. Some MPS have even experienced military detention themselves during the early course of their career.

A robust and independent inspection regime has played a critical role in the success of the MCTC. Since 2004, the MCTC has been overseen by Her Majesty's Inspectorate of Prisons. In the early days this was quite a novel concept and sometimes the Army was told things it did not necessarily want to hear. However, this process has allowed the MCTC to demonstrate its continuous improvement which has been hugely beneficial for the DUS.

There have been many changes throughout the last decade as the MCTC has striven to deliver, where appropriate, the improvements suggested by HMIP. These have invariably been supported by the Army chain of command and the MoD.

As previously stated, the changing ethos of the MCTC is in some way a reflection of society's changing position on detention, evolving as it does from an emphasis on punishment, then rehabilitation, and then resettlement – something undreamt of in 1947 when the MCE (Military Corrective Establishment) first opened its doors to military detainees.

The focus is firmly on trying to resolve the issues that have led DUS here and then help them to either return to their units (RTU) or ease them back into civilian life. But is this an entirely new idea?

All those coming into the MCTC today, whether awaiting courts martial or sentence, are interviewed extensively - 'death by interview' as WO2 Mark Doors once described it. This gives staff the opportunity to identify any needs or special problems DUS might have before they enter the main establishment and enables them to provide the right help as soon as possible.

Once detainees are sentenced, they are re-interviewed to make sure their needs are fully understood. Every Friday all new DUS attend the induction day when they receive briefings on debt management, sexual health, the dangers of drugs and alcohol, and how to find civilian housing. All those at MCTC have access to counselling for drug and alcohol problems as well as anger management. When deemed necessary, there is also access to the resources of the Department of Community Mental Health.

Detainees can request to speak to the padre in confidence at any time or to the welfare officers who can help with anything from family problems to finance. There are regular family days so that contact is maintained with children, and classes in parenting and 'thinking skills'. There is also a free half-hour legal clinic where detainees receive advice on matters not relating to their sentence, such as child custody and access matters. The CAB (Citizens Advice Bureau) helps with more complex financial problems.

For those going back to their units, the emphasis is on retraining and improving the military skills they already have. Regular access to the gym, lectures in the training wing, fieldcraft and training exercises – either in the MCTC or at outside locations – has meant some DUS have been promoted not long after returning to their units. Others, including three current members of staff, have so enjoyed their time here, that once they reached the level of Sergeant they requested a transfer to the MPSC (Military Provost Staff Corp).

But the biggest changes are in the way those who are leaving the services are treated. They now have numerous opportunities to gain skills and undertake training specifically designed to give them qualifications for civilian life. All DUS in D Company attend the 'First Steps Course' at the beginning of their sentence and finish with employment preparation and job searches. They can gain literacy and numeracy NVQs at levels one to three, have help to write CVs and assistance with job seeking. They also receive help in registering with organizations such as the Regular Forces Employment Association which has dedicated officers to aid those not entitled to normal Forces resettlement.

There are work placements available at places like Colchester Zoo or local fitness establishments, or at the MCTC's Fresh Start Farm, where detainees can gain skills to help them find employment in livestock and agricultural work. They can undergo training to become fitness instructors and some even attend the local university. DUS are also involved in several outside community projects, the success of which is borne out by the various photos adorning the walls in D Company. It is therefore not surprising that some detainees have commented: 'If my unit was like this I'd want to stay in.'

Lack of social housing and ever tighter restrictions on who councils will accept as statutory homeless, means those leaving the services have concerns about their post-discharge accommodation. Those who are homeless must look at other options. There is a full-time housing officer in the Welfare Department to advise DUS on any housing issues and to help them seek available accommodation. Homeless detainees are also entitled to a government discharge grant which goes towards paying for bed and breakfast for the night or weekend on which they are released. However, there is invariably a shortfall, and so the balance has to be provided by the service charities The Soldiers' Charity (Army Benevolent Fund), RNBT (Royal Naval Benevolent Trust) and RABF (Royal Air Force Benevolent Fund).

All departments of the MCTC ensure that DUS leave with the skills, training, and motivation needed to either become more efficient members of their units or responsible citizens. It is testament to the centre that many who have had a forced stay there say it is the best thing that ever happened to them. Others feel it was the turning point in their lives. Indeed many, as the title of this chapter suggests, wish their units were more like the MCTC – a sentiment the detainees of the Military Corrective Establishment (MCE) of 1947 would be most unlikely to identify with. For them, the current MCTC would be totally unrecognizable. For those detained in military prisons or Provost prisons before the Monkswell Report of 1895, the current regime is something they could have only dreamed of. With this in mind it follows that no historical account of the MCTC could begin without providing a brief history of military punishment and detention prior to 1947.

Chapter 1

Military Punishments
Prior to 1907

By virtue of the Royal prerogative enacted through a statute of Edward I in 1279, the Sovereign of England had the right to command all the military forces of the nation. This gave the Crown exclusive jurisdiction over military offences, but shared jurisdiction with civil authorities of any civilian offences committed by soldiers. Military law was administered through the Court of the Constable (The Commander of the King's armies) and Marshal (the second-in-command). On the advice of the Constable and Marshal, the King would issue a list of Rules and Ordinance of War at the start of any expedition or campaign and this formed the basis of the code of military law. These became known as Articles of War and set out purely military offences such as desertion, cowardice and disobedience, for which the main punishments were flogging, mutilation, forfeiture of possessions or even death. In the Articles of 1642, for instance, the punishment for forty-three different offences alone was death, imprisonment, burning the tongue with a hot iron and flogging.

Through the centuries the power of the Constable and Marshal began to decline and then, in 1521, after a quarrel with Henry VII, the Lord High Constable was tried for treason and beheaded. The office of Constable reverted to the Crown and was then only bestowed on a temporary basis. Although the Marshal continued to convene the Court on his own authority, the frequency of sittings decreased. Eventually the right to try military offences was taken over by committees of officers and became known initially as Marshal Courts and eventually as Courts Martial.

Because the inner workings of the Army was of little interest to the wider public and was seen as emanating from the King rather than Parliament, military justice continued to be viewed separately from civilian justice. Thus, during the seventeenth century, military courts began to develop their own set procedures and also split into two kinds, the General or High Court and the Regimental or Low Court. The General Court could try officers and soldiers of any rank and was advised on legal matters by a Judge-Advocate, who was normally a civilian lawyer. The Regimental Court could not try an officer above Captain and received no legal guidance.

The first Mutiny Act in 1689 provided parliamentary recognition of the legality of both types of military courts. Of these, most Army officers preferred the informality of the Regimental Court to General Courts Martial. Convened by commanding officers, composing of a captain and four lieutenants, they were usually brief and sentences were imposed immediately. They kept no written record until 1805 and no witnesses, defendants or the members of the court, took any oaths. Although they were intended for lesser disciplinary matters, there was no defined jurisdiction so commanding officers frequently used vague charges to cover more serious breaches of discipline allowing them to try defendants through these courts instead of the General Courts Martial. In the early eighteenth century there were several complaints by the Advocate General that not only were regimental courts being used for serious military offences, but also that they were imposing unnecessarily severe Corporal punishments on those convicted.

By contrast, General Courts Martial were much more formal, could only be convened by an Army commander and comprised at least thirteen officers. Full transcripts were taken and witnesses and other members of the court were sworn in. Any decisions taken had to be agreed by the sovereign or commander in chief – either of whom could reverse or change the decisions – and the Judge-Advocate General who had to check the legality of the proceedings.

Flogging, hanging or death by firing squad were still the normal punishments and were usually administered at the barracks or in the field. Flogging ranged from twenty-five lashes to 1,200, a sentence that would almost certainly permanently disable and probably kill the recipient. The Mutiny Act of 1765 also included branding as a form of punishment. This was done using needles and gunpowder to tattoo the letters BC for 'Bad Character' on the chests of transgressors. Some regiments provided a basic cell called a black hole which was completely empty of furniture and had no windows or source of light. Others also had a dry hole which was mainly for those who were drunk. Here they were just left to dry out, often in their own vomit. Given the choice, men would often prefer the lash, delivered in full view of the rest of the regiment, to solitary incarceration in the black hole.

However, by the time of the Peninsula Wars in the late eighteenth and early nineteenth centuries, questions were beginning to be asked in Parliament about the brutality of flogging as a punishment in the Navy and Army. But, as no immediate alternative was suggested, the debate continued, as did flogging. Military detention as a punishment did not really take hold until the latter part of the nineteenth century after the Army returned home from the Napoleonic Wars.

These ended in 1815 and, apart from the overseas garrison and the Army of occupation, the rest of the Army came home. As usual, once the Army had served its immediate purpose, the government began disbanding regiments and cutting costs, but there were still considerable numbers of men in uniform on British soil. Apart from the small percentage of 'ne'er do wells' who were useful to the Army during wars but a burden in peacetime, there were also a larger percentage of soldiers who had joined up for adventure and excitement and to see action. Being garrisoned at home with little to do, some became bored, got into fights, and generally caused a fair amount of trouble in the areas they were stationed.

Needing some kind of sanction or punishment more civilized than flogging, the local population and the Army looked around for alternative solutions to dealing with those society considered 'badly behaved' or those who had simply 'gone off the rails'. Eventually, the normal punishment was to lock them up in local jails with those accused of desertion branded by a tattooed 'D' on the top of each arm. However, in the nineteenth century there was no nationwide prison system. Jails were administered by local justices aided by the parson and paid for by local taxes. Income tax had already been introduced as a temporary measure to raise money and was universally hated, so the idea of imposing more taxes was anathema and it was decided that the best way to increase the number of jails was to take over existing buildings and convert them into prisons. Prison warders were not paid and raised money by utilizing the labour available to them. This was done by hiring out the men to work in the fields and offering the women as prostitutes to anyone who could afford to pay. The whole point was to make money out of the prisoners meaning they lived in appalling cramped common rooms in extremely basic conditions. The food provided was little more than swill, although prisoners could buy in their own from outside if they had money. Very few people left the prisons without increasing their criminal knowledge. Thus, for many military offenders whose only crime was transgressing military rules such as being absent without leave (AWOL) or insubordination, being locked up with hardened criminals was hardly an ideal solution.

Finally, the government was compelled by social reformers to take more control so visitors were introduced and warders were paid. Local Justices were now responsible for regularly inspecting the conditions of local jails, and warders at those near garrison towns were delighted to identify the proximity of garrisons as the main reason for the overcrowding and rowdy behaviour in the jail they were responsible for.

Eventually, in 1836, a Committee of Investigation was appointed which stated that soldiers should be confined separately. The reason given was that 'a soldier, though under punishment, should not lose sight of the profession against

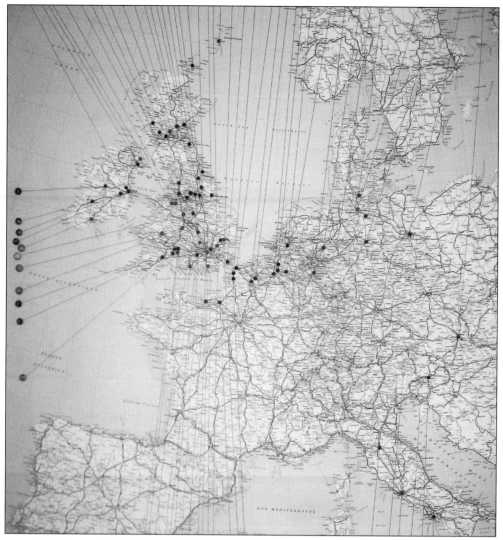

This is a map showing the locations of the MPSC throughout Britain and Europe. Picture courtesy of WO2 Craig Patterson.

whose rules he has offended, nor should he be placed in contact with other men, whose notions of crime are not very strict and have none whatever of the nature of the military offence.'

Although the committee's recommendations were noted, for several years nothing was done to implement them and the situation remained the same. Then, in 1844, a Royal Commission, chaired by Lieutenant General Earl Cathcart, was set up to examine whether it was feasible to establish separate prisons for military offenders. These would replace imprisonment in civil jails with military discipline of 'shot drill, breaking stones or other hard labour.' Its remit also included making recommendations on the diet, bedding and clothes that should be provided. After considerable investigation, the final conclusion was that military offenders should be incarcerated in military prisons and that there should be two types of punishment – solitary confinement and hard labour.

By 1850, society's aversion to the use of the lash meant it was normally only applied in military prisons. Initially, those sentenced to transportation were sent to Australia's convict prisons in New South Wales. If the sentence was just transportation they went as guards, but if it was with hard labour they travelled as ordinary convicts. But after the Royal Commission's report, new military prisons were built in Chatham, Kent, and at the Hampshire bases of Gosport and Southsea Castle in Portsmouth. A large section of the ordnance stores in Weedon, Northamptonshire, was converted into cells, and a hospital building attached to the barracks at Greenlaw, on the Scottish border, was converted into an Army prison. In Ireland four prisons were converted from Provost cells and as Robert Boyes records in his book *In Glasshouses*, others were built in Nova Scotia and Quebec and on Barbados, Bermuda, Mauritius, the Ionian Islands and Malta, at St Elmo.

The inmates of these new prisons were invariably young and most had served less than two years. Some were not regular soldiers but militia men who had failed to attend their training. Others had not completed training and had been absent for so long they had already forgotten the little they had learned. Literacy and numeracy levels were low and most were there for absence or desertion, drunkenness, insubordination, violence or fraud. Somewhat surprisingly, fraudulent enlistment also figured quite high on the list with men enlisting in one regiment, deserting, and then re-enlisting elsewhere. Those unlucky enough to be sent to these new military prisons soon learned that this was not the easy option and many may have wished they had been incarcerated in civilian jails.

The men's uniforms were taken away from them at the gate as they arrived, leaving them shivering in their socks and braces. The uniforms were taken back to the regiment by the escort to be sold and the proceeds given to public funds. The prisoners had to share a compulsory bath in cold, dirty water with all the others who had arrived with them. They were then searched and issued with a grey, cloth jacket, grey waistcoat and trousers. Those in Britain were given a Glengarry Infantry coat without the ribbons. Those in warmer climates had blue jeans and a straw hat. In colder climates they would be issued with a used greatcoat, fur hat, knee boots and a jumper.

The day began at 0600 when prisoners slopped out and were given their clothes and water for washing. Those entering the prison would remain at Stage One for at least twenty-eight days and after being weighed by the medical officer they would be allocated work. Stage 1 was extremely unpleasant and deterred prisoners from committing any misdemeanours which meant they would have

The Crank. This was the crank prisoners turned air – a way of making sure they were not idle when in their cells.

to return to it. Other than exercise and meals, days were spent carrying out shot drill and oakum picking.

Shot drill meant prisoners were commanded to take heavy metal balls from a pyramid heap at one end of the yard, carry them to the other end and pile them on another heap. They then had to move them back. This was normally done for an hour and a half in the morning and afternoon. Men weighing less than ten stone carried 12lb shot, while others carried 14lb shot. When not doing this, the prisoner would be returned to his cell. Stage One prisoners were not allowed mattresses and all prisoners handed over their clothes at night. These were labelled and tied in neat bundles to be re-allocated the next morning when the cell doors were once again opened.

While in his cell, each prisoner was expected to undertake a certain amount of oakum-picking so that he was doing something productive. The raw material for oakum was old rope that could no longer be used in dockyards. Most of it was stiffened by tar and each individual fibre or strand had to be teased out and softened without tools. The finished product was sent back to the dockyards to be used in caulking of wooden vessels. An even more useless activity was to sit and grind air with an £8 10s patent crank designed by a Mr Underhay. The crank was a simple handle with a dial which recorded the number of times the prisoner turned it. The pressure could be changed to make it harder or easier and the prisoner had to complete a set number of revolutions. The use of this crank led to the colloquial name for prison officers (screws).

After a while other work was introduced which was rather more productive and helped to pay towards the costs of the prison. The type of work largely depended on where the prisoner was. In some prisons laundries were introduced so the men washed their own clothes and those of the garrison's hospital. In others, stones were broken down to a set size for the Royal Engineers to use in making roads. Chopping wood and providing kindling was gradually introduced. This was not an easy option as the wood sent was often oak from hulk ships or from gun carriages from which the iron and rivets had to first be removed. Other work in the UK and abroad included making prison clothes and palliasse (straw mattress) covers, quarrying and clearing jungles.

Although a proposal in 1879 to abolish flogging was defeated by 106 votes, it was finally abolished in 1882. In 1894, the Inspectorate of Military Prisons and a committee headed by Lord Monkswell produced a report that suggested different ways of operating within military prisons and by 1896 changes began to slowly filter through. Squad drill was introduced and physical training replaced the walking exercise. Shot drill was relegated to a punishment rather than a normal part of the daily routine. Prisoners were now allowed to have one library book a week from a centrally approved list and to have their cell light on an hour later to allow them to read. They could also receive elementary schooling if they needed it. Previously, only those already in education would be allowed this – and only if their Commanding Officer had given his written permission.

Food was still monotonous and consisted of 10oz of bread and one pint of cocoa for breakfast. Dinner was 5oz of bread and 5oz of meat served in its own liquor with onion and flour to thicken it. Supper consisted of 9oz of bread and a pint of porridge. The meat varied from day to day. On Mondays and Fridays it was beef on its own, whereas on Tuesdays and Saturdays it was served with vegetables and 2oz of cheese. On Thursday it was mutton and on Sundays there was suet pudding as well. Most prisoners actually gained weight during their time in prison, possibly due to the time spent in their cells. Food was also used as a punishment. No 1 Punishment Diet was 1lb of bread and unlimited water to be served consecutively for three days. If the prisoner was put on this for longer, it was alternated with three days of normal diet. The No 2 Punishment Diet was more substantial with dinner consisting of 3oz oatmeal, 3oz Indian meal, 8oz of bread and salt and potatoes. Breakfast and supper consisted of more bread (8oz). Flogging still took place although it was now restricted to twenty-five lashes with either the cat or birch and had to be carried out in the presence of three visitors in addition to the governor and medical officer. The use of irons was also no longer used as punishment and was now solely for restraint purposes.

Dan Cowley (former Staff Sergeant from the1970s):

'In 1894 the Clothing Regulations authorized the issue of carpet slippers for warders on night duty within military prisons. Previously, ammunition boots within the C block meant the approach of staff was unmistakable. With the issue of DMS and patrol boots this advance warning was eliminated.

'As the gate lodge was outside the cell blocks, the prisoners had devised an early-warning system of their own. On the last night of lock-up it was customary to allow a mug of water to be taken into the night cell to eliminate the request,"Staff, I want a drink of water". This would mean a call for the keys from the main gate lodge and an "unlock". As the night staff passed out of the cell block the air pressure stabilized. This allowed those inside to move about without upsetting the pressure. As the member of night staff entered the cell block the air pressure was increased until he was fully in the block. The pressure then returned to a state of equilibrium. Over this time the pressure changes caused the water surface within the mug to vibrate in concentric circles. This also occurred when night staff exited the cell block and warned that they were within the block or had just left it.'

On discharge the men were now allowed to keep their boots, socks and braces and were issued with a cap, jacket, waistcoat, trousers, neckerchief and a warrant for their journey home. They were also given the address of the Discharged Prisoners Aid Society in London's Charing Cross.

Another recommendation of the Monkswell Report concerned barrack cells – or regimental guardrooms as they are known today – and Provost prisons which were staffed by garrison troops and could detain a man for up to forty-two days. While in detention, the prisoner had his hair cropped and spent his days on pack drill, shot drill and fatigues. The idea was to make the stay as unpleasant as possible. The Monkswell Report also suggested there should be a much closer look at Provost prisons, that hair should no longer be cropped, lighting should be improved and gym training given.

Things were gradually changing, but there was still a long way to go and it was left to the new Inspector General of Military Prisons, Lieutenant Colonel

Michael Clare Garsia, to implement the recommendations when he took office in 1898.

His first report recommended that all future prisoners arrive at the military prison in their uniforms and carrying their kit as part of their training was the maintenance of their uniforms and kit. Governors would hold parades and inspect the men as soldiers, and all the military prisons would have gyms. The whole aim of military detention should now be to 'return the young soldier to the colours in every sense improved and better fitted to resume his place in the ranks'.[1]

Garsia realized his reforms would have little effect if he didn't have the right people in place to deliver them, so he suggested that prison officers should be selected NCOs. This would reduce manpower and save money, an idea that naturally met with government approval. His next argument in 1899 was that as many of those delivering his reforms had little knowledge of changes in military training and, in fact, were civil servants with no military status or rank, it might be better to staff the prisons with military staff. These should be a distinct corps of warrant officers and non-commissioned soldiers, their rank no lower than a sergeant. Garsia's report also recommended that prisoners should have their own military uniform ' … to distinguish them as members of an honourable service in which they are entrusted with very important, difficult and responsible duties.' In 1900 he went one step further when he recommended that each military prison should be supplied with a field gun and machine gun for training and that training should also include digging shelter trenches, first aid and ambulance drill.

In December 1901, Army Order 241 announced the inception of the Military Prison Staff Corps and, in 1906, Army Order 114 Army Act Amendments made several changes to the nomenclature and introduced the term 'detention' to replace 'prison', thus reducing the stigma of those returning to their units afterwards. Other changes included replacing the term 'prisoner' with 'soldier in arrest', 'prisoner at large' with 'soldier in open arrest' and 'soldiers after sentencing by court martial or commanding officer' with 'soldier under sentence' (SUS). The term SUS remained in use for several years until it was changed to Detainee under Sentence (DUS) in 1992. It reverted back to SUS a few years later, a change that was reasonably short-lived. In 2008 it became DUS again.

More importantly perhaps was the change from Military Prison Staff Corps to Military Provost Staff Corp.

Chapter 2

The Military Provost Staff Corps, Military Prisons and Detention Barracks 1907 – 1939

Up until 1914 the staff of the military prisons continued to wear blue uniforms with red braid and sling belts. They taught a variety of skills including building bridges, knotting and lashing, making beds and mats and making head ropes (for sails) and fenders for ships, and so had to be proficient in several skills themselves. This continued until the outbreak of war in 1914. The men were now required overseas so new training was introduced which concentrated on honing their military skills and this took up most of the day.

Life for the staff was quite hard. They came on duty at 0530 in the summer and 0600 in the winter, and finished work at 1715. Breakfast began at 0800 and finished at 0845. Dinner was at 1245 until 1345. The SUS worked even harder, beginning at 0600 in the summer and 0630 in the winter. At 0745 they had a twenty-minute stop for breakfast before returning to their rooms to work until 0900. They then began their toil again until 1215 when, after another twenty-minute break, they had to go back to their rooms to work until 1400. There was another break, then work again until 1600, followed by a further twenty-minute break. The working day finally finished at 1930. The diet for the men was the same every day and consisted of porridge, bread, margarine and cocoa for breakfast, stew with potatoes and rice and a small piece of bread for dinner, and bread, margarine, cheese and tea for supper. They received nothing in between supper and breakfast. This led to the early-morning period being the most common for suicide attempts and violence between detainees.

Once the Great War started, preparations were made for staffing the military prisons in the BEF (British Expeditionary Force). Although statistics show there were misdemeanours in the Army, most of them were of a non-serious nature.

This is a map showing the location of the MPSC throughout the world. Both this and the map on p.4 show the extent of British troop locations before WW2. Picture courtesy of WO2 Craig Patterson.

Methods employed in maintaining discipline were the traditional ones of encouraging regimental loyalty and punishment within the regiment, or at special Field Punishment Centres supervised by the Provost Marshal. Minor offences such as being unshaven or untidy or losing kit, not saluting or addressing superiors correctly, having dirty or incorrect equipment, being late on parade or after curfew, would be dealt with by the NCOs and officers of a man's own unit. NCOs often gave men extra fatigues or exercise as punishment for small matters. Being confined to barracks or losing a day's pay was usually a torment too far for men who were eager for rest and amusement.

For moderately serious crimes, a man could elect to be tried by a district Court Martial, or be 'convicted' and sentenced by his Commanding Officer (CO). The CO could sanction detention or field punishment for up to twenty-eight days, deduct all pay for up to twenty-eight days, and impose fines of up to ten shillings. The CO could also inflict minor punishments, with the offender having no right to a Court Martial. These included confinement to camp for up to fourteen days, extra guard duty, reprimand, severe reprimand, or admonition. He could also sanction Field Punishment No1, during which a standing soldier was tied to a fixed object, such as a gun wheel or post, for up to two hours a day for a maximum of twenty-one days. If this was carried out in sunshine, the soldier suffered even more indignity and discomfort as it would aggravate the constant problem of trench lice. This particular punishment once included

11

flogging which was abolished in 1881. However, numerous stories circulated about recalcitrant soldiers being positioned facing the enemy lines and not always out of the range of enemy fire. Similarly, there were numerous reports of commanding officers abusing the regulations by tying soldiers' hands behind their back and suspending them so that their feet barely touched the ground. As these stories gradually reached Britain, the War Office reacted by issuing an advisory in 1917 which standardized the form the punishment should take:

12th January 1917

Sir,

I am commanded by the Army Council to inform you that they have had under consideration the question of the method of carrying out Field Punishment No 1, with special reference to paragraphs 2 (b) and 2 (c) of the Rules for Field Punishment (Manual of Military Law, page 721), and they have decided that, with a view to standardising the method in accordance with which a soldier may be attached to a fixed object, the following instructions will, in future, be strictly adhered to:-

With reference to paragraph 2 (b), the soldier must be attached so as to be standing firmly on his feet, which if tied, must not be more than twelve inches apart, and it must be possible for him to move each foot at least three inches. If he is tied round the body there must be no restriction of his breathing. If his arms or wrists are tied, there must be six inches of play between them and the fixed object. His arms must hang either by the side of his body or behind his back.

With reference to paragraph 2 (c), irons should be used when available, but straps or ropes may be used in lieu of them when necessary. Any straps or ropes used for this purpose must be of sufficient width that they inflict no bodily harm, and leave no permanent mark on the offender.

Field Punishment No 2 was similar, except the man was shackled but not fixed to anything. Both forms of punishment were carried out by the office of the Provost Marshal unless the soldier's unit was officially on the move. Then it would be carried out by his own unit. Field punishments inevitably caused considerable resentment and led to at least one mutiny at Blargies in northern France where the ringleaders were sentenced to death and one was actually executed. In another case, at No 9 Stationary Hospital at Le Havre, patients attempted to free prisoners who had been tied for punishment. Both civilians and many commanders objected to Field Punishment No 1, but it was only removed from the Army Act in 1923.

There were four different types of Courts Martial in 1914. The Regimental Court had the least powers. It had a minimum of three members who normally belonged to the same unit as the accused and who could not try an officer or warrant officer.

A District Courts Martial also had a minimum of three members – one of whom must have served in a different unit to the accused. Although it had wider powers, it could not try a commissioned officer.

The General Courts Martial had the widest powers. It had a minimum of either five or nine members (depending on where it was), could try officers and soldiers of any rank, and could impose the death sentence. There was, however, a legal requirement that none of the members were serving in the same unit as the accused unless there were no other officers available.

The fourth type was the Field General Courts Martial which only convened in the field for those serving or stationed overseas where there was no practical alternative. Needing only three members, or two if no other officers were available, these courts martial became notorious during the First World War for sentencing over 3,000 men to death, of which eleven per cent were later confirmed by a higher authority. Although acquittal by Courts Martial is binding, sentences are not valid until confirmed.

Incarceration for the more obdurate and serious offenders took place in the British military prisons manned by the Military Provost Staff Corps. Extra provision was made during the Great War by establishing two[2] military prison ships and five military prison establishments in the rear areas of the Western Front.

The military prison regime was deliberately severe with the aim of making conditions at least as harsh as those faced by soldiers serving at the Front, and included hard labour such as digging entrenchments.

Those with short sentences were kept in Europe in prisons at the centre of theatre so that they could be set to work constructively for the war effort. Because of a lack of suitable accommodation, the first two prisons were on ships, one at the port at Le Havre and the other on the river at Rouen. By 25 January 1915, both ships were full up, with 700 SUS at Rouen and 500 at Le Havre. By the end of the war there were five military prisons in the rear areas.

Some prisoners were sent to work on various tasks at the docks. They were accompanied by a small number of staff who had to guard large numbers of detainees. Both detainees and staff were required to work from dawn to dusk and always arrived at the docks with their rations for the day. The staff were armed with revolvers as there were many escape attempts. If a member of staff could prove he had fired at an escapee by showing the empty case, it was assumed he had done his best. There actually appears to have been few escapes, although in *In Glasshouses*, Robert Boyes talks of a prisoner who rode to freedom on the axle of a railway wagon.

Others were sent to railheads and advanced depots, or set to work digging entrenchments, stone breaking or on sanitary duties. Should work not be available at any of these places, then shot drill for a maximum of three hours a day was substituted. According to the 1913 Rules for Military Prisons, a hard day's work was scientifically defined as the equivalent of 450-foot tons. A table was attached to the rules explaining how this should be worked out. For instance, marching a mile with a sixty-pound pack would equal 25.93-foot tons.

Diet also came under scrutiny as the food had to be no better than that given to the soldiers in the field. Any luxuries such as jam, cheese, tobacco, rum, pepper, tea and coffee were excluded. This meant meals consisted mainly of tinned beef or mutton, biscuit or bread, small amounts of potato or rice, and one ounce of suet, lard or dripping, to be spread on the biscuits or bread. Half an ounce of lime juice was served daily, or half a pound of vegetables twice a week, but only when available. Punishment diets were also allowed by the Governor as 'only by restricted diet can the worst offenders be bought into subjection'.[3] The stage system was also suspended, although it was still possible to earn remission.

In the early days of the war most conscientious objectors served sentences in military prisons or detention barracks rather than in civilian prisons. They were given very long sentences – ten years' penal servitude in some cases – and were also subjected to field punishments.

Those given longer sentences were sent home to Britain to serve them, some spending time in Wandsworth, south London, where the prison had been converted to detention barracks in 1915. However, the treatment meted out to conscientious objectors there led to questions being asked in Parliament and the subsequent dismissal of the Governor. This treatment included feeding the prisoners bread and water and leaving them naked in single cells with their only choice of clothes being the full Army uniform laid out in front of them.

The number of soldiers under detention was still considerably more than those of the regular peacetime Army and additional accommodation was needed. The 1914 Prison Report listed the following military prisons and detention barracks: Aldershot, Colchester, Gosport, York Castle, Cork, Dublin, Stirling, Bermuda, Cairo, Gibraltar, Hong Kong, Jamaica, Kandy (Ceylon), Malta, Mauritius, Pretoria, Sierra Leone, Singapore, Tientsin and Wynberg.

As well as taking over part of Wandsworth Prison to cope with the increase in numbers, the Director of Detention Barracks, Colonel Ralph Turton, also took over Kilmainham in Dublin. The whole of Wakefield Prison was requisitioned, although it was returned to the Home Office in 1916.

Stafford Prison had one wing appropriated. Staff were a combination of military and civilian, with civilians carrying out gate duties, ground patrols and supervision in the industrial workshops. The grounds were so large it was possible to carry out route marches without leaving the area. These marches took place on Thursdays and the prisoners were marched past the burial ground of the murderers who had been executed there. Next door to the prison was an asylum from which shouting and yelling could be heard. Stones and other articles were often thrown over the wall.

D block in Barlinnie Prison, near Glasgow, joined the list, together with Hereford, Brecon and Chelmsford prisons. The Criminal Lunatic Asylum attached to Parkhurst Prison on the Isle of Wight became a detention barracks, as did St Paul's School, West Hartlepool, and St David's Convent in Mold, Flintshire, Wales. Many of these were only short-lived detention barracks, but some did not close until 1919.

By early 1915 however, some military prisoners were taken prematurely out of custody and returned to military units for active service at the Front. The best of the regular Army had been almost wiped out by now and, with no conscription, the manpower situation was becoming desperate. So desperate in fact, that a Suspension of Sentence Act was passed. This ensured that after sentencing, the soldier could remain at the Front, but with the knowledge that any future transgressions would be punished by as much as ten years in prison, whether the war had finished or not. Colonel Turton was also so concerned about the thousands of soldiers serving short sentences in detention barracks that he complained to the War Office.

The result was permission to draft SUS from Aldershot over to France each week. Every Monday around 150 fit men arrived from other detention barracks and were shipped out the following Friday. Those who were untrained underwent a course of musketry, signalling and bayonet fighting as well as being taught how to throw live bombs. Over 40,000 men were sent to France and many thousands more returned to their units fit for transfer overseas.

In all, just over three per cent of the total of men who joined the Army were court-martialled - 5,952 officers and 298,310 other ranks. Eighty-nine per cent of those who were tried were convicted and eight per cent were acquitted. The rest were either convicted without the conviction being confirmed, or the conviction was subsequently quashed. Thirty per cent of convictions were for absence without leave and fourteen per cent for desertion (although only three per cent were actually in the field at the time). Fifteen per cent were convicted for drunkenness, eleven per cent for insubordination and eleven per cent for loss of Army property. The remaining nineteen per cent were convicted of various other crimes. Twenty-four per cent were given three months detention in a military compound while twenty-two per cent were given Field Punishment No 1. Another twelve per cent were fined, while ten per cent received six months detention and ten per cent were reduced in rank. Eight per cent were given Field Punishment No 2 and just over one per cent of those convicted - 3,080 men – were sentenced to death. Although eighty-nine per cent were reprieved and had their sentence converted to something else, 346 men were executed – 266 for desertion, thirty-seven for murder, eighteen for cowardice in the face of the enemy, seven for quitting their post, six for striking or offering violence to their superiors, five for disobedience, three for mutiny, two for sleeping at post, and two for casting away arms. Ninety-one of the 346 who were executed were already under a suspended sentence from an earlier conviction and forty of these were already under a suspended death sentence.

After the war finished, many of the military Provost staff wanted to leave the Army so new staff were recruited from the units to replace them. In 1919 there were still over thirty detention barracks and branch detention barracks in the UK. Promotion for the staff came quickly and they were often allowed to choose where they were posted to. In addition to the existing prisons and detention barracks, in 1920 an Army Order set aside the ground floor of the east and west wings of the prison at Bonner Wall, Cologne, Germany, as a military prison and the second, third and fourth floors as detention barracks. But new regulations meant all recruits had to undergo six months' probation at the detention barracks in Aldershot – the 'Glasshouse' – before being posted.

Opened in 1890, Aldershot quickly grew to three times its initial size. There were three types of rooms. The original ones by the gatehouse had wooden floors and low ceilings. The centre part was added later, as was the far end which had dark composition floors, high ceilings and shelves.

For the new recruits the six months' probation was a time to watch and learn from the more experienced guards and also to learn how to judge situations. Many found the first few days daunting as during lock-up everything was quiet, but as soon as the staff entered the hall the noise became deafening until all the men were on parade. To the new recruits it was as if the guards were competing to see who could make the most noise. Whistles blew constantly and shouted orders echoed round the barracks. Other recruits felt that it took them the whole six months to fall into the routine.

One of the biggest challenges was ensuring all prisoners received their meals. At that time these were drawn from the kitchen in round, prison diet tins with one portion on the top and the other underneath. They were taken to the landings on trays and, as one member of staff supervised the issue of the food, another locked and unlocked the door. It seemed to the probationers that there was always one meal missing. A search would ensue and normally an empty tin found. This meant the NCO was 'on the mat' the next morning and the

Commandant would write up a report in his probationer report exercise book. Although these records were destroyed before the recruit was transferred, many worried that it would damage their chances of being accepted. However, very few were returned to their units, and this attention to detail invariably helped many to become better NCOs when they were transferred to other detention barracks.

For new detainees at Aldershot conditions were still strict. On arrival they were searched and their kits checked in the reception room. Once undressed, they had to take a bath in cold water in the presence of the reception cleaner. Their training was just as strict as it had been pre-war and no time was lost during the day. All parades were in full marching order and except for drill, all movements were carried out at the double. For those who did not keep up, sanctions included press-ups in marching order until they dropped.

In the mornings the SUS were taught musketry, PT, signals, semaphore, gas training and bridge building and were made to practise on the assault course. Special squads also continued with the same training in the afternoon. During the dinner hour and lock-up period at night, the men on bed-making and mat-making duties were given tasks such as 'sewing up' (four inches of mat an hour) and 'tabbing biscuits' (six beds in an hour). Each morning the Staff Sergeant, the Industrial NCO, would go round and check that the tasks had been completed satisfactorily with the required number of inches sewn.

Those not capable of such work would be employed cleaning rusty tins. Four dirty meat dishes or sixteen diet tins had to be completed by1930hrs. The materials supplied to complete the tasks were a bath brick, soap and a rag. Rooms had to be kept spotless and the men never entered them with their boots on. They preferred to put them on a piece of blanket inside the door before entering. The prisoners were continually monitored and checked as they worked, or when they were in their rooms. On Sundays they paraded for church, had an hour's exercise and were then locked up for the rest of the day. Staff often heard the men talking to photographs of their loved ones whilst they were locked in their rooms from 1615 to 0600 the next morning. Such a harsh regime meant that very few came back a second time.

In 1921 it was decided that the MPSC should take over the staffing of military prisons in Iraq and, according to *The Journal of the Military Provost Staff Corp* in 1954, 'in consequence the staffs for these were collected in Aldershot to be fitted out and medically examined. They were quartered out in Marlborough Lines and eventually sailed in the troopships *Princess* and *Brandenburg*.'

But things were about to change. Many of the detention barracks which had opened for the war began to close. So too did military prisons as the Army was drastically reduced in size. In 1922 the two old established prisons in Cork and

Dublin disappeared from the lists and in 1924 Colchester, which together with York Castle had only opened in 1897, also closed.

In 1925 the DPS (Directorate of Personnel Service) visited England's detention barracks, extolled the virtues of the military detention system and its staff and told them what good prospects there were for their future promotions. Thus, it came as a rather nasty shock when, not long afterwards, due to the falling military prison population, many of the detention barracks were closed. Gosport, the oldest prison, closed in 1927 leaving only three – Aldershot, York and Stirling. The detention barracks at York had a circular tower with steel balconies on each floor inside. All the doors, including those that led downstairs, looked exactly the same so if they were all closed it was very difficult to know which was which.

Stirling was one of the more popular postings because, as former Major W. J. Watson recalled: 'It possessed a splendid Sergeants' Mess and the Commandant took a keen interest in it.' Quoted in *The Journal of the Military Provost Staff* of 1954, Major Watson added: 'The Mess had a large contingent of honorary members and bowling was our most popular game during off-duty hours. We had a competition for the Davidson Cup, presented a few years previously by Captain D. A. Davidson, OBE, Commandant of Stirling.'

York detention barracks was eventually closed in the 1930s and the building was demolished as part of the city improvement scheme. The MPSC began to seriously worry about their futures as in October 1935, after a good deal of protest and press comment, Stirling also closed. At one time it had served the whole of Scotland and some of the north of England.

However, some of the overseas detention barracks were still thriving although Mauritius and Kandy, both of which had often suffered with outbreaks of fever, had closed much earlier. The remaining detention barracks in Tientsin, Shanghai, Singapore, Khartoum, Egypt, and on the islands of Gibraltar, Malta and Jamaica, were still in existence by 1937.

The most popular pre-war posting of these for the staff was the detention barracks in the Citadel, Cairo. It was situated in the old Turkish prison and comprised forty-eight single rooms, plus extra rooms for association. Located high above the city it looked out over the whole of Cairo.

Next door was the Mohamed Ali Mosque to which tourists came from all round the world. On its ramparts was a horseshoe cut out in stone about three-quarters of an inch thick. The tour guides related how it was the imprint of a horse which had escaped the slaughter of the ruling Mamelukes nearly two centuries earlier. Unfortunately the truth was slightly less romantic. It would appear that the horseshoe had, in fact, been cut out by a member of the MPSC who was taken round there every day for exercise whilst awaiting court martial. There was also a small branch of the Cairo detention barracks in Khartoum which comprised eight rooms, two members of staff, a Staff Sergeant and an NCO.

For staff and SUS, life in military detention barracks and military prisons between the wars still followed much of the strict Victorian pre-Garcia rules. The 1937 *Rules for Military Detention Barracks and Military Prisons* provided the Commandant with nineteen paragraphs of instruction which, as stated by Robert Boyes in his book *In Glasshouses*, required him '... to exercise his authority with firmness, good temper and humanity and to enforce similar conduct in his staff. It is his duty to endeavour to instil soldier-like and moral principles into the mind of every soldier under sentence, letting him see that he takes an interest in his welfare, and by his good advice and kindly admonition to endeavour to convince him of his error'.

Medical officers had seventeen paragraphs of instruction and even the Chaplain had instructions, the most prominent being, said Boyes, 'to be careful not to interfere with the rules and regulation of the detention barrack or prison or the routine of discipline and work.' He was further required to keep a journal of any points he wished to raise with the Commandant who would then record any action to be taken. However, he was also required to report any impropriety or abuse immediately. The Chaplain still retained the right to ban any library books that he considered unsuitable, although he was not allowed to communicate with any SUS who were not of his own religious persuasion.

The MPSC, said Boyes, were exhorted to 'strive to acquire a moral influence over the soldier under sentence put under them, and to raise the mind of the soldier to a proper feeling of moral obligation by their own example. This will secure the respect and confidence of soldiers and will make the duties of the staff more satisfactory to themselves.'

When off duty, the staff were required to be in their quarters and available on call, and the quarters had to be within reasonable distance from the detention barracks or prison. When on duty, they had to ensure there was no communication between those under sentence, and that no items which could be used in escape were left in open view. The staff all had to be capable of instructing and supervising any types of industrial work undertaken by the detainees. Overseeing more skilful work attracted additional pay for the MPSC instructor which ranged from £3 to as much as £12 per year. This work included cooperage, twine making, weaving, and making baskets and hammocks. Additional pay was also offered to those who trained as physical training instructors. Less skilful work such as sorting peas, chopping wood, shelling nuts and breaking stones did not attract additional payments.

All staff sergeants and sergeants also received clerical training so that the standards of the DBs and MPs could be maintained. Half of the staff were able to go off duty at dinner time on Saturday until 0630 the following Monday, were allowed one night in seven free if on night duty, and were permitted free time on bank holidays at the Commandant's discretion. During this time the SUS were given work to do in their cells. Civilian employees were also required to salute any commissioned officer, regardless of whether the officer was in uniform, and could be dismissed for drunkenness. Swearing was frowned on, as was incurring debts, frequenting public houses, keeping bad company, gambling and any other disreputable conduct, all of which could result in dismissal for the civilian and a return to the former corps for the MPSC member.

A bell rang at 0630 and all staff paraded to be inspected by the Sergeant Major, after which keys were issued. Breakfast was at 0800 for all those not on duty patrol and dinner was at 1230. Duty then continued until either 1615 or 1930 when the night watch took over. Life was run by the clock, punctuality was essential, and those who were late were severely punished.

The SUS arrived in uniform, minus weapons, and under full marching orders. He was searched, said Boyes, 'in a manner with due regard to decency and self-respect' and weighed, photographed and measured. The rules now stipulated that the photograph must not be given to anyone not officially authorized to receive it. If he was in a detention barracks, the new detainee's day would start at 0600 when he would get up and clean his cell. Roll call and slopping out was at 0635 followed by work until breakfast at 0800. He then cleaned and prepared his equipment, was 'closetted' and on parade at 0930 for military training which included drill, with and without arms, weapon training, miniature cartridge practice, morse signalling, tactics and lectures on various subjects including camouflage. The men were also taught how to pitch and strike tents and anti-gas drill. Those who were trained used the firing range once a week. Dinner was at 1230 followed by work back in the cells and then afternoon parade. Following this, some carried on military training and others did school work until tea. They were then returned to their cells to work and had to clean their equipment. They were allowed to read but lights went out at 2000hrs.

Life in the military prisons was almost identical except work replaced military training. Sundays for both consisted of 0630 reveille, cleaning of cells and corridors, a compulsory church service and long periods of being locked up. A stage system was now in use and a detainee could attain Stage 2 by good behaviour and hard work. This allowed him to sleep on a mattress and write and receive more letters. He was also allowed to communicate with other SUS for twenty minutes daily, split into two periods of ten minutes and within hearing range of a member of staff. There were eighteen named punishable offences. These included singing and whistling to trying to escape, and the final category included any behaviour that was prejudicial against good order and discipline. Punishments ranged from close confinement, loss of remission and the deprivation of library books, to loss of mattress and use of punishment diets.

The use of handcuffs was restricted to cases of extreme violence and had to be reported to the General Officer Commanding, as did the use of body belts and strait waistcoats.

Until 1930, soldiers returning to their units were usually escorted. It was then decided that it was more dignified to discharge them from the nearest railway station. In 1935 soldiers were discharged from the gate of the detention barrack or military prison.

They were given their dinner before leaving and recommended for a gratuity from the nearest branch of the Discharged Prisoners Aid Society. If there was not one available '… the Commandant may expend a sum not exceeding £1 as subsistence money to keep the man while seeking work …'.

For Regimental NCOs there was now a three-week course, after which they returned to their units and supervised their barrack detention rooms. In 1935 'doubling' was done away with, cocoa was issued to the SUS before breakfast, and staff came on duty at 0700. By 1939 there was only one remaining military prison and detention barracks in the whole of the UK. This was at Aldershot and proved to be adequate to accommodate the number of men sent to undergo longer sentences.

Things became much easier and continued in this vein until September 1939.

Chapter 3

Military Detention
1939 – 1947

The outbreak of the Second World War led, almost immediately, to increased staff being recruited for military prisons and detention barracks. Aldershot was the only remaining detention barracks in England and became the mobilization centre. As well as the activity from new and returning members of staff, preparations were made to take over Shepton Mallet for military use.

Plans were also made for two military prisons in the field which would be commanded by Lieutenant Colonel James McGordon, even though regulations for these went back to 1912 and had never been updated. A Major Ross commanded one and McGordon was in command of No1 Military Prison at Arras in northern France.

The Field Punishment Centre (FPC) in Arras was only big enough for twenty men. The second was set up in an agricultural college. This had a central courtyard which was adapted into a drill square. A third was set up in a factory and a fourth in a large house in Lens. Wally Watson, RSM, was instructed to rewrite the regulations in his spare time, but on 10 May 1940, the phoney war came to an abrupt end. The current detainees were quickly returned to their units but the FPCs soon began to fill up again. Within days the men were ordered home. Staff and SUS made their way towards the coast, finally arriving in Calais where they boarded a ship that had just unloaded armoured cars and was heading back to Southampton. On arrival back in Aldershot, they found the waste ground outside the prison filled with French and Belgian soldiers lying around on groundsheets and covered by greatcoats. Colonel McGordon was then detailed to be commandant of the new military prison in Hull which had just opened. It was bombed soon after and staff and SUS were transferred to Yorkshire's Northallerton Prison.

Parliament had passed the Military Training Act on 27 April 1939. This introduced conscription for men aged twenty and twenty-one who were now required to undertake six months' military training. The National Service (Armed Forces) Act 1939 was enacted on 3 September 1939, the day Britain declared war on Germany. This meant men between the ages of eighteen and forty-one were liable for call-up, with single men prioritized over those who were married. One of the side effects of these two Acts was that it brought men from all over the country with different backgrounds and abilities into military service. These included those with criminal tendencies and those who had fundamental objections to war: conscientious objectors.

By the end of 1939, over one and a half million men had been recruited – and not all of them wanted to be there. Desertion was a common problem and one that grew worse when soldiers knew they were to be sent abroad. At one stage there were over 24,500 men wanted for desertion. This, together with the conscientious objectors and those committing more minor offences, inevitably led to an increase in the number of detention facilities required.

By 1940 space in Aldershot was at a premium with three SUS sharing a single Victorian cell. This meant an urgent search for temporary alternatives. Two mills, called ironically enough, 'Perseverance' and 'Prospect', were selected to become Number 10 MPDB (Military Prison Detention Barracks). They were located in Sowerby Bridge in the Calder Valley between Halifax and the Lancashire border. The extensive floors of the mills were converted by constructing wire and wood cages, each of which was capable of holding up to thirty men. Each cage held two-tier bunks, highly polished night buckets and very little else. The men were categorized and segregated according to training, age and the degree of seriousness for which they were incarcerated. All the lower windows were bricked up and the areas used for administration. A member of staff slept on each floor and his only connection to the administrative area was a bell. If there were any problems he would press the bell and any free staff would rush to his aid. Sowerby Bridge had a fearsome reputation and those SUS who had experienced Barlinnie, Fort Darland and Colchester, maintain it was the worst one of all. Discipline was fierce and one man remembers wetting himself on parade rather than move a muscle.[4] Many of those held at Sowerby Bridge were little more than criminals in uniform who would isolate themselves from the rest of the prisoners and remain in tightly knit gangs. When posted overseas, many of these men would remain in handcuffs until they were safely on board and the ship had left port. As Cecil Newton (4th/7th Royal Dragoon Guards) recalls of detention barracks: 'In the Second World War I remember they had a formidable reputation and were best to be avoided.'

'Mr T.B.' was given twenty-eight days for continually overstaying his leave. He contacted Robert Boyes when he was writing *In Glasshouses* and contributed the following:

'There were cages made for six men in each and you were put inside with villains from every regiment. I was put in with two from Liverpool, two Cockneys and a Jock, and I can still recall the fights we used to have over one cig. As regards punishment, you were never still; three drills a day with full kit and all your webbing had to be scrubbed white, and your brasses polished back and front. Being a guardsman, that part was easy for me. Then there was PT twice a day.

'But the worst part was when you were locked up after your tea meal. They used to throw all the dirty pans and mess tins from the cookhouse into the cages and all you had to clean them with were a bucket of sand, cold water and rags and, believe me Major, those pans had to shine like silver. That was in addition to your own kit and there had to be dead silence. If it was raining they used to throw all the tins outside. When the tins were rusty the guards gave them back and said you hadn't touched them. In fact, some of the younger prisoners used to crack and cry.

'If you answered back, the guards had a favourite trick of making you run on the spot while you were having your meal. Just try having a plate of stew while you are running on the spot! I was there was in November and the weather was always damp and cold and the problem was how to get warm with only two blankets. There was also an outbreak of scabies at the time and nearly everyone had the itch. Luckily I escaped that bit but some of them were in a fair old state. It was the same on punishment drill. You could always tell the weak from the strong. Some used to stagger and crawl after twenty minutes. There was no end to it, just go, go, go. I might add that it taught me a lot. I saw things and did things that I thought weren't possible, and when I went back to my battalion I was a whole lot wiser and fitter. I went right through Germany and eventually, after VE Day, I went into another battalion and ended up in Palestine where I finished my seven years.'

Despite the seriousness of Britain's position and the ever-present threat of invasion, in 1941 a committee was convened 'to enquire and report as to whether the treatment, training, accommodation and feeding of soldiers under sentence in military prisons and detention barracks, is in accordance with modern standards and satisfies the requirements of a war-time Army'.

This committee was headed by Major General Miles Christopher Dempsey DSO MC, (later to be General Sir Miles Dempsey) the Commander of the Second Army from D Day onwards. He was joined by Colonel J.A. Fraser DSO DCM, Inspector of Military Prisons and Detention Barracks, Mr Alex Peterson MC, Commissioner of Civil Prisons, Wing Commander E.L. Ardley from the Air Ministry, and Major Geoffrey Gilbey MC, who was currently commanding the new Young Soldiers Training Unit (YSTU) Northern Command ,which had also started in 1941.

The Committee called five Commanding Officers as witnesses and were also advised by the governor of Wandsworth Civil Prison. The witnesses visited Aldershot, Fort Darland, Chorley, Sowerby Bridge, Maidstone Civil Prison and Stakehill, which was then in the process of opening. Their report started with a shrewd analysis of its clients[5] and then looked at the methods currently employed. They concluded that:

'In the mind of the ordinary soldier these places should have a definitely unpleasant association. We cannot afford at this stage to dispense altogether with the preventative value of deterrence. On the other hand, a purely punitive system will not transform a bad soldier into a good one.'

The report further identified that:

'A programme of training, more accurately described as retraining requires a period of time … Where the more unpleasant shock of punishment alone is needed this should be inflicted in a sharp dose, for a man in the course of months can get so used to Hell, as to be hardened rather than shaped by it.'

The report recommended that all corps should have a Corps guardroom, staffed by NCOs from its battalions and regiments and used for purely punitive purposes with the maximum sentence of ten to fourteen days. The military prison detention barracks were to increase the number of officers, thus ensuring one company commander for every fifty SUS. These should be changed frequently and comprise a mix of older experienced officers and younger officers to provide more empathy with the younger soldier. The number of NCOs should be increased by twenty-five per cent. Any establishment holding more than 500 prisoners must automatically have a resident medical officer and a chaplain who should always be able to conduct interviews in private in all establishments, regardless of size. Psychiatrists would also be employed in detention barracks, something that Major Wally Watson, who joined the MPSC in 1919, remembers happening immediately after the Dempsey Report was published, but which was short lived.

One recommendation followed up was the new post of Welfare Officer, intended at the time to be a combination of Education and Entertainments Officer. The training provided in the barracks had come under attack for being out of touch with both current weapons and training methods, and for lack of up to date equipment. Three of the barracks had only two Bren guns and Fort Darland did not have any. Furthermore, Aldershot and Sowerby had no assault courses and Chorley was too small to accommodate one. The report concluded that training should, in future, become the responsibility of the Director of Military Training. It also stressed the need for the Commandant and staff to know each SUS personally and to form regular boards to assess their progress.

One area that did meet with the approval of the committee was the Young Soldiers Training Unit (YSTU). This was the forerunner of the Military Corrective Establishment (MCE) that would be set up after the war and would later become the current Military Corrective Training Centre (MCTC). The YSTUs were set up to deal with young soldiers considered to be 'beyond redemption' despite previous punishments and detentions. In Number 10 MPDB (the mills in Sowerby Bridge) the most troublesome area was No 3 Company which was on the top floor and consisted of young soldiers from the YSTU. The soldiers were considered to have little military value, were frequently AWOL and, when on camp, were a bad influence to others and an administrative burden. However, they could not be discharged because this would have set the wrong example to others. These soldiers were initially sent to Pontefract Racecourse which was set up as a YSTU for 240 trainees with sixty staff. The aim was to treat each soldier as an individual, try and find the cause of his behaviour and then set him on the right path. The Dempsey Report suggested setting up three YSTUs. The initial one at Pontefract, West Yorkshire, was later moved to Wetherby, Yorkshire, and two more were set up in Lowestoft, Suffolk, and Redhill in Surrey. The system did not, of course, work for everyone who went there and although each YSTU was originally set up to support its own area, by 1944 it had become common practice to send the worst offenders to Wetherby, the doubtful ones to Lowestoft and those with potential to become good soldiers to Redhill.

The final answer was removal to Labour Battalions. Used for those aged twenty-one to twenty-eight, for whom punishment within their battalion or detention had not produced any discernible improvement, the regimes were similar to that of the YSTUs. The emphasis was on the knowledge of the individual, and the allocation to Companies was dependant on whether they were considered to be of any military value. The worst were sent to join No 10 Company which was based in Braal Castle in Caithness. Its location made desertion virtually impossible. The company was unarmed and did virtually no military training.

The other companies were based in open camps with no perimeter fences. Both YSTUs and Labour Battalions were considered to be unsuccessful by the Labour Government and were closed down in 1945.

Hard as the conditions were in Army detention barracks and prisons, the discipline and conditions were often worse in the four naval detention quarters (NDQs). There was very little attempt at education or training here. Men were housed in separate cells surrounded by high walls and no communication was allowed between them except on drill and exercise. At night they lay on bare boards without blankets – unless the weather was exceptionally cold – until they had earned 112 good conduct marks. This took at least fourteen days to achieve. During this time they could only send letters on compassionate grounds. Those in Army detention barracks slept in long dormitories ranging from twenty to seventy beds in hutted camps encircled by barbed wire.

Despite the report's findings there were no major changes during the war, although there was a general improvement after its publication.

Chapter 4

Detention in Colchester –
Camp 186

Prior to 1900 there was a Provost prison in Colchester in the North East corner of Hyderabad Barracks. It was exactly the type of prison that Lieutenant Colonel Garsia objected to and was eventually eliminated by Army Order 123 in 1897 when, together with York, it was appointed as a military prison which meant it could be regulated. It could house forty-seven prisoners in single cells and at first it was under the control of a Head Warder with NCOs from the garrison. These were soon replaced by the MPSC and shot drill was replaced with oakum

This picture is believed to have been made by a German POW using toothpaste and brickdust. This is a photo taken of the original picture some time ago. Unfortunately, because of the possible composition of the picture, it has not been possible to restore the original for fear of completely destroying it. Sadly the original, which has hung in the Sergeants' Mess for many years is now suffering badly from a combination of old age and cigarette smoke.

Prisoners of War boot repairs 1945.

picking and stone breaking. Drill and physical training were introduced, although there were difficulties because the shot yard was too small to allow proper drill to take place. The only PT possible was static exercises with dumbbells.

Initially the prisoners were allowed to attend church parade with the garrison, but their grey, shoddy clothing and prison caps over cropped hair were considered to be a danger to others, so, after 1900, church services were held in the prison. In 1901 efforts were made to modernize the old restricted Provost premises by extending the outer wall westwards and raising its height. Sixteen new cells were built and a laundry and gymnasium were added. Oakum picking had now virtually disappeared and been replaced by 'wood-chopping boxes'. These were designed rather like stalls in a stable so that the prisoners could not communicate with each other while working. Other activities still included making beds and pillows as well as repairing tents and horse blankets. The records show that at least one enterprising prisoner tried to escape while the building was in progress, but was caught three hours later.

In 1904 the government bought Reed Hall and Bee Hive farms. Together these comprised some 785 acres south-west of the garrison. By 1908 the detention barracks, as it was known, had sixty-three cells but at times as few as six prisoners. By this time, all MPSC staff were qualified, training either at the Small Arms School in Hythe, Kent, or the School of Physical Training in Aldershot, Hampshire. In 1910 the new king, George V, granted a Royal Pardon and instant release to all those sentenced to fifty-six days or less. Those with longer sentences had them reduced by half. By 1913, training had been expanded to include drill, PT, building trenches, signalling and scout and outpost work.

Thus, prior to 1947, military detention in Colchester consisted of Reed Hall and the detention cells in the garrison barracks. Wooden huts were put up at Reed Hall in 1914 when between 30,000 and 40,000 men were in training there. A military airfield was established on several acres of land at Blackheath which after the war was transferred to Friday Wood.

Between 1926 and 1933, large areas of Colchester's Berechurch parish, including Berechurch Hall, were bought for the Army. During the 1930s Kirkee and McMunn barracks were built at Reed Hall, Roman Way and Cherry Tree, and camps were established south-east of the main camp.

In 1939 emergency barracks were built on various sites in the garrison area including the field at Colchester Abbey, at Blackheath and Berechurch, and the detention barracks at Reed Hall became No 19 Detention Barracks. In 1946 Major Bob Firmstone was its Commandant and it held 200 prisoners. There were two education instructors permanently attached to the camp who taught during the day and ran woodwork and leatherwork classes in the evening. There was a radio in all rooms and a training cinema – the most effective punishment was to forbid the showing of a cartoon film.

There seems to be some confusion as to when Camp 186, the POW Camp, first opened and for whom. Although *The Victoria History of the County of Essex* refers to a camp of Nissen huts opening for Italian prisoners of war in 1943, the first German POWs to arrive in 1944 do not remember any form of built structure, only lines of poles and rows of folded tents in a large meadow enclosed by a barbed wire fence.

Great care was taken during the war to keep POW camps well away from any military activity. Three separate groups of 500 Essex Army cadets each spent a week camping in Berechurch Hall in July 1944. It therefore seems unlikely there was any formal POW structure there then, or any POWs. The confusion may have arisen because there was an established base camp in the Halstead area from which Italians and German POWs were then employed on local farms. Many may have lived on the farms in which they worked or in small hostels.

Camp 186 appears to have first opened on the night of 19/20 September 1944 with the arrival of 1,500 German prisoners. They were placed in large tents and issued with boilers, cooking pots and coal which they used to set up the first kitchen. Numbers increased daily and by 24 September there were upwards of 6,000 Germans living in the camp. The process of replacing the tents with permanent structures did not start until the following year and not all the tents were replaced with Nissen huts until 1946. [6]

As well as SS men there were also German soldiers and a group of Germans

C Lager in background of Camp 186 and the oak tree.

who had been studying for the priesthood. They requested that they be allowed to continue their studies whilst in Camp 186. Realizing that there were probably other Germans in other POW camps who also wanted to be priests, the British transferred them all to Colchester. Here they continued their study, helped by local Catholic church members who provided them with notebooks and pencils. Other churches and chapels also visited the camp to provide pastoral care or to take services. One priest cycled 167 miles from Birmingham each week. The resident priest was Father Grones who was helped by Father Schilling, a POW who was brave enough to teach Hebrew to the Germans of Camp 186.

According to records, eight POWs died in the first three months Camp 186 was open, and in Colchester's Cemetery Internment Register there are seventeen deaths recorded in total. Of these, three were from natural causes, one from a gunshot wound and two from hanging. Eleven had no cause recorded so may have been suicide or murder. It is also recorded that three POWs were murdered by fanatical Nazis[7] and their bodies dumped in the ditches within the camp.

The first three Nissen huts were finally erected in February 1945. These were each about thirty-seven feet long with corrugated asbestos roofs and housed about eighteen men. Washing and toilet blocks were built and stoves provided heating in the barrack blocks, albeit only in the evening. But within a year there was electricity in all the essential areas. According to former Staff Sergeant Dan Cowley, the electrical wiring was installed by German and Italian electricians who used the continental wiring system of green for neutral. In the 1970s this caused some problems in the 'Piggery' when English electricians replaced the wiring causing the system to short. (In England, the earth wire was green.)

By 1946 there were 1,340 buildings on the site and it was these that would later be taken over and used by the MCE when it opened as the new military detention centre in 1947.

The proliferation of prefabricated huts across the country was the result of the Burt Committee and the Housing (Temporary Accommodation) Act 1944. The Military Corrective Training Centre was in receipt of some of them. A total of four were built – the Armory, Pioneer Shop and two Close Confinement cell blocks. All of these had small high windows on each side and were of reinforced concrete construction. The two Close Confinement Blocks were enclosed in an eighteen foot wriggly tin fence with outer wooden support, this making it a sun trap.

Source: Dan Cowley (former Staff Sergeant from the 1970s)

Now the war was finished the vast numbers of German and Austrian POWs who had been held in America and Canada throughout the war began returning to the UK. This led to a shortage of SNCOs to man the increasing numbers of prison camps. As the infantry were no longer involved in fighting many were seconded to bolster the numbers of the Pioneer Corps who were struggling to cope:

As Sergeant Stanley Featherstone recalls:

'I was sent from Norway in January 1946 to Camp 186 and was billeted in Berechurch Hall House next door to the camp. I remember two huge compounds full of POWs surrounded by two banks of barbed wire fences with floodlights and a catwalk in between. The main guardhouse was located near Berechurch Hall House with a second one located near the back of the camp, behind which was a large wooded area where there were frequent searches for escapees. There was also a main camp within the compound with cells full of prisoners waiting to be interviewed by the Intelligence Corps. At the time many suspected war criminals, and those responsible for the concentration camps, were known to be swapping their ID with ordinary serving soldiers in an attempt to avoid justice. Camp 186 was also used as a transit camp, with the emphasis on identifying these Nazis so they could be tried as war criminals.

'I can remember members of the Intelligence Corps based in Camp 186 having strange names like 'Kent' and 'Suffolk' as they were really German and Austrian Jews. Any suspects considered to warrant further investigation were sent to the London Cage[8] and subject to vigorous questioning.

'One German spoke good English and was just your normal sort of chap really. Then I checked with my colleagues in the Intelligence Corps and discovered the man was one of the senior guards from Ravensbruck Concentration Camp and that his speciality was flogging women.'[9]

Camp 186 finally closed in September 1947 and the remaining POWs were transferred to Fornham Hall near Bury St Edmonds. The priests who were ordained while in Colchester formed a group called 'Colcestrianer' once they returned home to Germany. They kept in contact with each other throughout the rest of their lives, even visiting Colchester in 1989, although by then there was little left of the original camp.

Its closure was immediately followed by considerable local discussion about its future. Colchester Borough Council requested permission to use the huts as accommodation to relieve the housing shortage in the town. But its future had already been decided, partly because of events elsewhere.

In 1944 the southern half of the top floor of Aldershot detention barracks, about the size of ten cells, had been converted away from single cells to an association area. The ground floor remained the same with single cells. By 1946 there were between 400 and 500 SUS, twice the number the building had been originally designed to accommodate. Men were sleeping three to a single cell and each association room held between twenty to twenty-five men. On 23/24 February 1946 rioting broke out and the main building was destroyed. The damage was made worse by the water used by the Army fire service to quell the disturbance. Ten soldiers and one Royal Marine were court-martialled and the remaining prisoners were transferred to other military and civil prisons. Although the War Office considered rebuilding, the cost was prohibitive (an estimated £18,000 in 1948) and eventually the prison was demolished in 1958. In the meantime somewhere else was needed.

By 1947 the number of those imprisoned had fallen to about 2,000 and a new system was introduced. Army Orders 151/47 classified military prisons into two categories: Type A, of which there were originally two, would take the recidivists (convicted criminals who reoffend repeatedly) and Type B, of which there were initially three, for those offenders deemed capable of returning to their units after a period of training. By 1949 there was only one of each category left; Shepton Mallet for those whose services the Army no longer wished to retain, and Colchester which had type A and B.

Type B prisons were named Military Corrective Establishments (MCE) and were based on the idea of the YSTUs. Sentences of fewer than twenty-eight days were served at the unit except in exceptional circumstances. The decision as to which prison was used was solely at the Commanding Officer's discretion, although the War Office had drawn up a list of criteria to guide this decision. The maximum sentence was two years.

Men could not be sent to Type A prison and detention barracks unless there had been at least two attempts to rehabilitate them at Type B establishments. Furthermore, they could not be classified as habitual offenders unless they had previously served two periods of detention totalling six months in the past two years, or had a previous record of imprisonment. Reviews were carried out one month after admission and then at two-month intervals to ensure anyone capable of being retained as a soldier was not kept there.

One recommendation of the Dempsey Report – that psychiatrists should examine those with mental health concerns – was now implemented. If a psychiatrist felt a soldier should be transferred to detention on mental health grounds this was normally done. However, if someone was transferred to the MCE and his behaviour deteriorated he would be returned to the prison. Although it was never official policy to interview all those entering prison, all those leaving were interviewed by psychiatrists as a preliminary to discharge.

Accommodation for those in Shepton Mallet, the only remaining Type A prison, was in small blocks of cells made of reinforced concrete. There was little military training and most were employed on various administrative duties, in the laundry or making and repairing coil mattresses. Others made rugs, or were employed on Perspex or woodwork and sign painting. The education facilities were good and there was a weekly cinema show.

A stage system was introduced in MCEs through which a man could become eligible for suspension of his sentence if he reached Stage 3. However, as it was expected that a soldier would pass through at least six squads before reaching this stage, a sentence of at least three months was needed. Stage 2 was comparable to a strict regime in the soldier's own unit, while Stage 3 afforded a much greater degree of freedom with permission to leave the camp on parole and a regular Army diet.

In *Crime and the Service* John Spencer describes the offences of fifty men during his visit to Colchester. 'The majority were there for absence and desertion (twenty-eight including those deserters who had surrendered), theft accounted for nine, assault, four and miscellaneous for nine.' [10]

In 1946 the DPS (Directorate of Personnel Services) decided that there was a need for Quarter Masters (QM) in the MPSC and three WO1s were offered emergency QM Commissions – Captains Lovegrove, Fazackerly and Jimmy James.

Chapter 5

'It was a mad, mad world'
1947 – 1950

Colchester's Military Corrective Establishment (MCE) opened its doors to military detainees at the end of November 1947. As the last of the POWs left, the camp was made ready to receive its new inmates. Meanwhile, the 200 British soldiers under sentence in Military Detention Centre 19 at Reed Hall started transferring to Berechurch, supervised by Lieutenant Colonel Maurice Saunders of the Essex Regiment. The MCE in Colchester was made up from two different detention barracks, the one from Reed Hall and one from Darland in Kent. Although 19 MCE and 14 MCE initially kept their separate identities they eventually merged to become the MCE Colchester.

WO1 Avery was posted to Reed Hall in 1947 after completing his Probationers' Course: 'I barely had time to settle in before being sent to the recently evacuated POW camp in Berechurch Hall Road, to prepare for the transfer of all soldiers under sentence to what was to become the new site of MCE 19. We were to be joined by MCE 14 from Fort Darland which was also being closed down.'

Major BO 'Jimmy' James:

'I remember the chaos of moving some 1,500 soldiers under sentence from Fort Darland to Colchester, the freezing cold unlined Nissen hut that was to be the Sergeants' Mess and the icy dash to the open ablutions.

'By the end of 1947 there were 1,600 men housed in the MCE in Colchester, and the MPSC had also found a permanent home – although 'home' may not be the word the majority of people used to describe the MCE.

'For most people their first sight of the MCE Colchester would have been the high barbed wire fences and the armed guards at the entrance.'

Frank Bell came back from the Second World War and decided he wanted to join the military police. 'There was obviously some mix up with the papers as instead I was sent to the MPSC in Colchester in November 1947, just after the camp opened. It was a mad, mad world. We were locking up over 900 soldiers in two compounds. It was horrible. I didn't like it at all. There were soldiers everywhere and not enough staff. You never knew if you were going to get attacked while on duty.'

Ken Sparks[11] was a member of the Corp of Military Police based in Colchester garrison across the road from the MCE in 1947 and remembers one special event. 'As the camp was to be officially opened by General Montgomery, I and five others were sent to meet Monty at Dover.'

Proud to have been chosen to be outriders, Ken and the others went off on their gleaming BSA 500 motorcycles wearing their dispatch rider boots which had been suitably cleaned before leaving Colchester. However, several miles of travelling on muddy country roads soon took its toll. On arrival at Dover they lined up ready to greet their hero only to be subjected to an impromptu inspection. Ken recalls: 'Because my mate's boots were dirty after the journey Monty put him on a charge. I never liked him much after that. I also remember seeing several Canadian soldiers who were being held there, break out of their huts and climb onto the roofs of the Nissen huts where they sat hurling down tiles. But their protest was short-lived as the Army Fire Service was soon called out and turned the hosepipes on them.'

Ronald Thirst, a young Royal Marine, went AWOL and was given six months in Colchester in 1947:

'I thought Colchester was just like an ordinary day in the barracks. Having heard all about Aldershot from my brother I was pleasantly surprised by my stay at Colchester and I thought it was rather like a holiday camp. I can't remember being made to double anywhere and the huts were a pleasant surprise as I had been expecting cells.

'I can still remember the staging system quite clearly. Stage 1 was the basic routine which I found easy. Once we reached Stage 2 we were allowed letters and magazines and by Stage 3 we could go into town on a Saturday. We were even allowed to fire rifles on the firing range.

'When I returned to my unit I was convinced that my Commanding Officer would discharge me but instead, to my surprise, I was told that I had a long way to go in the service. Three weeks later I was posted to Singapore for two and a half years – not exactly what I thought the CO had meant! I went on to complete twelve years in the Royal Marines and my abiding memories of time in uniform were that the pay wasn't that good and the food was so bad I bought a big tin of curry powder and covered everything in it.'

John Ticker, an RAF Policeman based at RAF Watnall near Nottingham, has a less pleasant memory of his visit to Colchester as an escort to a prisoner in 1948:

'This young RAF National Serviceman had been caught by a Warrant Officer putting a lump of ham in a bush so that he could take it home to his mother. I felt sorry for him, as I thought he really didn't deserve fifty-six days in Colchester. I was sure this wouldn't have happened if he had been a regular airman rather than a National Serviceman.

'On arrival at Colchester both I and my prisoner were made to double everywhere. The young airman's kit was emptied on the floor and kicked around. He was then stripped and cold water thrown over him. But just when I thought it couldn't get any worse I was asked for the man's pay book. To my horror I realized that I had left it behind. Thinking quickly I explained that the Adjutant had locked it up at the base and that I would post it on as soon as I arrived back. Fortunately for me my explanation was accepted and I left hastily, hoping I would never have to return there again.'

Sid Young was called up in 1948 to do his National Service. As a young RAF Policeman he was initially based in the dog training unit until he was posted to Westmorland in Kent to help increase security on the airfield there. 'At the time a number of aircraft had gone missing, believed to be the work of one "Sidney Stanley" who was suspected of being connected to the newly formed Israeli state.'

Sid was curious about the 'Glasshouse', as Colchester was colloquially known, after hearing various conversations on the base. The opportunity for him to slake his curiosity came when, because there was a shortage of staff, he volunteered to take a young airman there to serve twenty-eight days for being AWOL for seven days, something considered to be very serious in those days. Recalls Sid: 'We travelled together to London Victoria and then across London to catch the train to Colchester. Once we reached London I had to handcuff the young man so that he didn't escape. If he had done I would have been in serious trouble. When we reached MCE Colchester I remember it being a frightening place and experience. The sergeants were all very smart, but they were all big chaps and they looked very fierce with their slashed peaks. I watched as they doubled the prisoner away and can remember thinking that I was glad to get away! When the airman returned to the base after his sentence he said to me "I never want to go there again"!'

Rupert Cooper remembers a friend from the RAF who decided to 'work his ticket' in 1948:

'He initially went AWOL for a short period and then gave what he considered to be a totally implausible reason for his absence. To his horror he was believed and only received a few days' jankers on the base. This would not be enough to get him out as the only way to be dismissed was to go through Colchester. Realizing he would have to try harder he disappeared again, this time for considerably longer and on his return his wish was granted. I remember my friend had to have his long, black hair cut on arrival. The person cutting it combed his hair forward and my friend said it all went dark, then suddenly light as his hair landed on the floor! His favourite time in Colchester was having lessons on the Bren guns, something the RAF would not normally have done.'

Brian Hartington, a Gunner in the Essex Regiment 1949-1951 also took a prisoner to MCE Colchester in 1949. 'I remember the enormous gate at the entrance. It was like a grim Fort Knox and the staff were a bit harsh. We were met at the gate by a gigantic Sergeant Major and I remember feeling sorry for the poor lad when his feet hit the ground running, and thinking I wouldn't like to be them!'

Christopher Clack abused a Corporal who caught him with his hands in his pockets when he came back from leave and asked him to remove them:

'As it was cold I refused and was sent to Colchester for twenty-eight days. My first impressions were that it looked just like pictures I'd seen of POW camps with wooden huts, barbed wire and runways everywhere. We slept forty to a hut on wooden boards with square mattresses called biscuits. There was one toilet bucket at the end of each hut. We were allowed one shower a week and each night two buckets of cold water were placed at both ends of the hut. I would take a mug of water at night and use it to clean my teeth and shave in the morning.

'Everywhere we went inside the camp was at the double, "run here, run there", and if you were out of line you would be sent to the doctor to see if you were fit enough to be punished.

'I remember being allowed one cigarette a day at 1400 in the cookhouse. On the way out you had to put out the cigarette in a bucket of water held by a guard at the door. As with most things there were ways round this and some would break the cigarette in half and put one part in their pocket to smoke later or use as currency. However, the penalties if you were caught were so severe that not many risked it. Those who did spent time in the padded cells on a punishment diet consisting of three days bread and water.

'We seemed to spend most days running backwards and forwards, to and round the Square. The rest was spent in our huts talking. It wasn't very pleasant and twenty-eight days was long enough!'

William Ravenscroft, a Corporal in REME (Royal Electrical Mechanical Engineers), took prisoners to Colchester three or four times by himself:

'Although I used to shout and scream at prisoners while they were in the guardroom, once we were on the train to Colchester I spoke to them normally. I remember going up to a big gate where both me and prisoners stood to attention. There was a guard box off to the right out of which would come the guard to open the gate. Once through, both I and the prisoner would be made to double to a big hall, rather like a hanger, and stand on the right side with the prisoner's kit on the floor. I would go off to the left with Document 1157 which was the custodial paperwork. Meanwhile, the prisoner would be made to strip and take a cold shower at the end of the room. On their return to unit prisoners would regale the others with tales of being made to cut grass with blunt knives and of sleeping on wooden beds with guards tipping them out in the middle of the night for no reason.'

The MCE gate in the 1950s – this was the first view for the detainees and their escorts.

39

Another detainee from 1949:

'I did fifty-six days there and I can tell you it was no holiday camp. I had a kit check and shower in less than twenty minutes, then we were doubled round to the cookhouse for a meal. My God, a meal! It comprised watery soup and four slices of bread. If you were a bit slow at eating the Staff Sergeant would make you light up your cigarette. If he decided to say "cigarettes out" you might only have had two puffs from it and they would come round with a bowl of water for you to put it out. If you got caught with a cigarette end in your pocket you would lose three days remission on your sentence. These are just a few things that went on in that hell hole.'

Robert Boyes includes a typical timetable for prisoners in his book *In Glasshouses*:

0530: Reveille
0600: Cold shower
0630: PT with additions
0700: Breakfast
0730: Kit check
0800: Parade
0830: Route march (between ten and fifteen miles a day)
1130: Shower (cold)
1200: PT
1230: Dinner

Chapter 6

'A bleak and dismal place'
1950 – 1952

In 1950 members of the MPSC were offered the chance to become commissioned into its corps. Previously they could only be commissioned into another corps or regiment, usually the one from which members had transferred originally.

At that time the MCE in Colchester held 770 SUS, many of whom were on National Service. There are numerous stories of men called up for two years who spent considerably more time in the Armed Forces because time spent in detention did not count towards National Service. 'I remember going to Munster in Germany where there was a man who was in his fourth year of his two years National Service!' recalls Gordon Davidson who did his National Service in 1957 with RASC (The Royal Army Service Corps).

One such National Serviceman tells his story in *In Glasshouses*[12]:

'During the summer of 1950, as a National Serviceman – a junior NCO – I was silly enough to get myself a district court martial. As a result, I was awarded six months at Colchester. My pal got the same. On arrival at the gates our escorts and the pair of us were screamed at, verbally abused and ordered to go away as we were improperly dressed. Our escorts' faces turned white with fear, so you can imagine how we felt peering through the December fog at the iron gates. Once inside we were hustled into the gatehouse, were read the riot act, and were told that a third of our sentence could be remitted but wc would serve the full time if there were any errors on our part. We had to strip and take a cold shower. I think it was 13 December! We were marched at the double for 400 yards to another wired-off compound just like those in the German films. I was terrified as the riot act was read to us once more while our heads were shaved.

'The compound was about 300 yards long with semi-circular asbestos huts on both sides and rolls and strands of barbed wire

The Oaktree and old Gate Lodge in the background c1950.

everywhere to about ten-foot high. The fear of God ran through me as I realized that human beings were kept there. The door of the hut was unlocked and I was ordered in by a red-necked screw who was just waiting to get at me. There was no glass in the windows, only wire mesh for obvious reasons. The stories the SUS told me would have scared James Bond because if you did manage to escape you would have to start again.

'Our beds were laid out to a specific order – full kit, everything square, bootlaces rolled, not one thing out of place. "Outside for parade now!" "Run, run run". "Line up". "Stand still for roll call". "Answer when your name is called!" A big fat screw looked at me and asked, "What's my name, lad?" "Don't know Staff", I replied to which he answered, "Go sick lad".

'This means seeing the Medical Officer to find out if you are fit enough to go on punishment diets PD2 – bread and water. I received three sessions of two days on bread and water and lost two days' remission on each count. One session was for having a few whiskers under my chin. PD 1 consisted of porridge for breakfast; lunch was mashed, watery dried potatoes, meat and cabbage. Tea was a one-inch diameter cheeseball and a two-inch cube of bread. On my first three days I refused to eat the filth. On the fourth day I ate the crumbs from the table.

'One day about thirty of us were running past the cookhouse and I saw the swill bins outside. There was an L-shaped crust half submerged in custard and slops. I grabbed it, roughly wiped it and ate it. This memory will be with me forever.

'It was a hundred per cent impossible to get through without loss of remission. I was ordered to sit in an empty hut, given a half brick and an old cement bucket, and told to wear a hole in it. I started to pound the bottom of the upside-down bucket. My greatcoat was covered in brick dust and I had a highly polished bucket. Another time I had to shift a large heap of sand to the far end and sweep the corner. Having done this I had to shift it to corner number three and then again for a fourth time. I thank God I haven't had to go near the place since.'

Major Chandler, originally from the Bedfordshire and Hertfordshire Regiment, joined the MCE in April 1950 and was Adjutant four times:

'It all began in January 1950 when a smiling CO at Kempston Barracks, Bedford, entered my office to tell me I was to be posted to the Glasshouse at Colchester on 1 April. (All Fools Day I thought – he must be joking!) I duly arrived and was politely told at the main gate that the Commandant's office was the Nissen hut just past the big oak. And so I was to take over C Company, a motley assembly of soldiers under sentence, all of CO awards. Everybody and everything moved fast and I had to learn quickly.

'My stay with C Company was short-lived as within a week or two I was to be thrown in at the deep end, and from then on, never had a dull moment. As Adjutant it was difficult to get away from the office; both wings were brimful and the singles block was never empty. The lock-up figure was about 770.

'Following the outbreak of hostilities in Korea, we had a spate of deserters committed to both wings, but we readily disposed of them when Captain Haseldine and a large escort took them to Southampton for embarkation. Their sentences were suspended after the troopship set sail.

'With all the routine training activities taking place and a full training programme to be followed, it was inevitable that escapes would take place. We were bombarded with Boards of Inquiry, Boards of Visitors and "Ministerials".

'I can remember one day asking WO1 Munday who the chap was at the main gate wearing a jerkin, wellington boots and carrying a shot gun. "Oh", he said. "He's the VCO". (Going back to the days of India I thought he meant Viceroy Commissioned Officer). "Yes sir, he's the Vermin Control Officer."

'Punishment diets were used quite regularly as sanctions. RD (Restricted Diet) 1 was bread and water, RD 2 was the same but with a reduced calorie ration as well. The MCE kept chickens and on one occasion they escaped during a Provost Marshal (PM) inspection. After being chased all over the square, the chickens were finally recaptured. Fortunately the PM had a good sense of humour, especially after he was given half a dozen eggs.'

Leslie Morgan (Corporal RAOC 1946-1952) recalls escorting a prisoner to Colchester in 1951:

'I was stationed with 15 Battalion RAOC at Bicester and was detailed, along with an escort, to take a squaddie to the military detention centre in Colchester to serve ninety-six days for going AWOL. All went well until we arrived at Liverpool Street Station. The prisoner was handcuffed to the escort and had a greatcoat over his wrist, while his other hand was used to balance his kitbag over his backpack. I was crossing the bridge between the platforms a little behind them when I was berated by an elderly lady wielding an umbrella who told me in no uncertain terms that I should carry some of the offender's kit.

'Arriving at Colchester we were met by a lorry and were transported to the detention centre. My escort was told to remain outside with all the other escorts who had arrived from various places.

'Once inside with the main gate finally closed behind us, we were "double double" marched to the Custody Office where I was handed a letter indicating that this prisoner had arrived.

'Marching smartly back to the entrance I was accosted by a bull-necked Sergeant of the Military Provost Staff Corps who told me in no uncertain terms, "We double double march in here Corporal!"

'I was in Colchester Detention Camp for no more than two hours, but that experience has left an indelible mark on my memory and sixty years later I have never forgotten it. There but for the grace of God! A most unpleasant experience.'

Another detainee remembers his time there in even more detail:

'On the afternoon of Monday, September 23, 1950, the troop carrier into which I had been crammed with about a score of other prisoners and escorts, lurched to a halt outside Colchester Military Corrective Training Establishment – the Glasshouse. It was an ex POW camp with around 300 asbestos huts entirely surrounded by barbed wire. Inside the main enclosure were four separate compounds containing four companies into which the camp was divided. We tumbled out of the truck and walked haphazardly up the short drive to the gate lodge, a small wooden hut beside the wire netting gate. A sergeant wearing the peaked cap and bright blue and red flashes of the MPSC let us in.

'"Get into two lines" he ordered. "Escorts on the left". The gate swung shut behind us. "Right first man – number, rank and name. How long have you got?" He passed down the line. One man called him "Sergeant". "In here you call everybody below Warrant Officer 'Staff'. You call WOs and above 'Sir'. That understood?" Quick March. Double March. He set us up marching to the reception office, a large corrugated Nissen hut about twenty yards away. Halfway across another sergeant took up the sharp "Left Right, Left Right" in double-quick time and marched us inside.

'Down each side, a series of oblong bays had been marked out. Each prisoner was assigned to a bay, ordered to strip to gym shoes and overcoat, and to "chase" to the building opposite for a shower. When we returned our kit was checked and searched. Everything not on the official list and especially prohibited articles such as tobacco, food, drink and valuables had to be stored away until our release. We were, however, allowed to keep three photographs.

'One by one we were called to a table where a Staff Sergeant checked our documents. With several other prisoners I was then quickly marched to B compound. In the company office our kit was checked yet again. We were each given five blankets, a mattress, a pillow, two sheets, a pillow case, two mugs (one for shaving, the other for drinking), two tin plates, sticks to make a laundry box and cardboard for squaring our kit. Under a load of kit I was double marched to my room. I dumped the kit on the vacant bed and was marched out for tea. After that I was locked up with the others for the night.

'I sat on my barrack box and looked miserably round my new home, a small asbestos hut with windows at both ends. Down one side of the central gangway were six beds. Down the other were four beds with a trestle table and two forms in between. In the centre was a stove which almost smothered the night's ration of three-quarters of a scuttle of coke. At the end was a recess with a latrine bucket. When our food was doctored, as occasionally it was, the stench was appalling.

'What depressed me most were the spotless Blanco and gleaming brasses of the kit laid out on the beds. I arranged mine as best I could but without cleaning materials this wasn't good. No one was inclined to help me, everyone was for himself. Suddenly, in desperation I threw the whole lot on the floor.'

Escapes were common and there were more than twenty recorded in 1951. Two of the escapees broke into a clothing store in Coggleshall and stole clothing valued at £20.6s.2d. They were caught after a policeman noticed their Army boots sticking out from under their brand-new overcoats. A young Pioneer was caught the same way after breaking into a house and stealing clothes in Layer-de-la-Haye. Another prisoner escaped in April 1951 in bare feet.

Such was the concern of local residents that questions were asked in Parliament by the MP for Colchester at the time, Mr (later Lord) Alport. Lancaster MP Fitzroy Maclean hastened to assure him that new security lights had been fitted and staff numbers were being increased.

Robert Whorley's National Service[13] was spent as a member of Adjutants staff and helping with the courts martial procedure. 'I remember going into the MCE as an onlooker and seeing the detainees doubling everywhere, cleaning dustbins inside and out with Duraglit, Blanco'ing their kit and scrubbing everything'.

Peter Pasola spent his National Service in the RASC (Royal Army Service Corps). In 1951 he was an ambulance driver for the British Military Hospital:

'I remember SUS regularly drinking metal polish and other things just to spend a few days in hospital. One time a man swallowed three bed springs and a bent fork. My overriding memory is that the detainees had to scrub all their kit white and double everywhere. They had no rights at all. One night I received a call to say someone had hung themselves. However, when I arrived at the camp it turned out to be some stuffed denims made to look like a body. Although I found this quite funny and was amazed that they had managed to find the material in such a strict environment, I recall that the staff were definitely not amused!'

David Biscombe spent fifty-six days in Colchester after he missed a Territorial Army (TA) Camp. Having already done two years of National Service he then had to do four years in the TA:

'I remember SUS scrubbing floors with toothbrushes. It was the same food every day, boiled potatoes, marrowfat peas and mutton followed by semolina cooked with water. The porridge had no milk or sugar and we were allowed two cigarettes a day. These had to be smoked in the Diets Hall and the butts dropped into a tin of water before the detainees left. Some risked breaking them in half and smuggling one half back to the huts to smoke later but the punishment for getting caught was fierce. Known as '3,7, and 10' it consisted of three days in a single cell with bread and water twice a day. On the next days porridge and a potato mix was added and you'd lose ten days remission. There were no visitors and the one letter a week had to be written in pencil and was censored.'

Lieutenant Colonel Jim Robinson was twenty-one when he arrived at the MCE in Colchester on a Sunday afternoon in September 1952 to attend the MPSC course:

'Someone directed me to a bus that dropped me off at the junction of Berechurch Hall Road and Mersea Road where I started to walk. Just a couple of hundred yards they said! There were only one or two houses and a farm, and it seemed ages before the camp came into view. I had been looking for a place with high walls or something similar but when I saw the camp it looked dreadful. The entrance was just a gap in the hedge, no gateway or anything like that, and certainly no high walls, though there was plenty of barbed wire. I discovered later that there was even a public right of way through the camp area, down the right hand side of the road and into Friday Woods.

'On turning into the camp there appeared to be a complete absence of personnel and all that could be seen was this small wooden hut at the right-hand side of this very long road. I went in there, thinking this was the place to report, but no it was the telephone exchange with a civilian operator. By this time my kit bag was beginning to feel heavy, but I went on for another quarter of a mile to find yet another wooden hut at the side of a very large, white-painted iron gate. Here at least was a military man. He passed some comment about boys being sent here for courses, but eventually showed me where to go – the depot!

'The depot was a mass of small huts lined internally with corrugated iron, as was the rest of the camp. At the top of the wall of each end of the hut, just above the doors, alternate bricks had been taken out to provide ventilation. A panel had been fitted in front of the gaps to prevent rain and snow from flying into the room, though this did nothing to prevent the wind from howling in. In the centre of the room was a small stove which burned coke and provided what little heat there was.

'A Staff Sergeant issued me with bedding etc. and a set of stripes which had to be sewn on as we were made local sergeants for this course. I was shown our dining room at the back of the junior ranks kitchen. We were not allowed to eat in the Sergeants' Mess, although we were allowed to use the bar there. When I looked for the toilets they seemed to be miles away. You needed a compass to find them and nearly froze to death when you used the urinal, a flat piece of concrete with a wall four feet high built down the centre with a gully on each side of the base of the wall. At least the toilets had a roof but they were just as draughty, as the cubicles had no doors!'

Jim's course, number 51, started the next day:

'There were about nine of us, mostly infantry. The instructors were Staff Sergeant Ernie Taylor and Staff Sergeant "Chippy" Reynolds – a judo enthusiast who had taught his wife the art. She regularly scared the garrison HQ Staff who hid out of sight and locked all the doors when they saw her coming. Staff Sergeant Preston, ex Guards, was our drill instructor, Sergeant Bill Jordan ran the office and Major Taffy Lloyd was OC of the depot.

'The first two weeks of the course concentrated mainly on drill and MPSC theory, with particular emphasis on the stage system which had been introduced a couple of years earlier. The next two weeks focused on weapons training and map reading.

'The depot MPSC contained not just our course and attached personnel. It also had those NCOs on Held Strength who were awaiting postings or were in transit from one station to another. It was a motley crowd and as the depot was a separate unit to the MCE, the NCOs did not work in the MCE, but passed their time carrying out any odd jobs that were given them.'

Jim had no intention of joining the MPSC until he realized he could get overseas quite quickly and get his third stripe, so he decided to transfer. 'I can remember to this day wearing my peaked hat for the first time. It felt huge and uncomfortable and took weeks for me to get used to it.'

At the end of the course Jim had two weeks' leave and on his return was posted to D Company:

'This was Stage 2 of the Type B, MCE. C and D Company were Stage 1 with Stage 3 as a separate block. A and B Companies were for recidivists and other bad characters, of which there was no shortage during those National Service days. The worst ones were in B Company while C and D Companies were for first-time offenders. The total lock-up figures at this time were between 800 and 900.

'My first duty was on morning shift and my first task was to supervise the "goldfish bowl". This involved standing near a raised manhole that had expanded mesh over it instead of a lid. At 0620 after unlock, the prisoners came running out of their rooms for a wash and shave, but two men from each room had to carry the latrine bucket between them. It was invariably filled to the brim – with ten men to a room this was not surprising. They would carry it to the bowl and slop it in. Then they had to use a stiff broom to mash all the solids through the mesh, finally rinsing out the bucket. This was not a job for anyone with a queasy stomach or if you'd had a rough night before. The two men carrying the bucket had to move fast and some of the contents would invariably slop over their trouser legs. They couldn't dawdle or they would not have had time to wash and shave.

'Routine in the companies was governed by whistle calls. One blast on the whistle and everyone stood still. A second blast meant that all prisoners stood outside their rooms and on the third blast they would form up as a company.'

The whistle calls carried on until the 1960s when Major Batchelder (then Second in Command) stopped it, together with the swearing that often went with the instructions. Many of the routines had simply been transferred from the civilian prison system; meals were called 'diets', charges against discipline were 'reports' and a soldier who wanted to see an officer would go 'on application'. This still continues today. Jim also remembers that no NCO would call another member of staff by his first name while on duty. If you were late for duty, even by just one minute, you would be locked out until the staff parade was over, automatically put on a charge, and taken in front of the Commandant.

After a while Jim was detailed to take over the main gate as relief NCO from Staff Sergeant Alec Pelling and recalls: 'The gate lodge was a little hut with just enough room for a bed, a desk and a chair. It had a wooden floor and a small iron stove that was permanently alight from September onwards.'

Jim also remembers that Pelling and another Staff Sergeant called Charlie Duthie devised their own shift system whereby they spent up to twenty-four hours in the hut at a time. 'Pelling seemed to alternate his time there with catching rabbits. His traps were set on the edge of the woodlands around the camp and he tried to collect his snared rabbits before Staff Sergeant McAndrews

Dent recording tell-tale clock – used by the MPSC – a way of making sure they checked on the detainees regularly during the night.

got them! These two were always arguing about whose rabbits were in the snares.'

They were not allowed to set snares. This was a perk of the Garrison Shooting Club, so it caused considerable trouble if they were caught by the garrison staff.

More memories from Jim:

'Another favourite task for new NCOs was to patrol the back wire just outside the compound. Often you would be forgotten and only when you realized how quiet the lines had become did you guess that the shift had gone to breakfast. There was no sympathy if you were late for your meals. Not that this seemed to be too big a loss as the meals were awful and as no one was prepared to pay extra messing charges we had to live on bare Army rations.

'Patrols and night watch meant pegging a tell-tale clock (a watchman's clock recording his rounds) which you carried with you. At various points around your beat there were brass pegs fitted to the wall. As you passed them you would insert the peg into the clock where it would register on a disc. At the end of your duty this disc would be removed from the clock by the CSM (Company Sergeant Major) and checked before you left the Company. You were in serious trouble if you missed any of the pegs.'

It wasn't only the detainees who looked for ways to beat the system. NCOs tried all sorts of ways to fiddle the clocks. Sometimes they had a spare key made out of a brass button stick and pegged the clock up for the night. This was fine unless the duty officer came in and checked the clock. It was difficult to explain at 0100 hours how your clock was pegged up to 0600! Some NCOs kept a spare set of pegs and others dropped the clock into a bucket of water which would turn the disc to pulp. They then blamed the rain! Dan Cowley:

'All of the gate lodge offices had two cabinets with double doors. One of these cabinets held the spare tell-tale clocks, clock keys, unrecorded clock discs and the carbon paper discs. I was intrigued to notice that some of the cabinets had had their hinge mandrels removed and the hinges "modified" by the use of a screw driver and some emery paper, then reassembled. This was done so that the mandrels could be removed from the doors and the doors opened without the padlock being undone.

'In some of the cabinets the locking bars had also been "modified" by removing the spot welds or rivets and replacing them with nuts and bolts. Removing the locking bar enabled both of the doors to be opened against the other hinges. This gave the night watch access to the clock accessories and other items and papers and, depending on their knowledge and ability, it was possible to fiddle the clocking system. My issue case key fitted one of the cabinet padlocks in D wing, but I kept this to myself and did not use it to fiddle the system. It was also possible to open the clocks with a paper clip. Sometimes a jewel case key was used by some with a little "modification".

'With the cabinet open and access to the clock accessories, it was possible to insert a further clock face and a carbon paper disc into the clock. This could be removed at the end of the night and substituted the following night for the new patrol disc. This meant there was no need to walk the lines and peg the clock, and possibly provided a few hours' sleep. With a doubled-staffed night duty it was possible to sleep alternate nights.

'Another ruse was for one of the staff to peg the clocks at the correct time by carrying the other clock alternatively. This removed the necessity of undoing the clocks and changing the clock patrol record disc. The following night the favour was returned by the other night-patrol staff. Sometimes one of the clocks was advanced by thirty minutes and both of the clocks were taken round at the same time. Again, the amount of rounds was decreased by half. In most of the night-watch clock fiddles it was necessary to have access to a nail file to secure the brass spinner disc against the built-in spring that rotated and cut the clock face record to show the time the clock was opened.

'I found a fiddle in D wing after the night watch had been reduced to one member of staff in each wing and a stand-by staff member

Colchester CWE 1953; Major Firmstone leading c1953.

sleeping in the main gate lodge. This was a unique method and only possible because the clock was worn in the key-pegging slot. The peg key could be inserted into the slot and moved from left to right for about half an inch. This enabled the key to be presented to the recording disc first to the right, and then to the left, giving two clocking times. There was a difference of about ten minutes which gave the impression that this time had passed between the two impressions. This allowed me to walk round the wing every thirty minutes and not every fifteen minutes. I got away with this a number of times. The last time I saw the tell-tale clock was on the penultimate night of a night watch in D wing after I had used it for six nights. On the last night I was presented with a "brand new just-out-of-the-box clock" with no play in the key way at all. I still think the WO II who was checking the clocking times did not understand the trick, but knew something was happening and that he was the fall guy.

'The same WO II had a method of catching out perpetrators of another con which involved collecting a full set of six pegging keys and seemed fool proof. A full set of keys was obtained from a store one at a time or when a unit was closing down, or by stealing them from the patrol route. The WO11 would select one of the key stations and rotate the pegging letter by ninety degrees. The next morning he would check that letter for its position. But he was so unpopular that all the night-watch staff were tipped off that he had changed a key station and which one it was. The retainers of the full sets of keys were old hands and they passed them on to a person of a reliable nature (depending how you looked at it) when they were de-mobbed. This gave the night watch the chance to sit at the gate lodge desk all night and to present the correct key at the appropriate time.

'An adaption of this was either removing all the keys from their stations on the first patrol and present them to the clock at the correct time, or just removing the out-of-the-way station keys. Both of these methods meant the keys were replaced on the last patrol in their correct station. I never used any of the "moved" or "retained" key tricks as the field officer's visits were so unpredictable and at times less than friendly. Few of them had a sense of humour.'

The Commandant at this time was Lieutenant Colonel Hose, and in 1952/53 a new uniform was introduced for ceremonial and formal occasions instead of battledress. No 1 Dress Uniform with its white pistol belts, holsters and cross belt was worn by a detachment of the MPSC when it marched in the Coronation Parade for Queen Elizabeth II. The badge was an old cipher of George VI.

There were visiting days for the SUS in the 1950s, but as few people had cars most would journey there by train and bus followed by a long walk up to the gate lodge. But not all visitors were poor. Some arrived in Bentleys and Jags, their occupants in mink coats and expensive jewels. In 1952 the Kray Twins spent a month in Colchester before being sentenced to nine months in Shepton Mallett and dismissal from the Armed Forces for breaking the jaw of a Corporal in the Royal Fusiliers.

Sgt Harry Knight by D Wing entrance 1952.

Chapter 7

'I couldn't hear myself think for all the shouting' 1952 – 1954

Douglas Corder was an RAF policeman in 1952-53:

'I escorted a Sergeant to Colchester under close arrest. His crime was the misappropriation of funds for which he received fifty-six days and was reduced in the ranks. I sat in the back with the prisoner all the way from Bedford. As we arrived in Essex I decided to stop at Braintree to see my parents, while the other soldier took the detainee to a cafe on the Coggleshall road, so he could have at least one good meal before arriving at Colchester.

'On arrival at the grim place I could see rows of Nissen huts and a nasty-looking man standing at the gate who barked at us to back the truck right up to the gate. The prisoner was made to double in with his kitbag above his head and once inside the reception area I couldn't hear myself think for all the shouting. The prisoner was made to empty everything out of his pockets while the member of staff tipped all his stuff from his bag all over the floor so that it was ready for evening inspection. I definitely didn't want to go there again.'

Corporal Alan MacDonald was in the RAF police based in Germany. Michael Foot MP threatened to raise the issue in the Houses of Parliament after a complaint about his ill treatment of a prisoner in the field punishment unit in Wahn. This led to a series of courts martial and MacDonald was sentenced to six months in the MCE in Colchester amid media headlines about brutal guards. He immediately became a target of aggression from other SUS and within the first week he lost his remission.

Bob Johnson, 5 Corp Signals Regiment, did his National Service between

Coronation party 1953.

November 1952 and November 1954 and was based at Cherry Tree Camp in Colchester. He recalls: 'It was opposite the Cherry Tree Pub. On a couple of occasions a group of us would have to pick up coal and deliver it to the MCE which was about a mile away from our camp. It was a bleak and forbidding place, not somewhere you wanted to hang around for long; the detainees had to do everything to double time. On release some of the men would temporarily join our unit. They were dressed in their own regiment's uniform and their hair was very short.'

Jim Robinson was still a member of staff, but the unit was now very much understaffed so a new shift system was introduced. 'The early shift would start at 0620 and finish at 1630. The late shift would start at 0800 and finish at 1800, with patrols to provide cover during the evenings and mealtimes for the staff.'

Although the shift system provided maximum coverage throughout the day it left the staff short in the mornings and evenings and was very tiring.

Jim's posting to the Middle East had now come through, but staffing levels were so low that he was posted to A Company and directed to take training:

'Although the square was in the same area as it is now, it was just hard-packed rubble, clinker and ash covered in large pools of water. Trying to teach forty reluctant prisoners to drill in these conditions in the cold of a February morning was not easy and we often ended up bayonet fighting as that at least kept them warm. On drill the men who were awkward would try to test the instructor by various tricks. One was to drag their feet every fourth step. The SUS knew it would drive you mad. But the instructors were not beaten. They had to find something that gave the men no chance to have four consecutive paces. This was turnings on the march, carried out in quick succession. They were never too happy about this.'

Although to a certain extent isolated from the local community, the MCE could still be relied on to play its part when needed. The detainees were sent to clear up after a myxomatosis outbreak and, in January 1953, when the east coast was hit by terrible storms and the sea wall on Fingringhoe ranges was breached, one hundred SUS were sent to repair the breaks. No escapes were recorded on either occasion.

Jim was one of the NCOs on security duty at Fingringhoe. 'The wind and the weather were bitterly cold and we were ankle deep in mud. The filling and carrying of sand bags did not help. There was no protective clothing except for a few pairs of wellington boots. The prisoners used their ordinary issue boots. The gaps in the wall were enormous and took a lot of filling. Dropping the sandbags into that hole was akin to dropping peas one by one to fill a large bucket. The men worked long and hard on that sea wall. They were on double rations and a rum ration all the time they were at Fingringhoe and they needed them.'

This was not their only contribution as the MPSC also sent £30 to the Mayor of Colchester for the National Fund that had been set up to help those displaced or bereaved by the devastation.

Another task for NCOs in A Company was to supervise parties of sentenced soldiers delivering coal to the married quarters. It appears the troops and their families were not high on the list of priorities then, any more than they are now, and Jim recalls: 'It was a dirty job! We collected the coal from a yard in the garrison where it had to be shovelled on to the back of a three-ton truck. It was of poor quality, consisting mainly of dust, and was issued by the tub full. Often NCOs or their wives would ask me to slip in an extra tub which I would normally do. It was of such poor quality that they needed extra to find some lumps in it.'

Brian Sutton was in the RAF police between 1953 and 1955. He describes Colchester MCE:

'... a grim and depressing place. In early 1954, I and an RAF police colleague had the misfortune to have to take a prisoner there who had been sentenced by court martial to 112 days detention. We were driven by one of our unit's duty drivers and on arrival were admitted through

56

the main gate by the soldier on guard duty and told to park on the roadside just inside the barrier. It was about then that I, and I think the other RAF Corporal and our prisoner, were somewhat dismayed by what we saw.

'It was indeed a forbidding place, much more like a prison than a military establishment. The boundary wall was topped with shards of glass and barbed wired. Not for nothing was it known as the 'Glasshouse'. It was not until much later that I learned the buildings had been used as a prisoner of war camp during the Second World War. I explained who we were and why we were there. The soldier told us to get out of the car and stand against the wall of the guardroom and wait.

'He reached across and pressed a bell push. A couple of minutes or so passed and then, some 100 or so yards down the road, another soldier appeared, pace stick under his arm, and yelled at us. "'Shun. Left turn, double time. Lef oit, lef oit, lef oit. Pick 'em up", etc, until we were level with him. "Mark time, 'alt".

'We then saw he was a Warrant Officer II, a Company Sergeant Major in the Royal Military Police, a redcap. We were mere Corporals and Royal Air Force police at that, but maybe he treated all escorts and their prisoners similarly. In any case it was clear that he did not like "Snowdrops". He asked where the papers relating to prisoner's sentence were, why he wasn't handcuffed, why his boots weren't as well polished as ours and when had he last had a haircut. He shouted his questions at us. We later had a laugh at the thought of having to double march with a prisoner handcuffed to us and him carrying his kitbag etc, and so realized that at least some of the CSM's style was put on for effect.

'Our prisoner was doubled away. The Sergeant Major told us to wait where we were until he dismissed us and then went into the building. We waited and waited and then he re-appeared. At that stage we wondered if it was just the unfortunate airman who was starting a spell of detention or whether we were to be incarcerated. This brown-job b****cked us up down and round the houses before doubling us back to the guardroom and our waiting vehicle. Were we pleased to get away from MCE Colchester! I do remember that when our prisoner returned to our unit he told of the "everything done at the double" philosophy with much bawling and shouting. We knew what he meant; we had experienced it.'

In 1954 Malcolm Wilson[14] spent his seventeenth birthday in MCE Colchester after being arrested for hitting a military policeman on St Patrick's Day:

'I was sentenced to fifty-six days and escorted across London through the underground in handcuffs. Arriving with my kitbag handcuffed to me, I was made to "double" to reception. Here I was made to strip and then "doubled" to the Company Commander who told me what to expect. From here I "doubled" to what would be my home for the next few weeks, a Nissen hut with wooden beds, mattresses known as biscuits, hospital corners and a board on top of the mattress.

'I remember having to bull my boots and put my kit away. I was then locked up over night with just a bucket for toiletry requirements. My first meal was some soup with bits of cabbage floating in it.

'In the morning I was woken by the sound of the screws running their batons down the side of the huts. Washing was done in cold water, then our kit was laid out on the bed for inspection and if it wasn't good enough a screw would take hold of a corner of the blanket and tip it all over the floor. We had to scrub off our own Blanco and put on the MCE Blanco which was very greasy, and we used Brasso to clean and polish our belt brasses and webbing. When inspection was over we began the day's physical training which was very hard.

'Breakfast was eggs floating in grease, and lunch every day was cobs of bread with tapioca. I didn't like tapioca so I gave it to one of the other lads who used it to spread on his bread to make a sandwich. I also remember the one cigarette we were given after lunch and that there was not enough time to smoke it before it was doused out in a bucket of water with the screws counting the butts. I remember too, the screws checking hair cream and the pockets of our battle dress for bits of tobacco that might have fallen out of cigarettes.

'Then there was more kit cleaning. The place was full of men who didn't want to do National Service and things were often so bad they had to separate the Scots and Irish from the English to stop them ganging up on the English. One of the punishments was to make us scrub six-foot tables with toothbrushes and other small brushes. At other times screws would hit people with batons. However, those with longer sentences had radios in their huts which we could just hear in the distance. I earned two days' remission and my abiding memory of Colchester was that it was the roughest place I've ever been. You were always hungry, so hungry you would eat anything, any scraps you could find.'

'J.E.P', an SUS serving two years for fraud, contempt of court and perjury, wrote to the *Journal of The Military Provost Staff Corps* in the Spring of 1955 and his 'Conducted Tour of the Military Corrective Establishment, Colchester' appears in full on page six. Here is a small part of it:

'Here then are the notorious half gates. They are now just high enough to deter any of the more adventurous of the "guests" from walking straight out and just low enough to deprive any of the heavy sleepers among the staff of the excuse that they were "locked out". This gentlemen, is the Old Oak Tree, the heated moisture below which is an accumulation of rain, emptied fire buckets and apprehensive perspiration … We are now passing the rear of the establishment with the fine contemporary style incinerators on our left and the most attractive barbed wire to our right…

'The staff, Sir? Quite a good crowd doing a not-too-pleasant job quite capably. The very nature of their work is not conducive generally to good humour and pleasantness.'

Wally Reeve joined the MPSC in 1953:

'My parents' home was visited by the civilian police who wanted to know if I had led a blameless life; rather funny as he had known me for twenty-odd years and lived three doors away! I first saw the MCTC in 1953 when I arrived to do the course for transfer to the MPSC. There seemed to be nothing but barbed wire and I wondered what I had let myself in for. Once the course was completed I was posted to A wing. The first morning after check and unlock there was a wild stampede by the prisoners to the bottom of the line where they washed and shaved in cold water in the open. The usual job for the newest member of staff was patrolling the bottom wire where the men tended to try and climb over. A truly soul-destroying job in all weathers.'

In 1954 young Irishman Alan Donovan (17/21 Lancers) also spent some time in Colchester for being AWOL:

'I joined the Army in 1952 because I was unable to find work, but soon found the constant drilling and discipline at odds with my free spirit. So, when I went on fourteen days' leave, I travelled home to Ireland where, back with all my old pals and with dances to go to, the idea of going back to England didn't seem quite so attractive. After some time working on a stud farm I was bored and decided to hand myself in. I caught the boat back to Liverpool and tried to hand myself into a lone policeman at the dock gates who, having been on duty all night, told me to "f…k off". I eventually went to a war office building and handed myself in there.

'After two months in Catterick Garrison Guardhouse with eight men to a cell, wooden beds and nothing to do, I had my court martial. I was initially charged with desertion. But as I had handed myself in, the charge was lessened to AWOL and I was sent to Colchester.

'I was told what it was like by my mates in the regiment. They told me what to try and smuggle into the nick. I had flints hidden in the cork of my water bottle; twenty cigarettes were smuggled in by breaking them up and scattering them amongst various pockets. When I was searched they did not find everything.

'I arrived at the nick wearing every bit of Army issue kit on my back like a bloody camel. I was shouted at to mark time and had to do so quite fast for about ten minutes. Marching, even walking, had to be at a fast pace. It was like a time warp with barbed wire everywhere. A long, paved path ran down between two pre-war huts and at the end was a row of toilets. There were no doors in case you hanged yourself. One prisoner decided to masturbate during his first couple of hours and was put on a charge of abusing the Queen's property!

'Another prisoner in a queue for lunch bent down to stroke a cat and was put on a charge for communicating with a cat on parade.

'One time I laid out my kit for daily inspection on my bed which was covered with a regulation green blanket. As I passed by the bed I brushed against it, putting a wrinkle in the blanket. I was charged with having an untidy bed and I had my mattress withdrawn for seven days. This meant sleeping on bare bedsprings.

'While doing "present arms drill" I moved two of my fingers together to improve my circulation. The screw spotted the movement and I was charged with being idle on parade. The punishment was seven days demolishing a brick wall and stacking the bricks. Then I had to break the bricks in half with a hammer and smash even more to make rubble and spread them to fill holes in the square. This punishment was carried out after you had done all your other things such as assault course and rifle drill.

'Even after all this time I still remember the daily routine. At 0630 you got out of bed, washed and shaved in cold water (one blade a week). You then made up your bed which consisted of every piece of equipment you were issued with and this was inspected every day. Then you had breakfast which was porridge made with water and salt to flavour it, a quarter of a loaf of bread, a small knob of butter and a mug of Army tea laced with bromide[15]. Prison food stank and resembled pig swill. You dreamt of food but thanks to bromide you couldn't dream of sex!

'After breakfast you went back to your hut. We all had various jobs to do before going out to be counted. Then came drill, infantry training etc. It was repetitive, but by God, you became a super-fit soldier. I swear if told to do so I could have walked up a wall, across a ceiling and down the other side!'

Like most SUS, past and present, Alan spent considerable time working out ways to beat the system:

'I remember having two cigarettes per day, one at lunchtime and one at teatime. You had to drop your dog end into a bucket of water, watched by a screw. My mate and I devised a scheme to smuggle a whole fag back to our cell. When it was my time to give the cigarette back I was taken to one side to be stripped naked. I had hidden the cigarette in one of my gaiters. The screw didn't find anything, but as he tossed the gaiter back to me it struck the edge of the table and out it fell onto the ground! I was put on a charge, lost seven days' remission and had to scrub the paving stones in between the huts. You had to fill a bucket with cold water, get a scrubbing brush and a rag and you scrubbed all day, even in the rain. If you allowed the water to get too dirty the screw kicked the bucket over and you had to dry it up. I was also put on RD 2 reduced rations and bread and water. After that I decided to register as a non-smoker!'

Colchester Officers c.1954.

The stage system was in operation and Alan was upgraded to Stage 2. This meant he was able to go out and deliver coal to the married quarters in Colchester. 'We filled sacks with coal, loaded them onto Army trucks and delivered house to house. On the way I picked up the dog ends and put them in my pocket. At dinner time I would go to the toilet, remove my boots, pack the shredded cigarette ends into toilet paper and push them tightly into the toes of my boots. Having declared myself a non-smoker I was taking a big risk, but although we were searched again after we showered before entering back into the MCTC, they never found my cigarettes.'

Having smuggled his cigarettes back in, Alan's next problem was how to light them as he had no access to lighters or matches. 'We all had polish brushes and used a razor blade to cut a 'v' shape in one end. We used our needles to make a hole in the centre of this into which we forced a smuggled flint. We then shaved fluff off our battledress, put it carefully in the top of a polish tin and took the lid off a tin of Brasso. The top half of a tin of Brasso had methylated spirits in it so by using a piece of grass or straw you could drop a tiny amount of the spirit on the fluff. Then, by carefully making a spark by flicking the razor blade on the flint, you got a flame to light your fag. This took two people. The brush with the flint in it was called a 'ticker' and had to be kept hidden or the whole room would be on a charge.'

Interestingly, and perhaps worryingly, Alan had to sign the Official Secrets Act before he was released.

The MCE was not just for detaining those who had been sentenced. In 1955 Sergeant Major Emmett-Dunn was found guilty of the murder of Sergeant Walters whom he believed was having an affair with his wife. The sergeant was found hanging from the bannister rail of the stairwell in Block 2 of Glamorgan Barracks in Germany. Although it was initially presumed to be suicide, persistent rumours, plus Emmett-Dunn's later marriage to Walters's widow, led to the case being reopened in 1954. Arrested in England and returned to Germany for the court martial, Emmett-Dunn was sentenced to death. However, there was no capital punishment in West Germany, and he could not be brought back to England to hang, so the sentence was commuted to life. Emmett-Dunn was taken under military escort to MCE Colchester where he was discharged from the Army and handed over to the civil police who took him to Exeter Prison. This process has changed little over the years and anyone who is dismissed before being sent to civilian prison still comes through Colchester to be discharged before being handed over to civilian authorities.

Chapter 8

'Everything at the double' 1955 – 1957

Wally Reeve returned to Colchester in January 1955:

'I went to work in the singles block with Bash Vernon in charge. I remember we had Emmett-Dunn passing in for a while before he went back to Germany for trial. One thing I do recall is cycling back to my quarter after night duty and going through the fields just before the Maypole and picking mushrooms for breakfast.

'Escapes were common in those days and residents in the neighbourhood must have got used to all the staff on their bikes haring round the countryside. In the 1950s every SUS who was placed in the singles block was handcuffed before leaving the block. I remember one day taking an SUS to appear before the Board of Visitors. When we marched him into the room the major in charge ordered me to take off the handcuffs. After checking with the RSM I removed the handcuffs and marched the SUS back into the room. As soon as I halted him he turned to face the table, grabbed it and upended it. The officer was covered in ink and was not amused. Needless to say the cuffs were replaced and the SUS faced a further charge!'

Wally recalls one attempted escape with amusement. 'Another day in the "singles" the gate was open because it was being painted by an SUS under supervision of a member of staff. Another SUS was being moved from one block to another and as soon as he came out he took off. I don't know whether he was ever entered for the Olympics but he cleared both the SUS and the member of staff who was an ex Guardsman and at least six feet tall. The escape was unsuccessful as he was caught before he reached the fence.'

In the 1950s National Service was still compulsory which, as in earlier times, produced several conscientious objectors (CO). Many were incarcerated in Colchester. Wally remembers one in particular:

'When they were admitted and refused to wear uniform they were dressed in a canvas suit. One day I went to Receptions where a CO refused to wear his uniform. I ordered him to put a canvas suit on and he refused. I repeated the order twice more and he still refused. I therefore marched him from Receptions to the block in just his underpants and carrying a bible. You can imagine the laughter of the SUS on the drill square. He put the suit on in the block without any protest; he had made his point. I must admit I admired some of those people who had the courage of their convictions.'

Things were not always peaceful however and Wally recalls:

'Rarely a week went past without a rough house of one sort or another in the singles block. I was once on duty in B wing at dinner time and for some reason they took a dislike to the food. They all had tin plates in those days and suddenly the mess hall was full of flying plates. There were only two of us on duty in the hall so for a time it was quite hectic. Then again, in those days, it was an accepted hazard. But it was not all doom and gloom. One day we dressed an SUS in a canvas suit and sent him to pick all the blackberries on the bushes round the singles block. These were then shared among the prisoners and staff.'

'Nobby' a bugler from 1st Battalion Durham Light Infantry, spent eight months in Colchester in 1955. 'I loved it there and thought it was an excellent way of getting fit.' As a tough twenty year old he had already spent twenty-eight days in Bielefeld for hitting an RSM who had tried to cut in on his dance with a rather attractive lady:

'When the 1st and 2nd Battalions were merged and sent back to Barnard Castle I became the bugler for the Battalion. As part of my regimental duties I was sent to take part in the York Tattoo. However, we weren't due on until 2330, so me and my friend went to get some fish and chips. Unfortunately the fish and chip shop just happened to be next to the Racehorse Pub so we had a quick pint as well. When we arrived back I was put on a charge for being drunk which I wasn't and we were taken back to Cavalry Barracks where a Corporal told me to stand to attention.
'Thoroughly fed up by now I told him to 'f**k off' and when the Corporal put his hand on my shoulder I gave him a left hook! I then refused to double back to the guardroom. I spent the next two months waiting for my court martial and was then given eight months in Colchester. Having spent twenty-eight days in the detention facility in

Bielefeld where the beds were very hard, I was delighted to find that the beds in Colchester had mattresses and springs and you could fire live rounds on the firing range.'

Ray, a national Service Corporal with RAOC (Royal Army Ordnance Corp), escorted a prisoner to Colchester in early 1955:

'I remember that outside the main gate a white line was drawn and all vehicles had to stop there. After my credentials were checked the prisoner had to get out of the truck and we entered through the gate. The guard indicated the building that I should escort the prisoner to for induction (medical etc.) and we started walking towards said building. Suddenly a sergeant appeared who bellowed at us, "you two double, you don't walk in here". We both had to double to the induction building, the unfortunate prisoner carrying his FSMO. Once all the paperwork had been completed and I had a receipt for the prisoner I left the building and the same sergeant was waiting for me to tell me again to double to the gate to leave, which I was very glad to do!'

Patrick Leonard was an NCO in the Grenadier Guards and in charge of an escort party taking two guardsmen to Colchester. They had both been convicted of desertion and had been absent for some time. The party consisted of two other guardsmen and the prisoners were handcuffed to each other:

'We had to get across London via the underground when I nearly lost a prisoner and escort as the train shut its doors before we could all get on. Fortunately for me I managed to keep my NCO stripes as they were both waiting on the platform when we arrived via the next train.

'It was the middle of winter and freezing cold, and on arrival at Colchester the reception was as frosty as the weather and a very aggressive attitude by the prison officers was soon apparent. We went, in very quick time, to a very long and wide corrugated building where both prisoners were taken for a cold shower. Inside the building it was bare apart from several long tables down the centre and benches against each wall but some distance from the tables. When the prisoners returned they were almost nude and shivering in the unheated building. They were then required to complete an itemised kit check. I decided there and then that this was not a place for me and, as soon as I got the prison officer's signature on my paperwork, I removed myself from that environment as quick as possible.'

On 1 January 1956, all MCEs became known as Military Corrective Training Centres. Jim Robinson returned to Colchester after British troops withdrew from Egypt. He was posted to 50 MCE which closed down on 31 December 1955. Arriving back at Colchester Jim was initially detailed for a two-week weapon training cadre, but halfway through was sent to be a training instructor:

'Training then was a mixture of weapon training, drill and route marches. The marches were anything up to fifteen miles. My squad was on the ranges one day when I noticed that a different SUS to the one I had detailed was issuing ammunition. On stopping the firing I went to check and was met by a wall of silence. It dawned on me that one of the detainees had run off. We formed up ready to march back when I discovered two sets of equipment spare and it became obvious I had not lost one prisoner but two! I was charged with negligence for allowing two men to escape, but cleared of all charges during the subsequent Board of Inquiry.'

Jim explained to the Board that he was concentrating on safety as the men were using live ammunition. As a result it was recommended that in future an extra NCO should accompany all range parties to act as security, a practice that still continues.

Peter Hunt was in the RAF and was attached to the MCE in Colchester in 1956 for a month's training, prior to being posted to a Detention Unit in Germany:

'Day one at the D unit was an eye opener for new prisoners. Everything was done at the double. A good, short haircut, body and kit searched for prohibited items, money, cigarettes and tobacco concealed in their clothing. Ten shilling notes tightly folded make a very small item. A flint embedded in the end of a shoe brush together with Duroglit wadding (brass cleaner) could be used to make ignition to smoke a cigarette. There was no physical ill treatment but all orders by the staff were in a firm, loud voice, not a method favoured by the RAF contingent employed on their staff. It was maximum control throughout every twenty-four hours, which was the strongest part of the system.

'The occasional attempt to escape caused the escape alarm to be sounded which was well recognized by Colchester town folk. There was a building in the MCE known as the "Singles". Housed there were attempted escapees, recovered prisoners and those who refused to wear uniform – commonly referred to as "kit rippers". They would be dressed in a coarse material suit in the form of a strait jacket. Over the years I have met a number of ex MCE guests who endured the physical and mental treatment, but who survived without too many scars.

'Our billeting was no different to that of the prisoners except that we were not locked in at night. The food was awful compared to RAF standard and the latrine was a row of thunder boxes with privacy provided by a hessian curtain. Part of the course was voice training, which was standing opposite a fellow trainee and just bawling at each other.'

Tony Ford was a recruit who underwent training at Colchester in 1956. He recalls:

'Preparations were being made for the shooting competition on the ranges where marquees had been erected for the staff and spectators. I was on guard one night just before the competition when high winds devastated the marquees. Prisoners and guards were called in to re-erect them and tidy up after the storm. The marquees were put back in a line and four or so prisoners took the opportunity to abscond by running from the inside of one marquee through to the next whilst the prison guards stood watch outside. Quite how many got away or whether they were caught in good time I do not know.'

Corporal Grahame Barclay of 90 Signal Regiment Royal Signals was billeted next door to the MCE at Cherry Tree Camp:

'I was told by our SSM (Squadron Sergeant Major) that I had been chosen for escort duty at the Glasshouse next door so I had to make arrangements for the journey next day. I booked out a three-ton Bedford QL truck and selected six guys to accompany me for the escort duty. What a horrible dismal place it was. We were immediately jumped on by prison staff who were mainly staff sergeants. You addressed them as Staff. They didn't seem to realize we were not part of the establishment's residents and proceeded to give us a big dressing down and a detailed inspection.

'It certainly was a grim-looking place with inmates walking round in fatigues carrying buckets and wearing no ties, belts or laces in their boots. You could always tell if one was coming because they had to shuffle about to stop their boots coming off, but their boots were still immaculate like black mirrors as per the required turnout in military establishments of the time. While we were waiting in reception I seem to recall seeing a small holding cell where the staff were actually hosing down a troublesome inmate with a high pressure water hose.'

Finally collecting an assortment of prisoners they set off for Shepton Mallet in Somerset:

'Our route took us through London of course. All the prisoners were handcuffed together and were moaning about the cuffs hurting their wrists. They asked if I would give the order to release them for just a few minutes. No way was I going to allow that to happen! We were in a place called Whipps Cross and I gave orders to stop and let the guys relieve themselves. In those days there were quite a few public toilets about and we stopped at a semi-subterranean toilet under the pavement. It was one of those buildings where you could go down one side using the steps and walk up the other side. As our prisoners numbered eight the last guy going down to the toilets could actually see the first guy coming up the other side. This amused the escort guys no end and helped to ease a sombre situation.'

As previously mentioned, time spent in detention did not count as time served during National Service and Grahame remembers with amusement, 'There was one Scotsman that had served over five years because he had been in trouble and detained … a right hard man he thought he was … who was the silly boy there then?'

Much later in life Grahame returned to the MCTC as a Warrant Officer (WO1). 'One of the senior NCOs mentioned that all escort duties were now carried out by Military Police who were based in the camp where I had been with the Royal Signals. The reason for the change was because some Signal personnel on escort duties had inadvertently let prisoners escape while travelling through London!'

The Commandant in 1956 was Lieutenant Colonel J. McDonald of the KOSB (Kings Own Scottish Borderers). He was known as 'Big Jock' and as well as being remembered by Jim Robinson for 'putting the Corps on its feet' he also spent considerable time putting the camp in better order. He had re organized the training set-up in 1955 and later arranged the planting of the lime trees that line the road into the MCTC. After several requests for a new drill square had been turned down, he sent a picture of a dead seagull floating in the large pools of water there to District HQ and his request was granted.

Jim Robinson had now moved to the QMs office:

'One morning the escape alarm was sounded. Travelling towards Birch somewhere near the zoo, I spotted one of the two escapees hiding under a hedge about a quarter of a mile away. He was in a red PT vest so he could hardly be missed. The three of us jumped out of the car to give chase while the second in command drove off to raise the alarm. We climbed over the fence and set off across the field which had just been ploughed in an attempt to catch him, then after a couple of hundred yards I realized I was on my own. The others were well behind. I continued on and having crossed Olivers Lane caught up with the prisoner after a further quarter of a mile. By this time he had a big pick in his hand which he must have found on the way across the fields. He was also bigger than me – much bigger! Knowing that help would soon be coming I tried to back the SUS towards the lane. But he knew what I was doing and kept swinging the pick helve. It flew out of his hand when he hit me the second time so I was able to dive in and swap punches. By now we were both so tired we could not possibly have hurt each other.'

A police car then turned up and the police officers helped Jim and the other members of staff put the SUS in the car. 'We finally got him on the cell block of the MCTC, but on the way there he complained to the Commandant that he had been struck, not by me, but by someone else.'

This was considered to be a frivolous complaint for which the punishment was loss of fourteen days' remission and Punishment Diet No 1 (bread and water) for three days. The escapee and striking of a member of staff would be dealt with at a later date and the SUS eventually had another nine months added to his sentence. Afterwards he said to Jim: 'To think I was caught by a Welshman. They'll never believe me back home!' Peter Hornsey:

'I was called up for National Service in January 1956, went for training and then to Bicester. I was a prisoner at the camp twice. Once for 112 days, the next time for six months around 1957 and 1959. I was in the RAOC and went absent twice and was sent to the camp first in A wing and then in B wing. The prisoners were housed in Nissen huts and it was cold in winter. The food was pretty awful too and punishments were PD 1 and PD 2 - Punishment Diets. I remember PD2 (or may have been 1) when you are moved into C block and you get bread and water and that was all you had for however many days you were sentenced to. You could also be sent to C block. They were single cells for as many days as you're sentenced to, and not in the huts with other prisoners, so this was a kind of solitary I guess.

'But the main problem why so many went absent was, like me. they had left a good job earning about £5 weekly then all of a sudden were in the Army getting thirty shillings a week for two years. Ok, if it had been war time fair enough, but there I was at a vehicle park in the freezing winter and crawling under lorries to drain out the petrol and then someone else put it all back again. So many went absent to go home and earn some money as some had families.

'You could get jobs easy in them days and a lot more money than the Army was paying. In the Army we spent the days working on lorries and the evening cleaning boots and cleaning your kit, so little wonder some went absent.

'So to the actual Colchester. I went absent for six months, came back, got 112 days in Colchester, then back to my camp, went absent again for about four months and got six months in Colchester again. The first time I was in A wing, the second time in B wing. They treated you like you were sub-human. Food was nowhere near enough. We lived in Nissen huts and were locked up at weekends at about 1600. It was crazy treatment and we all used to say we were probably treated worse than when the war was on and they had German prisoners.

'The RSM was quite funny really. He was in the Guards and he was about 6ft 7ins.[16] On the parade ground he used to find a small stone on the ground and stand on it. We never knew quite why. Maybe he thought he needed another inch on his height. He would scream at us and his nickname was "Big Mary" as he had a shrill voice.

'The second time I was at Colchester me and four others decided we would never get out the Army as after that six months we all had to go back to our camps and serve the time over again. I joined in January 1956 and never got out until June 1959, so I finished up doing three and a half years instead of the usual two years so I never really gained much at all.

'One night we decided we had to do something so they would throw us out of the service. So we burnt all our kit. They watched through the door, but would not open it as it was a weekend and they had few staff on duty. The next day we refused to soldier and we were taken off to C block. We refused to march and just strolled over there. Eventually we got told we were to be sent to Shepton Mallet and would then be discharged from the Army. We "got our ticket" which means not having to go back to camp and serve more time. We just got a railway ticket after we served our sentence. I seem to remember they added some time to our six months, but we got out and back to civvy life and jobs again.

'There was a lot more to it of course. They threatened us with causing a mutiny as there was more than three of us, but we stuck to it and refused to soldier. If we hadn't done this we would have been back to where we were, so we just had to stick to it and they said we could get five years, but we got maybe an extra month or two.

'I went to Shepton Mallet in about April 1959. In March 1959 there had been a riot and some of the prisoners got three years for the rioting over food etc.

'So there you are. My National Service went from two years to three and a half, which was pretty silly of me, but then, when you're eighteen, you do not think too well about things.

'I would love to get in touch with some of the old crowd to see how life treated them when they got out and how they are now.'

By 1957 PT was a regular part of the MCTC training. The PT Staff at this time consisted of a WO1(SMI) APTC, WO2 (SMI) APTC, an RAF PT Sergeant, four MPSC Sergeants and eight Corporals. All marches and runs had to be timed to the minute and you could not be more than one minute early or late. In the evening the two companies would be trained for the Corps Weekend Display. B Company performed log exercises while C Company did straightforward PT exercises. One or two Stage 3 men put on a gymnastic display which was later performed at Colchester's Castle Park under floodlights and became the first military tattoo there.

With the men dressed in white and the equipment painted black, the effect was of the men jumping over nothing.

Recalls Jim Robinson, 'I was the idiot who remained on top of the box and was knocked off backwards. I often knocked my head on the side of the box during practice so it was no wonder I was never that keen on gymnastics!'

Gordon Davidson did his National Service in 1957. He initially joined 2 Royal Tank Regiment. But because he was colour blind he was transferred to the RASC (Royal Army Service Corps). He remembers escorting two men from Germany as second in command:

'One of the men was a clerk who had trained with me and while waiting for his court martial he somehow managed to get hold of some fat from the cookhouse and heated it in his billycan and then poured it over his foot. He was still limping when they took him to Colchester. He was released after two months because of his foot. I remember the Nissen huts with fencing all around and a sign in reception that read "It's easy to escape but harder when you come back."'

Chapter 9

'Quite harrowing'
1957 – 1960

In 1957 the training area was gradually improved and, needing some very long logs for a rope climbing area, the men decided to source a couple of trees from Friday Woods. Jim Robinson remembers:

'One day a couple of us went into the wood and chopped down the first one. We brought it back into camp and hid it, knowing quite well that the Lands people would notice it missing. We covered our tracks pretty well or so we thought. It took them a long while but they knew who was to blame and eventually discovered the tree concealed behind the church. They sent a bill to the Commandant for him to pay personally. He came to us afterwards and said: "If I have to pay for this tree then I want it sawn into logs for my fire." After that, any SUS excused PT would end up sawing this tree into logs.'

Dan Cowley retells the story of how MCTC's obstacle course was improved, thanks to some clever manoeuvering by the then Adjutant, Major Stan Chandler:

'Prior to Christmas 1957 the MCTC had been trying, without any visible success, to obtain a quantity of scaffolding to bring the obstacles in the training area up to a state of difficulty and proficiency. Like the MCTC, the other units were trying to decrease the numbers in detention over the Christmas period. Although the administration in the MCTC knew the rules, the administration in other units did not seem to. It so happened that during the last few working days before the holiday period, the Adjutant's phone rang and the Adjutant of a Royal Engineer Unit at RAF Stradishall, near Sudbury, requested that the MCTC take a seven-day SUS. The Adjutant refused as it was contrary to the rules and suggested he contact the Suffolk Regimental Depot at Bury St

Edmonds. As adjutants didn't have a lot to do, they passed the time in general jargon and it transpired that the Royal Engineer Unit was closing down, no longer to exist after Christmas.

'"Have you any scaffolding in the unit?" asked Major Chandler. He was told, "Tons of it". Said Chandler, "You let me have the scaffolding and I will take your seven-day man." And that is exactly what happened. When the SUS arrived the Commandant contacted the Adjutant to point out that he had contravened existing policy. But when it was pointed out why he had consented to take the SUS, the Commandant's comment was "Good one Stan". The SUS was at the main gate in no time, followed the next day by two ten-ton vehicles filled with scaffolding and all their fixing clamps.'

The assault course was also improved and had several new obstacles ending in a tunnel followed by a log over a pond. In the summer the detainees would deliberately fall off the log so that they could go and get changed, but strangely enough that didn't happen in the winter.

Those waiting for court martial or in safe custody also did battle PT every morning and sometimes there were upwards of twenty men. Recalls Jim Robinson, 'Whilst demonstrating an exercise one morning the SUS I was using suddenly pushed forward on me and took me to the ground. Then he started to bounce my head on the concrete slabs. It was only a few seconds before the security NCOs grabbed him. I had to give evidence against him at his Courts Martial.'

Roy Rogers of 1 Battalion Royal Ulster Rifles spent three months in Colchester in 1957:

'My main memories are of daily kit inspections with all the kit laid out on the bed, sheets and blankets having to be squared off, having to double everywhere and being shouted at to "get them knees up". It was also the time I was at my fittest because every day we trained on the assault course over the six-foot wall and fences, and through the second biggest scramble net in Europe with a twenty or thirty foot drop.

'After training like this on a daily basis I became rather over confident and the day before I was due to leave I decided to do a lap of honour. As I threw myself over the top and my feet landed on the ropes, for some reason I let go. I landed on the ground, winded and moaning and groaning. The duty Corporal fetched a ten-ton truck and took me to Colchester General Hospital with me screaming every time we went over a bump. The hospital did not bother to x-ray me and said I had just bruised my kidneys. Despite this I enjoyed my time there!'

John Belcher, of the Royal Army Ordnance Corps (RAOC), escorted a prisoner to Colchester in 1957, two days before he was due to be discharged after the end of his National Service:

'It was normal practice for those nearing the end of their National Service to try and grow their hair before they left and I was no different. A sergeant and I left Warwickshire with me handcuffed to his prisoner and headed towards Colchester. On arrival we saw people scrubbing the guardhouse with toothbrushes, but before I could really take that in I was shouted at because of the length of my hair and, to my horror, I was taken off to have a very short haircut! I can remember people shaking at the mention of Colchester. My lasting memory? That is was quite harrowing!'

Another recollection from Jim Robinson:

'I was working in B Company one weekend. My job was to stand at the back wire, just outside the showers, to make sure the men did not dawdle. One man came out very slowly. I told him to start running but he ignored me. I again told him to run. He turned and said, "You can't make me run". For some reason I started to run after him. He ran like mad, at the same time waving his arms in the air and shouting "you can't make me run". The SUS in Section 4, which was where the very hard nuts were kept, were in hysterics when they saw him running and shouting.'

The education section in the 1950s was very active. One young SUS, who came in unable to read or write, left having reached First Class Standard. However, Jim Robinson remembers that not all achieved this. 'One question from the Third Class Education Certificate in the 1950s was "Who was Queen Salote?" She was actually one of the visiting royalty at the Coronation of Queen Elizabeth. The answer given by one SUS was "Queen Salote is what we give the Queen. If we had a King it would be a King Salote!"'

Iain Stewart was a Royal Army Medical Corps Officer (RAMC) in October 1958. He was expecting to be posted somewhere exciting like Singapore, Hong Kong or Cyprus, so to say he was rather disappointed to be posted to Colchester was an understatement:

'I arrived at Colchester knowing next to nothing about MCTC. The very title sounded a bit intimidating – as indeed the place turned out to be for many of the unfortunate inmates. I was billeted in B-Officers' Mess,

74

Cavalry Barracks, with a large number of Roman Catholic padres who dominated the bar in the late evening. Each morning I reported to the Medical Centre, MCTC. There was a senior MO in charge and a visiting RAMC psychiatrist. I was given the task of early morning sick parades at around 0630 on occasions, and sometimes these were rather perfunctorily conducted in an old prison hut next to the charcoal burning stove. The patients marched in and out at the double by intimidating Lieutenant Corporals with canes under their arms. They looked like robotic clones.

'One of my other tasks was to visit the sinister C block. In this clanging steel compound were housed men, for example, who refused to wear the Queen's uniform and who refused to eat. The latter I tried my best to charm out of this useless exercise and do not know if I succeeded, although in my short time at MCTC I did not see any who came to any harm.

'The uniform-deniers were interesting because the authorities clothed them in ridiculous coarse canvas suits with locked steel collars at the neck. Some years later I saw a newspaper report about a question being raised in Parliament about these punitive suits and being *denied* by the Armed Forces Minister of the time.

'Most of the SUS during my short association with the MCTC were young men who did not want to be in the forces, and many just kept absconding after the Military Police bought them back to complete National Service. Some had been on the books for five years and still had eighteen months National Service to complete. A lot of them were seemingly tough northerners, including a rugby league player.'

Pete Thomas (BAOR from 1958 to 1964) was sentenced to 112 days in Colchester in Minden and reduced in rank in July 1958:

'We travelled through Germany and Holland by train under escort to the Hook of Holland and then took a troop ship to the UK. My first impression of Colchester Detention Centre (gulp) was the high fencing which looked like a prisoner of war camp. I jumped out of the vehicle and was immediately jumped on and double marched through the gates carrying every scrap of my equipment (my escort also had to double march).

'I got through reception, had a strip medical and was given denim clothing. Then it was on to a hut which had about sixteen beds in it. I was marched for a haircut and joined a queue of about thirty men. I waited my turn and was told "no sideburns" so they shaved off all my

Overhead view of the MCTC before the rebuild – probably not long after it opened.

hair up to about two inches above my ears leaving me looking like a monk or friar! I was then taken back to the billet, where most of us being new, began to unpack. All our other clothes were taken away at night leaving us only with pyjamas, three photos and plimsolls.

'The toilet in the billet was a large metal bucket stuck in a small alcove. You took it in turns to empty it in the morning. There was a bright ceiling light on all night.

'Reveille was at 0600 when you got up and stood by your beds and were then marched across to the ablutions and toilets. The toilets and bathrooms had no doors and you were constantly told by staff to get a move on. You were issued with a razor blade which you had to return. There were a few suicide attempts when I was there. You then picked up your clothing, doubled back to your billet and got ready for breakfast and parade. But you also had to box your blankets and lay out all equipment for inspection on your bed.

'Then it was off to have your food, which you guarded with your life. If you didn't, someone would take it from you. To this day I still tend to protect my plate! After breakfast, which used to be awful, it was back to the hut to stand by your bed and a member of staff would inspect you and have great fun tossing everything into the middle of the hut and giving you ten minutes to sort it out.

'After parade the whole centre would line up and march at the double to the square where you would do a period of PT then drill, then another period of PT and then drill, on and off all day. If you weren't quick enough you ended up running round the square with your rifle at arm's length in front of you.

'You stopped for thirty minutes to have your lunch and then were off for a five-mile march with an "eyes right" or "eyes left" to every pub we passed! Then it was back to the centre, a quick shower, back into denims and dinner.

'After dinner you did your washing, Blanco'd your equipment and bulled your boots. At about 1900 you were locked in, got ready for bed, wrote a letter which had to be read by the staff, your equipment was taken off you and you were locked in again. You killed time by telling stories, talking about your problems or just keeping quiet.

'At about 1930 they came round with a type of tea urn full of steaming hot food. It consisted of all the left-overs of every meal, so you had cornflakes, porridge, eggs, bacon, fish, bread, meat pies, vegetables, gravy, custard, apples, anything which was left. It was all mixed up and you dipped your tin mug in for your supper. Plenty of strange noises came from the huts at night.

'Volunteers were required for special jobs, such as cleaning out mains drains and sewers. It was a filthy job, but I did it several times, mainly for the extra pint of milk and shower you would get at the end of the day. Sometimes a member of staff would give you a sweet – lovely! Any disobedience ended up with you cutting grass with scissors or painting coal white.

'I played cricket for the Army in those days and I used to sign myself out, be picked up by Army transport, taken to the location to play the game, mixed and ate with the colonels and majors for a while and then went back to the Glasshouse and sign myself back in at night.

'Some staff were power crazy, but most were OK especially the RAF sergeants. Loyalty was also there in the Glasshouse and I made some good friends.

'Visiting times were horrific. Everything that was brought in for you was opened including packets of washing powder. Biscuits and chocolates you never saw again.

'On my release with thirty-five days remission for good behaviour, three of us were dropped at the railway station and the first thing we did was to empty the chocolate machine on the station and bloat ourselves out. Then we walked all over our kit! Sounds silly but it felt good!

'We were returned to our original units and carried on with our lives.

Within six weeks I was a full Corporal again and within a year I was married to my sweetheart who stuck by me while I was in Colchester. We are now in our fifty-third year of married life.'

Major (Retd) Patrick Graham was a sergeant in the RASC at the time he was posted to the MCE. He was a Clerk there for approximately two years in 1958:

'The MPSC were low in numbers but why was not explained as the MCTC Bielefeld in Germany had closed down. Senior NCOs were posted into Colchester from Army units to run the centre. I was in administration and was not involved with the detainees except all those other than the MPSC who worked on a set cycle and were required to help out on various duties during weekends every three weeks. All MPSC staff were Senior NCOs.

'The CO was a colonel from a Scottish regiment. His table was firmly secured to the floor. At the time there was a large enquiry going on within the War Office. The Colonel had to prepare a report which he dictated to me because I was a fast typist. I remember several problems with SUS including one father punching his son, saying: "If I can fight a war he can do National Service."

'We had a period of swallowing pins and needles which was eventually stopped by the hospital staff saying that one man was close to death (whether true or not I was not sure). After that, all who claimed to swallow had to eat cotton wool sandwiches.

'Cigarettes were rationed to three a day. Everything was done at a fast pace but running was illegal. Solitary was only given for specific crimes and two staff had to be present at all times with the inmates.

'One of the Infantry Sergeants lost two men from the barracks while teaching a group how to locate hidden soldiers. When he went to call them in they had vanished!'

George Henderson describes this in more detail:

'One incident that caused some amusement and alarm was when a fairly new member of staff took a group of SUS into Friday Woods to give them a camouflage lesson. He chose one SUS and told him to turn his back on the rest. They were told to go into the wood and conceal themselves and to stand up when he blew his whistle. After a short period he told his chosen soldier to turn around and try and point out the hidden men. I think he spotted one or two. Then he blew his whistle and told them to stand up. No one did; they had slipped out the back of the wood! The alarm was raised and over the next few days most were recaptured or gave themselves up. The member of staff had a quick move and no more trips into the woods with the prisoners took place!'

Major (Retd) L. W. Prescott was stationed in Colchester during 1958 and worked in the Military Court:

'Everyone had to do two years National Service, but time spent in detention did not count towards this. However, if the men were given imprisonment, they were sent to Shepton Mallet prison and given a dishonourable discharge at the end of their sentence. Those in detention in the MCTC used to try and get out by burning their kit and getting another court martial and a sentence of imprisonment.

'I can remember on one occasion reporting to the Adjutant of the MCE and being told to go to the singles block and tell the offending soldier that I had been appointed as his Defending Officer, to which he replied, "I don't want no f*****g defending officer. I want my MP to defend me." Whereupon the Provo sergeant pulled me out of the cell, slammed the door and said: "We've never had this one before".'

'I reported this to the Adjutant who, after consulting the *Manual of Military Law*, said that he could be represented by his MP, either as a friend of the accused or legally if he qualifies as Counsel. The Adjutant told me to go back and find out who his MP was. This turned out to be Bessie Braddock. The Adjutant wrote to her but she replied there was no way she would represent him and that he deserved all he got. Our opinion of Bessie Braddock went up enormously.

'I remember another time when there were two QARANC (Queen Alexander's Royal Army Nursing Corps) officers from the hospital as members of the Court under Instruction. The president's dislike of women was obvious when he told them to sit in the corner and keep quiet.

'One case of mine concerned a soldier who had escaped from MCE but been recaptured. On being asked if he had anything to say in mitigation the Defending Officer replied, "The soldier escaped because he was very worried about his mother who has remarried. Her new husband has a wooden leg which he regularly takes off and uses to beat his wife." The two QARANC officers burst into tears! I have never seen a court cleared so fast!

'If a soldier did escape most of them thought that being near the sea meant the best thing to do was steal a boat. When the alarm was raised the local police used to send a patrol car to wait at the edge of the

Causeway to West Mersea and within a few moments they were recaptured!

'When sentencing a soldier already under sentence the Court had to add on any unexpired sentence. To help the court the Prosecuting Officer (The Adjutant of MCE) used to give a statement to this effect. Once, just for the hell of it, I pointed out to the prosecutor that the statement was illegal and that if he submitted it I would object. In the event he did not submit it, the court forgot about the unexpired sentence and the soldier got just eight days for escaping. The Adjutant was not pleased with me!'

Roger Taylor was a trooper from 15/19 Kings Royal Hussars, stationed at the RAC (Royal Armoured Corps) Training centre in Bovington:

'I was asked to accompany a Corporal to Colchester to collect a detainee 'serving' there. His regiment (RTR-Royal Tank Regiment) required him back urgently as they were shortly to deploy to Akaba on the Red Sea and this man was apparently an outstanding tank driver. The Corporal was told in all sincerity by the RSM that if said detainee escaped he and I would be required, according to the *Manual of Military Law*, to complete his sentence. This was a load of bunkum but neither of us knew that. We were sent off with warrants for the rail journey, but no extra funds other than that left over from our weekly pay – in my case virtually nothing – and a two sandwich packed lunch.

'At the detention centre the Corporal went in with the paperwork to affect the detainee's release and I was told to wait outside the main gate on the public approach road. It was cold and windy and after some time I wanted a smoke. I had just had my first puff when an irate MPSC Staff Sergeant erupted out of the small door shouting obscenities, which was not unusual in those days. He marched me in double time a good half-mile down the road and almost out of sight of the gates where I had to wait until called forward.

'Eventually the Corporal reappeared and I ran back to the gates and was handcuffed to the detainee. We were then driven to Colchester railway station to catch the train to London and had a wait of about three hours. We were out of cigarettes and could barely scrape up enough for a cup of tea. My mother was luckily at home in New Cross when I phoned. I explained the situation and within an hour or so she arrived with a basket containing sandwiches and thermos flasks of soup and tea for the journey, and money for us to buy cigarettes and fill up at the Wimpey Bar before the train left.'

Another detainee from RASC in Minden Germany (BAOR) was there for three months in 1959. 'I remember huts with fourteen to sixteen men all using one bucket and our clothes being taken away at night to be locked up leaving us only our pyjamas. There were no doors on the toilets. We were issued with razor blades as and when needed, and one day we were being lined up when a captain asked if anyone there was from the RASC. When I said "yes" I was told to wash his car!'

Peter Mallet was chaplain at Colchester from 1957 to 1959. By then National Service was almost finished but there were still 450-500 detainees there. His wife Joan recalls:

'The Church was a Nissen hut just outside the perimeter fence. Though dedicated as a church, it was not open to the public or licensed for weddings. I remember my husband sticking his neck out and getting the reluctant agreement of the Commandant, Colonel Jock McLeod, to take one of the SUS (with no escort) to the Garrison Church in Colchester so he could marry his pregnant fiancée from the North of England, before returning to camp to complete his lengthy sentence.

'The bride's family and friends travelled down by coach and came to our house before the service, so the bride could change into her wedding dress. Most of the staff thought the groom was unlikely to return and would abscond. When my husband dropped him off after the ceremony and short family reception in the Garrison church hall, he deliberately left him across the road from the main gate and watched as the man banged on the door and shouted "let me in Staff!" I think a lot of people lost a lot of betting money!

'We used to go visiting on Sunday afternoons. A wing tended to be for first offenders serving short sentences. B wing was for those serving longer sentences, habitual reoffenders and old lags. It was interesting to chat to folk visiting their sons.'

Chapter 10

'Never again'
1960 – 1965

Jim Broadstock was a member of the MPSC from 1960-1969:

'My Probationer Course lasted six weeks with lots of drill, but a high eighty-seven per cent of those applying passed. I was then sent to A Wing where the shifts ran from 0620 to 1330 and from 1330 to 2000. The night shifts were from 2030 to 0630 and there was a seven-day rota. Detainees were housed in Nissen huts with concrete floors and a coke-burning stove in the middle. There were twelve beds and the men were locked up at 1930 and given mugs of soup at 2000. All clothes were taken away at lock-up and the detainees were left with just their pyjamas and slippers.

'When I first arrived there were 1,227 SUS, many of whom were Jehovah Witnesses who refused to wear uniforms. They were given camp suits which were thick canvas suits with a key that locked at the back. This rather barbaric treatment was stopped by parliament during my time there, as were the punishment diets of three days of bread and water. One punishment that did continue was the loss of mattress.

'The stage system was active then; Stage 1 SUS were locked in but those in Stage 2 were not. Stage 3 prisoners received ten shillings a week and were allowed to wander around the camp with minimal supervision. The days would begin at 0800 with training and weapons drill and at the weekends the men would do gardening. If it was wet they were allowed to watch films.

'The oak tree outside the CO's hut was something we will all remember as this was where we had to wait if we were in trouble! I spent the last three years at the centre in the kitchens where the food was not great, bland with little variety.

'My most memorable night there was one cold February when two inmates escaped and got stuck in the sewers and I had to rescue them.'

Liverpool Street Station in the 1960s through which many a prisoner and escort travelled on their way to the MCTC.

Wally Reeve recalls, 'We had an SUS in the early 1960s who had been sentenced to two years detention for selling ammunition in the Middle East. He protested his innocence and in the end was given leave to have his conviction reviewed by the Appeal Court. I, together with Sergeant Jack Train, escorted him to London for his appeal. At the end of his hearing the conviction and sentence were quashed and he was reinstated in his old rank of Sergeant.'

Barry Sillitoe was stationed at Cherry Tree Camp which was virtually next door to the MCTC. 'I was a Corporal draughtsman RE, serving with the Intelligence Section of Brigade Headquarters. My job every afternoon was to take sacks of classified waste in a Land Rover to the MCTC incinerator and burn every sheet by hand. I was always glad to get out of there. At the time I was branch secretary of SASRA (The Soldiers and Airmen Scripture Association) and the Scripture reader, a Mr Brockies, used to visit the MCTC at least once a week to speak with the SUS. The Commandant at the time was a devout Catholic and encouraged Mr Brockies to visit the lads undergoing sentence there.' Geoff Phillips:

'I had the pleasure of escorting an airman once and also saw three airmen from my unit pay a long visit. I met one several years later who testified that it was the best thing that ever happened to him.

'The escorts were treated like dogs. There was probably some rationale behind it, but I am not sure what it was. I was a junior NCO, but it counted for nothing. The guy I escorted was a former colleague, intelligent, well-educated and highly principled (which is the reason he was there). It totally broke him and he could not wait to leave the RAF.

'I had dealings with another airman whom I believe actually beat the regime. He acted totally thick and behaved as if he did not understand whatever orders he was given. For example, when ordered to double march, which as you probably know means virtually running at 240 paces per minute, he just took huge strides of about forty-eight inches at the normal pace! He lost his remission and sometime later he was sentenced to a further fifty-six days. Colchester refused to have him back......so he wasn't stupid!

'I also had very close dealings with a guy who was court martialled in Singapore for being gay. He committed a series of indecent assaults on sleeping airmen intending to get caught so that he could be ignominiously discharged. Spending 180 days at Colchester first seemed a rather extreme way of terminating your contract to me!'

Jim Robinson returned from Malaya in July 1962:
'We lived in Eight Acre Lane for about twelve months and were then moved to a new quarter on Lethe Grove. This was a new estate built by the Army with the intention of housing all the families from the MCTC.

St Michael's Church c.1960.

84

They had even fitted alarm bells in each quarter. As always, the people who designed the estate failed to do their homework and got the combination of two and three-bedroom houses wrong. As a result, they had to allocate most of the two-bedroom flats to other units and they were never able to use the alarm bells. Still, it was a good estate and the residents got along well together, despite reports in the local newspaper many years later.

'Our first move was to number ninety-seven. Number 97 had one resident shortly after we moved out. It was a Corporal in the ACC who was also based in the MCTC. He went out on the ranges and murdered his wife by strangling her with her own bra, then went off to work leaving his young child in bed. The next door neighbour reported the child in distress. The Corporal was contacted but claimed his wife was still in the house when he left. He ended up serving a life sentence.

'I went to work in what was now A wing. The wing Commander was, I think, a Major Rickord. As CQMS you dealt with all the usual tricks that soldiers attempted. The worst one was in winter when they would tear strips off the sheets to make handkerchiefs, and then claim that the sheet was torn on issue.

'Whilst I was acting as CQMS, the Army decided once more not to rebuild the MCTC, but to improve the buildings instead. All the huts were given new linings, hardboard instead of corrugated iron sheeting and strip lighting instead of bulkhead lights. The outsides were given a waterproof skin. WCs had already been fitted in the SUS accommodation, so by this time there was no need for latrine buckets. It was certainly a better system and more hygienic, but still primitive.'

One Northumberland Fusilier spent six months in Colchester in 1963:

'Colchester was all right but you didn't light the fire in case it got dirty and you had two cigs a day.

'I had a tinderbox and flint; the box was just an old tin with a bit of old duster. You then hit the flint with a razor blade to light your cigarette which would often only consist of grass cuttings and toilet paper. One of the worst parts was the morning inspection where you had to have all your kit laid out on the bed. If there was one thing out of place, or a bit of Blanco on it, they would tip it all on the floor. They would stand right in front of you and shout. You could smell the alcohol from the night before and it was often hard not to laugh as someone would always be standing behind them making faces.

'Although I had some laughs, there were also more serious things such as a friend I made there, an ex-borstal boy. He had been given the option of joining the Army or going to prison. He ended up in the block for three days on bread and water and had to wear a strait jacket over his underwear which had horsehair inside.

'Church was every Sunday and for those who opted out there would be fatigues. Delousing also took place regularly with the men lined up at the back of the hut, stripped naked and standing in a star shape. I can remember one lad from Blackpool arrived with lice and it spread like wild fire. There were two escapes while I was there despite the ten-foot barbed wire fence that surrounded the camp. At the time I was in Colchester I remember a proud Staff Sergeant who was always immaculately dressed. He had been captured in Burma and tortured so he had trouble pronouncing his words which often caused the men to laugh whilst on parade, even though they had considerable respect for him.'

John Corley:

'I was called up into the RASC just two weeks before the end of National Service. I was even more unfortunate as I then had my time extended to two and a half years because of the Cuban Missile Crisis. I escorted a prisoner there for a six-month stay in 1963. I took him across London from a small camp in Framington near Barnstaple in Devon. I didn't use handcuffs for the journey and found myself treated exactly like the prisoner on arrival. In this case the prisoner, who was from an Irish Regiment, had asked to go to his own barber for a haircut as there were no barbers on the camp. He was given permission, went to London and went AWOL for two years, eventually handing himself in at the Guards Depot in London.

'I also remember hearing about two matelots who were sentenced abroad and then given train warrants and told to go to Colchester. It would be fascinating to know if they ever turned up!'

Gerry White was an RAF Policeman in 1963, stationed in Dishforth in Yorkshire:

'An airman absentee from the unit was the subject of an investigation into a homosexual relationship with another airman from RAF station Church Fenton.[17] During the enquiry, he went absent without leave (AWOL) to Dublin. The Irish Police, the Guarda, arrested the airman and he was placed into Mount Joy prison, in Dublin. RAF police from

Bisley Staff & School Cup c1962.

RAF Aldergrove in Northern Ireland provided an escort and the absconder was returned to Dishforth. The Commanding Officer awarded twenty-eight days detention to be served according to Queen's regulations at the Military Corrective Training Establishment (MCTE) at Colchester.

'I was detailed with an airman of the same rank as the airman concerned. It was Senior Air Craftsman. I should add I was a Corporal. A railway warrant for the airman under sentence (AUS, as they were called) and escort, was provided together with seating on the train. On arrival at the MCTE we reported to a wooden hut, a short distance from the main gate. A telephone in the box rang. I answered and a voice said, "Bring the airman to the main gate". We duly reported, the gate opened and we were all escorted into a guardroom.

'A sergeant asked for the live airman certificate, which he signed and returned to me. Our AUS was then ordered to empty his kit onto the floor, whereupon the sergeant kicked it all over the place and ordered the AUS to pick it up. We waited until the kit was checked off against a kit list. The airman escort and I marched smartly back to the gate and the outside.

'Just twenty-eight days later, armed with appropriate travel warrants and the same airman escort, we reported to the MCTC to charge our AUS with the offence of having buggery with the airman from Church Fenton. When I read out the charge, the releasing officer, a WO, confided to me that our man had definite feminine tendencies and was not surprised he was being re-arrested.

'The smartness and improvement in drill and deportment was obvious as we escorted our airman in close arrest awaiting trial by court martial, back to RAF Dishforth. The MCTC had earned its name of the "Glasshouse". I was quite impressed with the conduct and training of the staff, there.'

In March 1964 Roger Tucker was a young Detective Constable in the Oxford City Police:

'At approximately 0100 two men in civilian clothes bought a third man, very drunk into the police station. The duo stated they were military police from the Army Depot in Bicester Oxfordshire. They stated they had arrested the drunk, a private in the Pioneer Corps, at Oxford Railway Station. The drunk was placed in the cells to await escort back to the barracks. I was suspicious, military police not in uniform? When the prisoner sobered up he said that his watch, lighter and wallet had gone missing. I searched the "MPs" and recovered his property. They were charged with robbery and bailed to appear at Oxfordshire Assizes. Meanwhile, the victim had become a prisoner at the Glasshouse detention barracks in Colchester. He was bought to court under escort by the Military Provost Staff Corps. They were shorthanded so I agreed to take him back.

'We went by train to Colchester and taxi to the detention barracks. The gate guard directed us to reception on the far side of the drill square which was about the size of a football pitch. For appearance sake I had handcuffed the prisoner and despite his pleas and protests set off diagonally across the square.

'A sergeant, all of 5ft 4ins, with a cap and a slashed peak over his nose, appeared. Screaming like a maniac he doubled us across. At this time the CID diet was best bitter, pork pie and too many ciggies during a sixteen-hour day. Out of breath, I obtained a body receipt and departed via a couple of pints in the Sergeants' Mess! The sergeant explained about the hallowed ground of the drill square and all was forgiven. I still tremble at the mention of Colchester today!'

Roger Ivermee was a driver with 1 Squadron based in Colchester from 1963 to 1966:

'I spent some time on driver detail at the MCTC which was virtually opposite our camp at Roman Way. This consisted of general transport duties of collection and delivery of various goods and on the odd occasion collecting prisoners from the main railway station.

'My first impression of the MCTC was how much it resembled a prisoner of war camp from the Second World War, and on entry to report for duty I was somewhat taken aback by the starkness of the place. I was soon aware that this was not a holiday camp from the manner in which the staff and SUS were behaving. Everything appeared to be carried out at the double. The camp itself, although very sparse and ancient, was immaculate.

'On my first visit I have to admit to being very apprehensive as I had heard stories from the other squaddies and it felt a bit like coming in through customs where you feel rather guilty, but haven't done anything wrong. I was actually welcomed and treated very well by the staff, albeit very formal as you would expect.

'Subsequent visits were fine and I was not bothered about working there again. I do recall collecting an escorted guardsman from the station and I made the mistake of helping him take his kitbag from the

Colchester escorting SUS Duty Staff Sgt John Bone MPSC.

tailboard of my truck. Big mistake and I was bawled out by the Staff who made him carry everything inside the reception centre. I was present in this office while he was being processed and I have never seen such activity and this guardsman was reduced to tears of frustration by the whole experience.

'There was also a square, corrugated iron compound within the camp which I was told was the solitary confinement area, but I never got to see it internally.

'I also remember removing all the horsehair mattresses and taking them up to Friday Woods and burning them. This was when the Army introduced the new Dunlopillo mattresses for all.

'I also remember a certain driver from my platoon from Birmingham who decided he no longer wished to remain in the Army and decided to take some drastic action to obtain his discharge as he did not have the funds to purchase his discharge in the normal fashion. Despite our reservations and protests he came up with the idea that if he went continually AWOL the Army would eventually discharge him. He embarked on this course of action and was soon serving seven days in our detention barracks. On completion he went AWOL again. He did this on several occasions, eventually ending up in MCTC. He persisted in this course of action for several months and eventually was granted a discharge from service.'

Jim Robinson was still on B wing in late 1965 and early 1966 when Shepton Mallett started to close down:

'Those soldiers sentenced to jail went to civilian prison and those sentenced to discharge were now dispatched to Colchester. It was decided that B wing should take them on a temporary basis until more permanent arrangements could be worked out. This gave considerable boost to wing numbers, but there was no corresponding increase in the number of staff! The wing had to perform as normal and yet keep the discharged men occupied. Often thirty to forty men were locked up in their rooms until staff were available to take them out on their jobs. I was often in trouble for this and was told I should have got staff from other wings, something I always tried to do, but normally without success.'

Mike Barry:

'I escorted prisoners on a couple of occasions. Escorts, one NCO and soldier, were either sent by train or by vehicle to MCTC. We were allowed to take over a train compartment after reporting to the RTO at the station and as designated by the RTO of that time. (Not sure what would happen today by train.) On arrival at MCTC we had to double with the prisoner to a reception area were we had to sign him over with his personal items and kit to the staff member.

'The prisoner was met by noisy staff and doubled away to an inner reception area out of our sight. Once we had signed over we departed quickly.

'I have spoken to soldiers who have been in MCTC and they tell me that at the inner reception area they had to stand to attention and await instructions. This could be from five to fifteen minutes. Then the shouting commenced with stripping, inspection by a medical person, a shower and the issue of clothes to wear, all at the double. The next stage was being taken to the area where a SUS was to be berthed/bedded down.'

Trevor Barlow spent twenty-eight days in Colchester in 1965. 'I lost a stone in weight while I was there. We were only given two cigarettes a day, one in the morning and one in the afternoon and they would count all the butts afterwards. The stoves in the huts were cast iron so we didn't light them in case they got dirty. We were locked away at 1700 and would drink water from the toilet cistern if we were thirsty in the night. There was one escape while I was there. The unfortunate man was caught in Clacton, but while he was missing we were all locked down. I remember being woken at 0500 and working until 2030 some nights. Some men ended up in hospital after only eighteen days.'

Neville Paddy:

'I was a regular in The Life Guards back in the 1950s and then joined the prison service where I served twenty-seven years. As an officer at Aylesbury YP Prison in 1960 to 1963, I had the duty on two occasions to escort a young prisoner/Army deserter to Colchester Military Prison after serving their civilian prison sentence. This was an exception as National Service soldiers who deserted during their service, committed criminal offences and faced Criminal Court sentences, were more often than not court martialled and discharged from further service. However, there were exceptions to the rule when it involved the committing of serious military offences while serving as a soldier.

'Those serving twelve months and under often served their sentence at Colchester, and sometimes due to character and progress reports etc. would continue to serve in the Army. Those serving longer sentences in civil prisons would be discharged from the Army either by court martial or with their services no longer required.

'Colchester's reputation as being a hard place put many off committing crime and having to go there. Young offenders used to comment about "Bloody Colchester", even though they had never set foot inside the place or served in the armed forces. They would pick up stories and rumours from other inmates who had served sentences there.

'When I went there on the escorts, I found its discipline very severe and greatly leaning towards the physical side of all punishments. Everything was done at treble time marching, doubling or constantly marking time. There was always a considerable amount of screaming and shouting at the offenders by the NCOs. There was, by far, more discipline than at the prison service's detention centres, of which Aylesbury Detention Centre, next door to the YP Prison, was considered to be one of the hardest by its detainees.

'It really was the case that when we got the prisoner into Colchester all that was required was a body and a property receipt duly signed. The prisoner was whisked away very smartly and we were treated well by the Army NCOs. In fact, on the occasions I was there, the escort was invited to retire to the mess for a cup of tea and a wad. I and most of the prison service were used to military service life. I had served as a regular in The Life Guards 3 Troop – Household Cavalry Mounted Squadrons at Knightsbridge Barracks. Sometimes when performing barrack guards at Knightsbridge, I and another trooper were ordered to accompany the then duty Humber driver – a Guards NCO – to collect guardsmen who had been arrested for desertion from London police stations. We were to escort them to the guards prison at Scotland Yard. Now that really was a frightening place to behold. If my memory serves me right, it was located somewhere beneath the Scotland Yard buildings. Anyone who was unfortunate enough to be taken there really weren't allowed to let their feet touch its holy ground.

'I remember two drunken sailors being there for molesting the Queens Mounted Guard at Whitehall by shoving ice cream down the top of his jack boots. One was lucky not to have been decapitated, for the LG trooper brought his sword down upon the sailor and knocked him to the ground. I believe they were arrested by off-duty guardsmen in uniform and taken over the road to Scotland Yard. During the same evening I was part of an escort handing over two Irish guardsmen who had been arrested by Richmond Police for fighting a gang of Teddy boys in Kew Gardens. The Admiralty Naval Police from Whitehall were there at the same time to collect the two sailors.

I know that I and the other part of the escort were relieved when let out of that place.'

Corps Weekend c1962-63 Colchester in the Ball Room.

Captain (Retd) D. Eeles MBE:

'I was an Army Catering Corps soldier and joined the Army in 1960. My first nine months were at Aldershot cookery school. I was posted to the military hospital in Nairobi and served in Kenya until 31 December 1963. Because I had been overseas for three years I had three months leave to come and was on leave to March 1964. I duly reported to Aldershot to hand in my tropical kit and get new issue for European theatre. I was called in by a very well-known and fierce RSM and he told me I was to go as escort to collect a prisoner from a police station in Hull and escort him to the MCTC in Colchester. This was unusual due to the fact that he was a civilian (albeit an Army deserter since 1944) who had not been sentenced by courts martial. It seems he had handed himself in to the police after working on trawlers for years without proper papers to enable pension etc.

'I and another Corporal were issued warrants and proceeded to Hull. We collected the prisoner and went by train to Colchester. The prisoner told us he had been wounded in the foot at Dunkirk and spent some weeks in hospital. He had been re-mustered and posted as an ACC cook to North Africa. He came home on leave in 1944 and then went AWOL as he was due to go out again to a battle area. He was a nice person and we were sorry to see the predicament he was in. On arrival at MCTC we reported to the guardroom and were met by a Sergeant Major and a drill Sergeant. We were all given a full kitbag and ordered to run two laps of

93

the parade square. We found this a problem but we were fit. The prisoner struggled to complete but eventually we all arrived back at guardroom. We signed him over and returned to base. The RSM told us he was discharged after thirty-six hours. He had been interviewed by RMP, signed his discharge, issued with a railway warrant and sent home.'

National Service finished in 1963 and the return to a professional Army encouraged changes at MCTC. It was now even more important to ensure the selection process for the staff reflected the changing nature of the recruits. All those applying to the Corps had to first send their documents to Sydney Harris. Sydney had arrived in the training wing in Colchester in 1960. By the time National Service ended he had the power to reject applications to the Corps on the application documents alone. If they were satisfactory they were interviewed and if they passed that they had to attend and pass a mandatory Probationers Course.

In 1964 Lieutenant Colonel Parker became Commandant and began to make changes. Detainees in A wing were now allowed to keep their night razors, table knives, pokers and floor bumpers in their rooms at night. However, detainees in B and D wings were still required to hand them in.

Alex Taylor, now editor of AVA Journal, *The Dhow*:

'I visited the centre in 1964, but only as an escort to a regimental boxer who was always going AWOL when he had to go to Germany because he was afraid of flying.

'We had driven all the way up from Yeovil in Somerset, me, a driver and an NCO (Corporal). When we reached the car park of the centre we got out and the Corporal decided that he would be a good fellow and assist the prisoner with his baggage. Wrong decision! The Colchester NCO said me and the driver should wait in the car park which we gladly did. The Corporal and his prisoner were shouted at by the prison NCO in a good military voice – in other words yelled at – and the last I saw of them was doubling away into the inner sanctum of the prison.

'When our NCO returned to our vehicle his words were something like, "Never again". I think he thought he was also going to be locked up!'

Gerry Phillips:

'I had the misfortune of spending eighty-four days at Colchester in 1964, something I am not proud of admitting, but in those days there seemed very little justice. I was in the RAF based at Little Rissington in the Cotswolds on my first tour out of doing an eighteen-month apprenticeship and was given the job of running the station post room. While on leave my replacement found a five-shilling postal order in a drawer and reported it. I pleaded innocence but was given the time anyway. I went on to spend twenty-four years in the RAF and reached the rank of Flight Sergeant and loved every minute of it, except Colchester.

'I remember arriving at the reception area in October 1964 and being escorted by two Corporals. It was freezing cold and I was petrified. Once signed in we were told to double quick march a quarter of a mile to where I was going to spend the next eighty-four days. The Corporals were horrified to learn they were expected to march Q/T too! We eventually got there only to be met by a hairy-arsed Staff Sergeant who screamed abuse at me before showing me my bed space and the lads who I would be living with. It was dark by now and there was no light in the toilet. It was depressing to say the least. The Nissen hut had one coal fire and eight beds. I didn't sleep that night and was woken at 0500 to be told to get outside and wash in ice cold water. As the winter progressed there was no water as it was frozen.

'Food was the only thing we looked forward to, especially lunch and dinner as this was when we were given the only two cigarettes of the day. For this we kept a small razor blade in our lapels and under the table you would see everybody that smoked cutting the cigarette in half to be smoked in our hut that night. We had to be careful as the cigarette had been lit by a screw and we had to hand in the butt before we left the mess hall. We did this by using toilet roll (the type used in those days was shiny) and we mixed the tobacco with (wait for it) blanket hair which we scraped off using our razor blade.

'I remember the mealtimes, especially when the CSM, who was a huge man, would come in and shout, "Any complaints?" There never was. Every day was much the same. We spent a lot of time drilling and weapon training. Many of the weapons were strange to me being a "blue job" as I was affectionately known. We were beasted until we dropped, had church parade every Sunday and received one letter a week which had been opened and read. We only had a pencil and one piece of paper to write on once a week. Maybe they thought we were spies?

'Did it do us any good? God knows. We were locked up, forgotten, brainwashed, a bit like a prisoner of war camp, barbed wire everywhere. I didn't want to go back.'

Another detainee recalls:

'While in Hohne in the middle 1960s I got 112 days for DD and did most of my time in Colly. In reception my escort was given a harder time than me and left a nervous wreck. A lad from our mob got six months. He pinched a stalwart from the tank park and motored down to Ostend. He tried to cross the Channel and got a couple of miles out but turned back and landed on a beach near Calais amongst all the Frog holidaymakers. He was quickly arrested by gendarmes but he made the headlines in most of the papers.'

The rigid rules were gradually beginning to relax. In 1965 Stage 2 detainees were allowed to watch selected TV programmes and were no longer locked in at night.

Perhaps more importantly the actions of one young man in 1965 bought about a much needed change in the law. A young airman who had served ten years in HM Forces, including two tours of Aden, applied to buy himself out. He had signed on at the age of fifteen for thirty years and now regretted that as he wanted to carry on with his education. His request was turned down because, according to Lynn Eldridge who later started a petition, his job was considered of value. An appeal was also refused. Deciding to take matters in his own hands

Colchester unit photo 1965.

the airman refused to obey orders, was court martialled and sent to Colchester.

The case attracted considerable media attention and Lynn Eldrige's petition in Edinburgh was supported by several people within the military who considered it an infringement of human rights and counter-productive to expect a boy of fifteen to sign a contract that effectively signed away the next thirty years of his life. Lynn Eldridge: 'The law was subsequently changed though to what extent this relied on publicity generated by the case I can't say.'

A television play appeared later that year in which a young recruit in a similar position finally commits suicide in desperation at being refused permission to leave the Forces in order to take up a place at university.

Chapter 11

'Bloody Red Caps!'
1966 – 1968

Billy Mitchell spent 112 days in Colchester in 1966. 'It was a tough place. Everything from your kitbag got emptied on to the floor and kicked about. They made what they called a wee man out of your pyjamas bottoms. Then you got doubled away to your wing and your hut. I was in B wing which was for second offenders, escapees. They took all your kit every night into another hut for the first three weeks. Your day was drill, PT, drill, PT, along with cleaning your kit and scrubbing floors. There was never a good word said to anybody.'

One escort recalls: 'I knew a couple (not SNCO) who were still shithouses when they came back from Colly. I acted as escort to a lad who had been caught trying to buy cannabis from an undercover copper. I got a nice cuppa off the staff after handing him over. Beforehand they marched me ragged.'

Sapper Barry Craig served five years with the Royal Engineers at 36 Regiment, Maidstone, Kent:

'I was due for posting to Aden but this was delayed slightly as I was required to attend a course at RSME Chatham. While this was arranged I was co-opted on to the regimental police and ordered to attend a Court Martial as an escort. The accused had been found guilty and sentenced to a term at Colchester Glasshouse. I was detailed to transport him there. It was a long and uncomfortable journey in a Humber armoured car with escorts carrying pick axe handles to deter any escape.

'Upon arrival we reported in and I asked for the location of the nearest toilet. I was approached by the largest and loudest sergeant I had ever seen who handed me this massive key more suited to the Tower of London, and promptly marched me there at the double. I protested I was the escort to no avail and was ordered off site never to return.'

Barry recalls with sadness:

'I visited Alrewas Arboretum to pay respects to my Army pal who was killed serving in Aden in June 1967. Prior to his posting there he had been charged with AWOL [again] and was told to choose court martial or a third posting to Aden. He chose the latter and died after running over a land mine. A sentence at Colchester would have saved his life.'

Jim Watters served in the Royal Army Service Corps:

'I entered Colchester on 6 April 1966, driving past those high metal gates with the initials MCTC. I was handed over by my escort to the Provost staff at the reception area where my belongings were separated. I only kept the gear that I required for my seventy-day term. We were immediately told that there was no rank, and that all the Provosts were to be called "staff".

'We were then escorted to the stores and issued with a black box in which to keep our stuff, a mattress, bedding and webbing. I was then taken to A wing, which, like all the others, was a compound of Nissen huts holding about ten men, with a solitary toilet at the back. The next morning after a bed check, I heard a loud voice shouting "get a wash" and everyone just charged out to the wash house, where we were expected to wash and shave in about thirty seconds. Then came the same voice shouting, "Get out". We got our knife, fork, spoon and mug and then "doubled" to the cookhouse for breakfast. After returning to the billet we prepared our bed spaces for morning inspection.

'If it was your first morning, you were taken on what was called "The Milk Run" when you saw the Padre and welfare officers. After this you joined the rest of your wing where, for the rest of the day – and every day thereafter – you had forty minutes of drill and forty minutes of PT.

'At lunchtime and teatime smokers were issued with a cigarette each. The staff collected the dog ends in a tin dish full of water. I never smoked myself thankfully, for at nights those who craved a smoke used to pluck the fluff off blankets and roll it in newspaper or any other kind of paper just to have a puff. At about 2000hrs, from Monday to Friday, the staff came to the billet door and ladled into your mug what they jokingly called soup, but which tasted more like cooking stock, but it was hot and we were hungry.

'At the weekends we got a treat and instead of "soup" we got a mug of cocoa made from water and no sugar. During the night a light would stay on. If you were thirsty you dipped your mug into the toilet cistern.

Children's Christmas party Colchester 1960 in the Ball Room.

'Anyone stepping out of line was told to "go sick" and the doctor examined them to ensure that they were fit for further punishment. Some were put on what was called RD1 or RD2 (restricted diets) which could include bread and water.

'Those who refused to soldier or who committed a serious breach, were sent to C block which was another compound where the infamous canvas suit had to be worn. Once a month we were shown a film which was usually a B-movie western, so any servicemen hoping to see some female flesh were bitterly disappointed. We squeezed toothpaste into spare denim buttons which we sucked like sweets during the film.

'Some of your other contributors may remember the PTI who was nicknamed "The Sadist," for his hard line when training. While men were hanging from the bars in the gym, he would walk up to those with hair on their chests – including me – and just pluck them out. He also made me laugh, especially when he ordered us to jump high into the air at the count of three, and then put his nose up to your ear and shout at the top of his voice, "Who told you to come down again?"

'Although the going was tough inside Colly and we spent endless hours bulling kit to the highest standard (even the coal burning stove that heated your billet during the night had to be polished until it gleamed) I found it quite enjoyable, probably because I was pretty fit when I went in, and even fitter and more disciplined when I left. But you were fully occupied every day, whereas sometimes in my own camp we would spend boring hours picking up litter and such. At the end of my confinement I earned twenty-three days remission for good behaviour, and was returned to my unit in Marchwood, Southampton, where I was put on the RP staff.'

Martin Hoare was sentenced to twenty-eight days in the MCTC in 1966:

'It would have been longer but I had been in the unit guardroom under close arrest for ten weeks waiting for the court martial and that time was taken into consideration. It was quite terrifying as I had heard many lurid tales of how tough life was in Colly. Two of our regimental police drove me there in a Land Rover. The booking-in process was completed efficiently and was less frightening than I had expected due to the very high level of professionalism of the staff.

'The accommodation consisted of huts with around twenty standard grey steel tubing beds in each. There was a black wooden locker at the foot of each bed and a solid fuel stove in the centre of the hut. The toilet was unusual because it had a low-level window next to it so that as you sat on it you could be seen from outside – a necessary device to counter any attempt at wrong doing such as smoking or suicide, both of which were forbidden.

'The intention at MCTC Colchester is simple – to turn bad soldiers back into good soldiers. To do that they start from scratch and it was just like going back to the beginning of basic training. Making the bed perfectly, cleaning the room immaculately and folding kit into a foot locker in an exactly prescribed layout. In an odd way it was quite comforting to me. Nothing was very difficult. You knew exactly what you were going to be doing for every minute of every day. The timetable was simple – get up, clean yourself and your room, march to breakfast, eat, march back, fall in outside, forty minutes of drill, ten minutes to change, forty minutes of PT, repeat until lunchtime. March to lunch, eat, march back, rest, then back to drill and PT until the evening meal. Smokers were allowed one cigarette after lunch and another after dinner. After the first week of just drill and PT more interesting training was added like arms drill and assault course work. All of this training was started from scratch, as if none of us were already soldiers.

'The atmosphere in the hut was great with a team spirit of us against the screws, although the screws were all excellent so there was no actual animosity at all. The way we got back at them was to be as good as possible to prove that we could take whatever they dished out which was never particularly difficult. It was simple, basic military training. It was very childish to think we were somehow "getting back" at them but I believe it was exactly what the staff were trying to achieve as it made us into a team. Pride in ourselves first and then in the Army. They were always addressed as "Staff" whatever rank they held. There was no bullying or cruelty, unlike my original basic training where there was quite a bit of both. The training to become a member of staff at Colchester must have been extremely good, and hopefully still is.

'I recall one lad who received a letter saying that a relation had died. He asked for leave to attend the funeral but was refused as it was not a close relative. He was very upset and the next day during PT, after a rocket from the Staff PT Corps Corporal, he ran away from the squad. The Corporal jumped on his bicycle and gave chase, cornering the lad among some buildings. The lad became violent and the Corporal picked up his bicycle and used it to trap him against a wall. Other staff arrived and took the lad in hand. The Corporal was later removed from Colly for using excessive violence, which seemed very harsh to the rest of us as he was a very good staff member. On reflection it was the best option as the story would quite likely have been distorted over time and the Corporal's authority could been undermined, or he may have faced repercussions from detainees later.

'MCTC Colchester did a lot for me and my memories of it are good ones. I wasn't a truly bad soldier and I don't think any of the detainees were either. The really bad ones would have been in civilian prison or discharged. We were recoverable. My sentence resulted from what even the courts martial described as a schoolboy prank, but it was against the rules. Colly was enjoyable. It was how basic training should have been with truly dedicated and highly skilled trainers.

'When I re-joined my regiment I was more of a soldier than before. I was also famous. Four of us had been involved in the incident that resulted in my CM. One man was discharged and the other two had not yet returned, so I got most of the "glory". Everywhere I went around the regiment I heard, "Aren't you that bloke that's just back from Colly? What was it like?"

'I remember going to the stores to try to beg a pair of socks, quite a difficult task in 1966. The store man wanted to hear about my escapade and was happy to hand over two brand-new pairs of socks while I told the tale. Many times I was invited to sit down and have a cup of tea and talk about Colly. It got me noticed, made me different and perhaps displayed spirit. It led to me being given more responsibility and certainly added enormously to my confidence and success from then on.

'I owe thanks to the other three men involved in the "crime", which incidentally would not be a crime outside of the Army. I would never have done it alone. It was because of the support of the group that it happened and it changed my life for the better.'

Stan Brown of 16/5 Queen's Royal Lancers was in Colchester a few months longer than Martin:

'We were both famous in our time as we went absent without leave while on a visit to Canada for training. I was away longer than Martin so got a longer sentence. I remember a few people shaving their greatcoats and smoking the bits in toilet paper. There used to be a sort of museum that displayed items people had tried to smuggle in. There were some very clever things.

'We didn't have showers in the 1960s, just four inches of tepid water in the bath. You had to get in the bath while it was running and a screw was standing outside shouting at you to hurry up. Five minutes from running the tap to out and dry. We had two baths a week, one on Sunday afternoon and one on Wednesday. A guard had the bath book and called your name and number when it was your turn and put a tick by your name.

'Getting to the next level, Stage 2 was an individual effort and only a few people every week made it. It was much easier to get down-graded. Restricted diet was the worst punishment, just bread and water, porridge and dry bread for breakfast. There were three stages, but only long-term men made stage three. There was the punishment block, C block, but there was no one in it while I was there, although there were lots of stories and rumours of canvas suits, hosepipes in the cell in the early hours, that sort of thing.'

Martin Bourke of 2nd Battalion Green Jackets (Kings Royal Rifle Corps) was stationed in Colchester. His widow, Jenny Bourke, recalls: 'Even when all he had to do was to take a message, he was made to double everywhere.'

Gareth Jaxon was in the MCTC in 1967. 'I was there for 154 days after being AWOL for the same amount of time. Although it was harsh I learnt a lot. I was in B wing and I have a lot of happy memories of my time there.'

Frank Bowron was neither a prisoner nor an escort:

'Although I was not at Colchester, either as staff or "customer", I have a story that perhaps illustrates the effectiveness of the regime employed

Colchester 1962 Annual Admin Inspection Parade. WO1 Ganner leads.

there. At RAF Waddington in 1967 we had an airman on Line Servicing Squadron that we called "Angry Frank" – his surname doesn't matter. Frank was determined to leave the RAF and pursue his budding career as a rock musician. He deserted the RAF by the simple means of no longer reporting for work and moved himself into the barrack block assigned to civilian working parties, leaving his uniforms behind in our barrack block. Wearing civilian clothes and with long hair, no one would have taken him for a serving RAF Senior Aircraftman. Three months later, when the RAF police eventually stopped watching his mother's house and discovered his true whereabouts, he was charged and sentenced to fifty-six days in Colchester.

'Arriving back from work one evening, I needed a light for a cigarette and wandered into one of the barrack rooms, where I found Angry Frank, freshly returned from Colchester, sitting on a bed. As I entered the room he sprang to attention. I asked him if he had a light and he shouted, "Yes Corporal!" and stamping his right foot behind his left, offered me his box of matches, stiff-armed at the present.

'At first I thought he was joking, but it was soon apparent that he was still under the effect of the disciplinary treatment he'd received in Colchester. It took quite a long time for this to wear off and he never did return to his rock star ambitions. In fact, two years later he was sent on a fitter's course after which he was promoted to Junior Technician. It seems to me that the regime employed at Colchester was very good at reforming bad characters, at least in this particular case.'

Richard Bennett was given six months:

'I arrived at Colchester on 18 January 1968. I was in the Royal Artillery. When I had done my time I was to be RTU (returned to unit). I was escorted to Colchester by two bombardiers. They were as nervous as I was because the staff at Colchester treat everyone in the same harsh way, prisoner or escort. If the escorts looked a mess they were told so in no uncertain terms.

'When we arrived at the gatehouse, me with a suitcase and kitbag, we were told to march to the time the Staff Sergeant called, which was more of a gallop. I could see the look of relief as my escorts left me and I made my way into Hell! After a few checks and a medical I was marched over to B wing, my home for the next four months. There were massive tin huts surrounded by a wire fence. I was shown to a billet and bed space and left to sort my kit out. The place was empty as it was mid-morning. Dinner time arrived and I met my roommates for the first time. There were all very friendly and there was no ill feeling at all. They put me in the picture.

'Mealtimes were strange. We were only allowed so much food a day, so it had to be rationed out. We were always starving. If you were a smoker you were allowed one fag a day at teatime. I've never smoked so it didn't bother me. It must have been hard for those who did smoke. When it was time for us to bed down we had to strip off and put our PJs on. Then we put our clothes onto a metal frame which we had to take to a different hut to be locked up overnight. If we were thirsty after lock-up, we got water by flushing the toilet and catching what we could before it hit the bowl. I kid you not.

'We were woken in the morning by "The Beast" as we called him, screaming at the windows and banging on the side of the tin hut. Once opened up we ran like hell down to the ablutions to wash and shave in cold water, to get our clothes, get ready for inspection, then breakfast. We had endless inspections, you name it, they inspected it!

'The regime was very physical. I remember running round country lanes with telegraph poles on our shoulders. It might have been January but we were never cold. There was endless drill instruction. They used to say all of the best drill instructors had done some time in Colchester and I can quite believe it.

'There were not only lads from the Army in Colchester. Navy and air force lads were naughty too. Friday night was haircut night whether you needed one or not. The barber had electric shears and it was a case of all off all the time. Those who were getting out asked him to go easy but it never worked. I think he got paid by the ton.

'Half way through my sentence I had settled into the routine, was as fit as a fiddle and was up to all the trick. One lunchtime my name was called out, so I leapt up (as you do) and was told to report to D wing after lunch. D wing is the discharge wing for those being chucked out. I was a bit puzzled, but on my arrival there I was told my CO did not want me back, so I was SNLR (services no longer required).

'D wing was not as harsh as B wing. There was still plenty of shouting and bawling, inspections and constant cleaning, but no drill or classroom work. I was given a job in the gardens which I hated. We were allowed to watch TV and even had a cup of cocoa before bed. We were well and truly spoilt. On Sundays we went to church parade wearing our No 2 uniforms.

'There were loads of different regiments in my hut, so one week I might go to church dressed as a sailor. I loved the Scottish No 2 Dress uniform with its tartan trousers and short jacket and wore that a few times. If we had been caught we could have been charged for attempting to escape but we didn't give a toss. There were plenty of laughs while getting ready. I had about six weeks left of my sentence when they made me a blue band meaning I could wander about the place.

'I was given a job in the gatehouse where I could swagger about and watch the new arrivals coming. I had to clean up after the night duty offices who slept in the gatehouse. I stripped the bed, put clean sheets on and took the dirty ones away. During the day I would make tea, constantly clean the floor and go to other parts of the camp with messages. The staff could have used the phone but why when they had me? They had a greenhouse and I was with the civvy gardener who gave me plants to look after. Sometimes as a treat I got to shift the piles of manure from one end of the plantation to the other, then, if it was a quiet day, put it back. All to get me ready for Civvy Street. I came from a shipbuilding background so it really helped.

'For some reason I developed a rash on the upper part of my body and was taken to the military hospital in Colchester where they kept me in. An officer from the prison came to see me and I had to sign a bit of paper to say I wouldn't run away. I had a great time as the nurses all felt sorry for me and the doctor said he would keep me in as long as he could. I still never found out what the rash was. I was discharged from hospital and a week later, on 9 May, I was no longer a gunner but was back to being a Mr.'

'Mac', a Royal Marine, escorted a prisoner to Colchester in 1968. He recalls:

'In 1968, at Stonehouse Barracks Plymouth, the Easter Rear Party called for volunteers to take a prisoner to Colchester. Me and a friend Nick volunteered on the basis that we would get a run ashore in London before reporting back to Plymouth. Usually Royal Marines went to Portsmouth Naval Detention Quarters, a place of foul reputation, but I recall there was either another enquiry into brutality going on or it was in the process of closing down. The prisoner, a Rhodesian, turned out to be a mate of ours and had been court martialled for absence. I think he got sixty days. We were dressed in No 2s, wore RP armbands and were equipped with truncheons and handcuffs. We had a compartment reserved on the train from Plymouth to Paddington and had strict orders not to let the prisoner out of the compartment. On arrival at Paddington we were to get the tube to Liverpool Street and catch a train to Colchester. At Colchester we were to call for transport to MCTC.

'As we had served together in Aden we decided to make the journey a memorable one for our mate. This involved pouring lots of beer down his throat and parading him through the train in handcuffs in an attempt to gain the sympathy of any young ladies who might respond to his predicament by offering their bodies to him. This ploy failed. We were quite happy by the time we reached London and enjoyed immensely our tube ride. We handcuffed our prisoner to the hand grips on the tube and stood next to him, growling at civilians and telling them to keep their distance as he was a very dangerous man. At Liverpool Street we decided to pop into "Dirty Dicks" for a farewell posset or two before proceeding to Colchester.

'We eventually boarded a Colly-bound train. Each of us were handcuffed to our, by now, quite happy "oppo". A couple of soldiers spoke to us on the train and when we said we were taking the prisoner to MCTC they gave us worried looks. Disembarking at Colly we discovered we had lost the telephone number we had been given for transport, but we managed to cadge a lift in a three-tonner outside the station. On arrival we brushed ourselves down, I picked up the prisoner's kitbag and we approached the entrance.

'A screaming skull of a Redcap Sergeant screamed at us. I was in trouble for carrying the prisoner's kitbag, we had not reported our arrival at the station, the prisoner looked drunk and we were not properly dressed for escort duty. When I pointed out to the officious falsetto-voiced pipsqueak that Royal Marines had a different order of dress from the Army, he went berserk threatening to charge me with insubordination. He grabbed our paper work, signed for the prisoner, called for an escort and proceeded to make us double mark time on the spot. Our prisoner was doubled away, kitbag over his shoulder, and we were subjected to a tirade of abuse. The sergeant then told us to dismiss. Marine drill is different from Army drill and we don't stamp our feet but he was unable to comprehend this simple fact. This provoked much more recrimination and foul language against us. We left on a nice note; he was going to report us to our unit for a list of various offences and misdemeanours.

'We eventually got back to Plymouth and duly had to report to the Sergeant Major. He waved a report in our faces and asked us what we had done to upset that paragon of military police virtue. We explained that it was all an inter-service misunderstanding about different dress, drill etc. The Sergeant Major smiled and asked, "Did you give X a good send off?" We told him we had and he binned the report with the comment, "Bloody Red Caps!"'

Chapter 12

'Don't let this bloke get away!'
1968 – 1970

Rod Rodway, ex 3rd Royal Green Jackets: 'It must have been in the late 1960s when I had the misfortune to be detailed to escort a prisoner from my battalion to the centre. I remember a formidable structure of concrete and barbwire and as I walked into the reception area I was immediately struck by a sense of depression and oppression. Although the staff were friendly enough to me, being of or above their rank, they instilled a sense of fear into me! It was only a visit of about twenty minutes, but I was really glad to get out of there and I certainly never wanted to return as an inmate!'

Harry Angier escorted two prisoners to Colchester:

'I have forgotten the exact year, but it was either 1967 or 1968 when I and another soldier were detailed to escort two prisoners from Germany to Colchester. We were due to go on a three-week leave to the UK when we were told but we were also informed we would gain two extra days leave. You don't argue with military orders!

'The two prisoners were well known to me as we all came from the same town in Wiltshire. They had spent quite a long time, on and off, in the guardroom within the barracks in Germany for constantly being bad boys. They were not being sent to Colchester because they were extremely naughty, but because they kept escaping from the guardroom. This earned them the nickname "The Great Houdinis" by the soldiers in the barracks. They went to Colchester in order to receive some severe discipline.

'We left the barracks one misty morning for Hanover Airport, handcuffed to the prisoners. The handcuffs came off once we were on board the plane, but were put back on once we landed at Gatwick Airport. The next mode of transport was a train from Gatwick to London. We stayed handcuffed together on the train as, although I knew them very well and sort of trusted them both, I thought it was too risky if one of them decided to run off suddenly. This would have resulted in our leave being cancelled, being sent back to Germany and being severely reprimanded.

'The prisoners had packed one very large suitcase between them as they lived in the same street in their home town. They requested that I look after it for them as they didn't want the contents falling into the wrong hands at Colchester. This I decided to do because I was sort of pally with them.

'We had been given orders to stop overnight in London and were to take the prisoners to Whitehall and hand them over to the Welsh Guards guardroom where we were to stay the night. As my parents were living in Dagenham, Essex, I asked if I could spend the night with them and also take my two suitcases to their house so that I wouldn't have to carry them to Colchester and back. The other suitcase of course, belonged to the prisoners, but I did not want the Welsh Guardsmen to know that. They granted my request after receiving forty cigarettes from me as they knew I would have plenty after returning from Germany.

'I spent the night at my parents' house and the next morning I left both suitcases there and returned to Whitehall to collect the prisoners. Handcuffed again we proceeded on the final leg of the journey from Liverpool Street station to Colchester where we were met by an escort and truck from the prison.

'Although we were the original escort from Germany and had done a very good job at getting these guys to Colchester, the military prison officers treated us with contempt and we were also shouted at occasionally.

'As I entered the prison the first thing I heard was the shouting as we were ushered towards the office for the final handing over of the prisoners. The prison at that time had many Nissen huts and it was around these that I saw squads of prisoners being bawled at and drilled. They came from all the services. The whole place had a sinister feel to it like it had its own secrets, and those in charge, from Officer down to NCOs seemed to be enjoying their task of disciplining the troops. No doubt they had some bad boys in there but I think the majority were in there for less serious reasons.

'The handover was dealt with quickly and the last time I saw those boys was when I glimpsed through the office window and saw them being chased in double time toward a hut.

'After some questioning by the officer in charge we were bawled at and told to go and wait at one of the huts until we had permission to leave the prison gates.

'I used to smoke in those days and the one thing that sticks in my mind is leaning up against the hut to have a cigarette and talking to my pal when a loud bellow came from two blocks away, "Stand up straight and put that bloody fag out." There on a push bike was a Sergeant Major who was going blue in face as he spat forth obscenities. Well, trouble was the last thing we wanted, so we hastily did as we were told and the Sergeant Major rode off.

'The time came when we could at last resume our leave and it was with relief when we finally left those gates. Never had I seen a more sinister and somewhat corrupt place. How those prisoners were treated inside is anybody's guess and I am certainly relieved that I sort of behaved myself while I served in the Army.

'I made my way to my parents' house in Dagenham, picked up the cases and made a hasty retreat to my home in Wiltshire. Two days later I handed the prisoners' suitcase over to the parents of one of them and related to them what I had seen and what their sons could expect to go through.

'Those two boys were kicked out of the regiment when they returned from Colchester. They are both now married with children and grandchildren.'

Jim Murray:

'I was from unit 1/DLI (Durham Light Infantry) which disbanded in 1968 and I had a year to decide where I wanted to go. I decided on the MCTC as I thought it would be a more settled lifestyle for my wife and daughters. I was a thirty-six-year-old recruiting sergeant and most of the others were Corporals who had been overlooked for promotion in their units. It was a basic course and I think we all passed. Being of the older staff I was posted to D wing.

'It was only a short time before I realized I had made a mistake. It was the most boring job I had ever had, counting heads in the morning, counting heads in the evening, counting heads at mealtimes, counting heads at wash times, and I told Major Milton that I felt more of a prisoner than a SUS.

'I was living in the mess at this time and really enjoyed the facilities and my comrades. On one weekend off I visited the pig farm and was disgusted at the way they were being kept. The Sergeant in charge said he didn't know much about them and didn't like the job. I had kept pigs before I joined the forces and he mentioned this to the CO and I was offered the Job. I organized an evening pig-husbandry course at Writtle

Agricultural College, followed by an artificial insemination course in Norfolk and then a basic slaughter course at the COOP Colchester. Within two years we had a top-quality herd of forty breeding sows and two boars producing 800 weaners per year. I had four blue bands to whom I taught the finer skills such as injecting iron and castrating, and four Stage 2 who carried out general labour such as mucking out.

'One day I gave a Polish man, Joseph Danilenko, a free load of manure. Over the years we became good friends. He told me that during the war he had run away from the Germans and joined the Brits. At the end of the war he was working with engineers clearing minefields at Mersea when he lifted an anti-personnel mine. The RE Staff Sergeant insisted he threw it over to him which he eventually did and it exploded and killed the NCO.

'Danilenko was thrown into the MCTC which, at that time, was full of German prisoners of war – his enemies. He spent two days with a QM's work party digging a great hole somewhere below where the kennels are now. A truck was loaded with new buckshee kit all preserve-wrapped. This included two brand new motorbikes with the same preserve wrapping. The hole was refilled and camouflaged over with turf and saplings.'

Captain Rod Leonard 42 Bde (NW and IOM) ACFA Regional Shooting Officer remembers an escort duty in 1968:

'In 1968 when I was twenty-one years old, I escorted the largest Jamaican soldier from 3 Royal Anglian Regiment stationed in Tidworth, by train, underground through London and on a further train journey to Colchester, where he was taken from the station by military police to the MCTC. Thankfully we got on well, but being handcuffed to him for the four-hour journey was to say the least, one of the most frightening things I did whilst serving as a regular soldier, despite having been wounded in action on a tour in Aden the previous year!'

Reg Lamb was an NCO in the RAF Police. He made several trips to Colchester from 1968-1971:

'On returning from a three-year tour in Cyprus I was posted to RAF Debden which housed an establishment known as D Unit, the RAF's Detention Unit. During my time on the staff we had to take any airmen sentenced to more than twenty-eight days to Colchester. We also had to go to airports to meet airmen coming back from overseas who had a sentence of more than twenty-eight days. I can remember that back then they were housed in Nissen huts, enclosed by high wire fences and we as escorts, had to double along with the prisoners until such time as the Staff signed for the prisoner.'

Bryan Morris Squadron Leader RAF (Retd) asked for contributions in the FPS Newsletter in February 2011 and kindly sent me this:

'In the 1960s I served with a Sergeant "Spud", in the Parachute Regiment who was attached to our RAF unit at Aldershot. He was a character never to be forgotten. From time to time he regaled us "crabs" with tales of his checkered and colourful career in the Paras. Two touched on a brief sojourn in MCTC Colchester.

'His first story went thus: "One of the activities to which we prisoners were assigned involved polishing rusty buckets with a tiny piece of wire-wool. Several hours a day were spent polishing the things inside and out. At the end of the day the now gleaming buckets were recovered by a screw who returned them from whence they came – a static water tank where all were submerged once more until they again became covered in rust. There appeared to be a never-ending supply of rusty buckets and an ever-diminishing stock of wire wool!"'

'Spud's second anecdote concerned the daily ration of a single cigarette to each of the smokers. "We were paraded in small groups and fell in in a single line. Each NCO in charge of a line handed out a cigarette to each individual in turn and lit it for him. When the end of the line had been reached, the NCO marched in quick time carrying a bucket of sand back to the first man in the line and promptly snatched what was left of the cigarette from his lips and stubbed it out in the sand. This "fag-snatching" was repeated until the end of the line was reached. Having a cigarette lit to having it snuffed out was very brief and there was no time at all to smoke it properly as there were only a few smokers. Consequently, in order to smoke as much tobacco and take in as much nicotine as possible, each man sucked as hard as possible to inhale mightily on his one and only fag of the day. This resulted in spinning eyeballs, loss of balance and feeling sick as a dog! It was an event to be eagerly anticipated day after day."'

Richard Hamilton:

'In the late 1960s I was tasked to be NCO escort for a prisoner from Gutersloh to Colchester. The other escort was a large gunner so the SUS was handcuffed to me! We flew RAF to Heathrow and took the train to London for an overnight stay in the Guards Brigade Cells in Whitehall. The SUS spent the evening pushing a heavy bumper up and down the corridor while the escort went out in No 2 Dress for fish and chips and a beer! Next day we caught the train to Colly and met a REME escort with his prisoner. The REME Corporal had lost the prisoner's documents so we vowed to stay away from them. There were two minibuses waiting at Colly station and we grabbed the first one and legged it to the Nick, where an enormous Staff Sergeant with a waxed moustache under a slashed peak shouted briefly until he realized we were smart and all accounted for! We escorts were put in a side room with a cuppa while the prisoner was marched off at a great rate of knots. Then we heard the fuss that ensued as the REME party arrived and confessed to having lost the paperwork. How we laughed, quietly, before creeping away, back to the minibus, onto the train, and home for a buckshee weekend at home!'

Benjamin Graham, an NCO in charge of the escort of a prisoner remembers:

'I received a very simple brief from my RSM – "Don't let this bloke get away. Get him to Colchester and get a signature for him!" In the mid-1960s the escort and I would go to the guardroom, sign for the live body of "Joe Bloggs", take him to the Land Rover and cuff him on. Sometimes the prisoner was handcuffed to the framework all the way to Colchester! I simply told the fellow that it was my job to bring him to the MCTC and that's what was going to happen.

'We would drive to the MCTC, hand the prisoner over (always with some measure of relief!) and get a receipt for him. Then we drove back to barracks, gave the receipt to the Provost Sergeant and the task was finished. Apart from the handcuffing I always treated the prisoner well. If we stopped for a coffee break I ensured he had one too. I really don't know how these fellows were treated in the MCTC. I never discussed it with them if or when they returned to the battalion. The fellow would not have been an associate of mine so I had no reason to chat with him afterwards.'

Alan Ford:

'I escorted two men to Colchester, both of whom had received six months detention plus a dishonourable discharge. "Brian" was a good and close friend and was victimised by a senior NCO who was, amongst

114

many things, a bully. One time Brian walked into the company office with a loaded rifle, pointed it above the NCO and opened fire. Alas, he missed and threw the rifle on the floor and walked away. He was arrested and was eventually court martialled.

'I escorted Brian to Colchester without worrying about him wanting to escape, but I did handcuff the other soldier to a roof rack in the train and to a Land Rover to and from the train. In the late 1960s Colchester was seen to be a bit of a rest camp compared to Shepton Mallet which certainly had a more frightening reputation. This would have made a much better story! On arrival the goons took over: strip search, clothes replaced with prison clothes, full medical and cropped haircut. My initial impression was of a very nice garden! After his release I did meet up with Brian and his view was very clear – the basic training at the guards' depot was significantly tougher than Colchester. The latter was no more than a holding centre with the maximum attendance being six months so the real challenge was to keep busy.'

Amanda Crampton recalls: 'My father Major John Crampton was the Welfare Officer in the late 1960s up to his retirement in 1974. He promoted a more humane approach to the SUS such as initiating and supporting family visits. He also arranged transport for wives and family from Colchester Station, not something that had happened before! He offered counselling, forged effective links with civilian social care and probation services and stopped the use of restraint. In 1973 he was awarded the MBE for his work at Colchester. Sadly he died in 1983.'

George Henderson, Sergeant, Royal Marines, served on the MCTC staff from July 1968 to August 1970. He was given a temporary home, a flat in Lethe Grove, Berechurch Hall Road:

'When we arrived I was very surprised when a Regimental Sergeant Major came to our door carrying a large tray with a pot of tea, cups and saucers and a selection of cakes. It was such a nice gesture from a member of the MCTC. This sort of kindness was to continue during my two years' service there.

'When I reported for duty I was included in a group of Sergeants and Corporals from different regiments and corps who were rebadging into the MCTC. The aim of the MCTC, under the guidance of the staff, is not to punish but to rehabilitate the soldiers under sentence and to return them as better men. The other newcomers and I were paraded in a large hall for the opening address by Camp Commandant, Lieutenant Colonel G. A. Coaker (Royal Artillery)

'I sat near the back and shortly after the address I felt a tap on my shoulder and was told to report to RSM P. Bunyan. As I made my way to his office I wondered what I had done wrong. I was invited in and told to take a seat. To my surprise he told me that he was short of staff and that Royal Marine Sergeants didn't need training in how to handle men. He told me to report to A wing.

'There were five wings which made up the MCTC. As well as the four other wings, E wing or "the block" as it was called, housed those who would not conform to discipline. This was surrounded by corrugated iron walls so that the men could not look out and they were segregated into separate cells.

'I reported to A wing and was paraded before Major David Livingstone, Royal Highland Fusiliers. He was a relative of Victorian missionary Sir David Livingstone and A wing Commander. The RSM was WO1 Jim Robinson.

'I joined a team led by WO2 J. Bourne, late Parachute Regiment and son of a Royal Marine RSM, so we hit it off straight away. Sergeant Sandy Sanderson was the wing clerk. Staff Sergeant Harry Parry was the wing CSM. The rest of the team were Staff Sergeant Harrigan, Staff Sergeant Harrison, Flight Sergeants Murray and "Paddy" O'Neil, Royal RAF. We worked a two-shift system: Week 1: 1300–1800 Monday to Friday, week 2: 0630–1630, Saturday and Sunday 0630–1745 with Monday to Friday and weekend off. The evening staff took over at 1800 and were relieved by the night staff at 2030.

'I was posted to MCTC to replace Sergeant *****.[18] He had been posted to MCTC straight from commanding a ship's detachment. He was a Platoon Weapons Instructor and wanted to get back to that and was determined to get out of MCTC so refused to take or give Army orders. He was in danger of getting himself into serious trouble as well as bringing the Royal Marines into disrepute.

'On my second morning I was in A wing gatehouse. We could see through the wire fence to the door of the Commandant's Office. Sergeant ***** was being marched into the office on a charge. The RSM had lined up the escort with him and one WO2 behind and one WO2 in front.

'The RSM gave the order, "By the front, quick march". The front WO2 shot off at 140 paces to the minute and Sergeant ***** stepped off at the Royal Marine pace of 120 paces per minute. The result was that the front WO2 disappeared into the office and the rear WO2 ended up stamping on the sergeant's heels. The RSM screamed at Sergeant *****. He continued at the marines' pace and entered the office.

116

Colchester A Wing on Training Parade; WO2 Gabbett MPSC.

'Inside, the two WO2s marked time at 140 paces to the minute while Sergeant***** came to halt and stood there. The RSM screamed at them to come out. Once again they were lined up and the RSM gave instructions on how he wanted the escort and accused to behave. They set off again and the same thing happened. The Commandant shouted, "Get him out of here". Sergeant ***** strolled out and that was the end of it. He left the MCTC that afternoon.

'Prisoners doing a long sentence could undertake advanced training and a six-mile run outside the camp. The run was under the control of the Regimental Physical Training Corporals with a member of MCTC staff in attendance for security. The staff member would collect a bicycle and a map of the route to be run. He also had a sixpenny coin to ring the camp from the nearest phone box should any of the men make a dash for freedom. This routine had gone on for years with no problems.

'Then one day a staff member was on his bike and shouting at the men at the rear to keep up. An old lady heard him and told him to get off his bike and run like the rest. He carried on and she complained to the Commandant. No action was taken but the woman contacted her MP and questions were asked in the House.

'As a result, bicycles were resigned to history and staff had to run the route with the prisoners. This meant they were as tired as the men and would take some time to reach the nearest phone box if the need arose. There was a rota of staff required for the runs and this caused a lot of trouble. There were a lot of staff nearing the end of their service who found it very difficult to keep up. The RAF staff had been posted in because of a shortage of Army personnel. The retirement age of the RAF was fifty-five years old. The RAF staff had been selected for the MCTC as they reached the end of their careers and most were in their fifties. They could not take their turn on the run. The RSM called for me

Commandant's Office and oak tree MCTC 1970.

and explained the situation. He said he could not make me do more than my share, but if I volunteered I could come in late in training uniform and go home afterwards to shower. I jumped at the chance as I would be keeping fit in their time and spending more time at home!

'One example of the problem with the RAF Staff was Flight Sergeant *****.[19] He was approaching fifty-five and nearing retirement. He had been a "tail-end Charlie", a rear gunner in Lancasters, flying over Germany in the war. He had a large beer belly and smoked a pipe. One day he was detailed to march a party of prisoners to the gym which was a fair distance. He decided to take a short cut across the parade ground. The men were required to march at 140 paces per minute and he couldn't keep up. So he would start them up and then halt them when they were some distance from him. He would then walk up to them smoking his pipe and start them off again. The training RSM saw him from the parade office and came out screaming at him to march the men properly. The RAF Flight Sergeant halted the party and replied that he was doing his best and if the RSM didn't like it he could do it himself. The RSM went red with rage but realized there was little he could do, although returning the flight sergeant to the RAF station would have suited him. He was never again given a party to march round the camp.'

Regimental dinners took place regularly and for George Henderson one in particular stands out. 'They were always grand and held at the Warrant Officers' and Sergeants' Mess. The one that stands out was the Burns Night Supper on Saturday, 25 January 1969. Staff Sergeant Jock *********[20] was chosen to pipe in the haggis and provide music for the Scottish reels and dances. He could be heard for weeks before the supper practising his bagpipes in Friday Woods. After we had dined, he drank deeply of the golden liquid. As the night went on he was found lying on the dance floor, still trying to play the pipes as the dancers went round him!'

By 1969, SUS in A and B wings who had reached Stage 3 were allowed three shillings a day, but their equivalent in D wing were still not allowed anything. However, trade courses had now been introduced and detainees were given the opportunity to attend half-day courses for fourteen days in motor maintenance, carpentry or brickwork. Civilian trade instructors had also been employed and, in 1969, painting and decorating was added to the list of courses.

Chapter 13

'I was left holding the baby while the newly-weds had half an hour together' 1970 – 1973

John E. Garner (Ex RAOC) remembers escorting prisoners on their way to Colchester:

'In May 1970 I was out in the field with 32 Heavy Regiment RA to which I was attached but was due to fly home to England before the end of the exercise. Just before I left to return to barracks I received a phone call informing me that I had been elected to act as an escort to some prisoners on their way from Germany to the military prison in Colchester and that I would have to travel in uniform. Well, you can imagine how that went down. I was not pleased.

'Back at barracks I went to the orderly room to find out what was what and was relieved to be told that my escort duties had been cancelled and I could proceed on leave as normal. I changed into civvies, grabbed my case and was off to the airport. When I arrived I checked in and settled down to await the flight. After a short while I became aware of a group of soldiers milling around on the opposite side of the room and that one of them kept looking at me. A feeling of apprehension descended upon me, a feeling not helped by the quick approach of the guy who had been looking at me.

'He asked me if I was Corporal Garner to which I replied, "Yes". I was then asked why I was not in uniform when I was due to escort some prisoners to Colchester. I gave him my version of events which turned out to be a cock-up by the orderly room and I found myself reluctantly crossing the room to join the group of soldiers I had earlier spotted.

'There appeared to be six prisoners, each attached to an escort, so I thought, "Oh well, at least I won't have to worry about the prisoners escaping or whatever." Silly me. After I formally identified myself, the escorts released their prisoners and I found myself signing for six live bodies who were handed over to me to look after on my own. I wasn't very chuffed about this turn of events. For one thing it meant delaying my journey home while I took these idiots to Colchester and, for another, it meant I would have to enter the military prison myself and I wasn't even in uniform. I thought that I would be lucky if I didn't end up in clink myself before the day was through. Then there was the horrible thought of what would happen if any of them decided to leg it on the way. Great start to my leave.

'Arriving at Luton I found a coach waiting to take us all to Colchester. We stopped at a cafe on the way for a bite to eat and a cup of tea. Naturally the guys wanted to use the toilet and I was on tenterhooks in case one of them made a run for it but they all behaved themselves and soon we were on our merry way.

'When we eventually arrived outside the main gate of the prison I was in a state of nerves having heard of its reputation and read about it. I wondered how I was going to fare with the staff who, as far as I knew, were all screaming and stamping at anything that moved or indeed didn't. As it turned out a Sergeant greeted me, accepted without any fuss my explanation for being out of uniform, and after signing for six live bodies was as nice as pie to me. Great relief. I can't say that he was quite so considerate towards the prisoners.

'Naturally nobody had any thoughts about me getting to London or had made arrangements. I did at last find a train to Manchester and went on leave.

'Thankfully that was my first and last appearance at the entrance to Colchester clink.'

There was often a lighter side to life in the MCTC. George Henderson:

'I had an unusual task given to me one day and that was to be a witness to a marriage between an SUS, an Irish Guardsman, and a Belfast girl, now a nurse in Leeds. They had a nine-month-old baby girl. The guardsman was a Protestant from Belfast and the bride was Roman Catholic from Belfast. Apart from the bride's sister who was also a nurse, their families had disowned them.

'The wedding took place in the MCTC church with the padre officiating. I acted as best man and signed the marriage certificate as a witness. After the ceremony the happy couple, padre, me, the bridesmaid and baby, went to a small room in the padre's office where a small wedding cake and soft drinks were provided. I was left holding the baby while the newly-weds had half an hour together.'

Geoff Thewlis (1097 Thewlis) of 1st Bn Prince of Wales's Own Regiment of Yorkshire 1967 – 1980, spent some time in Colchester in 1970:

'I was stationed in Cyprus after being in the Army for only three years. One night, me and two friends were out with our wives having a drink in a bar near Limassol. A Canadian chap came in worse for wear through drink and started telling everybody how the Yanks, along with the Canadians, had won the Second World War for England. After a while we left and went further into Limassol to another bar, only to be joined by this Canadian who again started spouting about the War. We left and he followed us outside, still shouting and carrying on, whereupon one of my mates hit him. Unbeknown to us, Mick took this man's wallet that had fallen out of his pocket.

'The next morning when we went into barracks the three of us were called into the RSM's office and he asked us individually if we had been drinking in town on the previous evening. We all answered "yes", whereupon three SIB (Special Investigation Branch) officers stepped up and arrested us. We were driven to the SIB HQ where we were interviewed and charged with robbery with violence and GBH. As I said before, me and Jerry knew nothing about Mick picking up the wallet. I was petrified. I was nineteen years old, had only been married for a year and my wife was expecting our first child. Now here I was facing two very serious charges.

'We were interviewed at length and then taken to our married quarters where the SIB asked for the clothes we had worn the night before. Blood was found on Mick's clothing, and that was all that they needed to charge all three of us.

'We went on CO's orders where we were remanded for court martial. After two days we were released from the battalion jail and told to await our trial. When we went on court martial we pleaded not guilty. Jerry, a Lance Corporal, was busted to private soldier, and all three of us were sentenced to an eight-month jail term each and a dishonourable discharge from the Army.

'We were flown back to the UK by RAF aircraft along with lots of other passengers from the RAF and Army who were all going on leave apart from us.

We were escorted onto the flight by RAF police who accompanied us all the way to Colchester. My wife had been flown home under medical evacuation because she was so far into her pregnancy.

'We were in D wing, the discharge wing, and had yellow tabs in our epaulets. Those in A, B and C wings had other colours in their epaulets.

'We were in ten-man cells which were old Nissen huts with bars on the windows. Unfortunately my bunk was next to the window the prison staff would bang on if one of the inmates had his head under the blankets (the lights were on all night) and I had to get out of bed and tell the lad to show himself because the Staff had to be able to see everybody's head. (That's what we had to address them as – "Yes Staff, no Staff, three bags full Staff.") They had to make sure there was a soldier in bed and not just pillows because the lad had escaped. Some chance.

'We had cell inspections every morning when the D wing Commander would walk round the beds and each inmate had to state his prisoner number, name and his EPDR (earliest possible date for release). If your block wasn't up to standard it all finished up on the floor along with everything else that was laid out on your bed. This included boot brushes which were sandpapered for effect, and a razor with the old Gillette '7 o'clock Blade'. Everything had to be immaculately clean, the towel had to be folded in a perfect square and numerous other items had to be laid out nice and neat. If it wasn't to the prison officer's liking, it all went wallop all over the floor. We also had what was called a "Soldier's Box" at the side of our bed and this too, had to be laid out very neat and tidy or be upturned onto the floor. Within the box we were allowed only three photos that were stuck to the inside of the lid.

'No matter where you went within the prison you were made to double march. It certainly kept you fit, the Durham Light Infantry had nothing on the speed that we were expected to move about at. I was certainly fitter and a lot slimmer than when I went in to the MCTC. Meals were collected from the cookhouse and then you had to walk about fifteen yards outside to the canteen to eat your meal – that's if the fat it had been cooked in hadn't congealed it too much. Breakfast was always solid. The food was terrible, honest.'

There may have been a reason why the food tasted so awful to the prisoners. Dan Cowley:

'During the middle 1970s it was discovered that a passable substitute for all forms of meat could be created from soya beans. The ratio was twenty-five per cent real meat to seventy-five per cent substitute. This did not detract from the accepted taste, texture and look of the dish, and lent itself particularly to mince recipes.

'The RAOC rationing depot issued a quantity of this soya substitute to most units on request, including the Military Corrective Training Centre. The soya was issued as a separate item and then mixed in the cookhouses. Detainees were employed to clean the wing kitchens and to prepare food and it did not take long for them to notice that the ration meat issue had changed. This passed relatively unnoticed in the three staff Messes but caused comment and disapproval in the cookhouses and lines accommodation .This was demonstrated during the Duty Field Officers' and the Duty Officers' inspections at mealtimes.

"Have you any complaints?"

"Yes there is something wrong with the meat."

'Nothing definite was ever said, only the inference that something was wrong with the prepared dish. Us staff knew what the problem was but were never asked. When they were investigated, all of the complaints were traced to dishes containing the soya substitute.

'Within a few weeks it disappeared from the ration store issues – either that or the mixing was carried out *before* the meat was issued to the wings. The original mistake had been getting the two items mixed together in the cookhouse.

'So, by a subtle form of complaining about a non-specific problem, the prisoners brought about a change in the strategy or the issuing of this item. Whether it was a cost-cutting idea or a good healthy substitute I do not know, but I know who came out on top. The now perfected meat substitute is sold under the trademark of "Quorn".'

Geoff Thewlis (1097 Thewlis):

'In prison I did a three-week decorator's course, a three-week mechanic's course and got a cushy job making coffee for the Staff on D wing. We had some civilians working on the wing doing some building work at the same time. I used to make these lads a drink and they would give me cigarettes, trouble for both of us if we were caught, but to be able to hide somewhere and smoke a cig without the Staff hanging round was heaven. I rolled cigarettes for the smokers in our cell but what they didn't know was that theirs were like matchsticks and mine were like cigars.

'The rest of the time was working in the Officers' and Sergeants' messes washing and scrubbing floors and walls. We had only been in the MCTC a couple of days when I was made to do some hoeing of the gardens near the main gate. I was looking over the road at Roman Barracks because it was where we were before being posted to Cyprus. One of the staff saw me looking across at the barracks and said: "Don't even think about it lad. This is a garrison town and you would be soon picked up if you escaped." Escaping hadn't even entered my mind because the wire and gate were far too high. I replied: "Oh, I know my way around Colchester because we were stationed over there in Roman Barracks before we went to Cyprus". His face was a picture, but I was taken back into D wing and ended up sweeping it. That taught me to keep my mouth shut.

'Every Sunday we had to attend the church within the camp, and as we were in D Wing we were always the last to be taken into the church. We were always in uniform. There we were with our yellow tabs in our epaulets and as we entered the church, the lads from the other wings were on the right hand side and D wing SUS were always seated on the left. We walked down the aisle and swaggered our shoulders at the other lads from the other wings to show them our yellow tabs signifying we were in the Discharge Wing and were not serving a prison sentence and then soldiering on ...'

D Wing Carol Singers led by Sgt Dave Chenier.

George Henderson also remembers church services:

'We often had guest preachers and once we had an Army Scripture Reader (ASR). He started to preach on the evils of drink and would shout, "How would you like it if your sister got drunk?" The inmates would shout back, "We would love it!" As the service went on so the noise level would rise until the RSM intervened and stopped it because he was concerned that things might get out of hand.

'On some Sunday afternoons several hundred SUS paraded on the gravel parade ground armed with their knives and forks and ordered on their knees. The order would be given to start weeding and the line would move forward, the direction controlled by the staff. Not one weed was left behind.

'Every Saturday and Sunday afternoon a barber came in to cut the detainees' hair. He had to cut around 500 over the two afternoons and was paid 6d per cut. To get through the large numbers he placed two chairs side by side and as he finished one he would switch straight to the other while another SUS took the empty chair. He also came in during the week to cut the hair of any new arrivals.'

Meanwhile Geoff Thewlis was looking forward to be discharged but he was about to get a shock:

'Having served three months, Mick decided to appeal against our sentence and it was reduced to six months and "soldier on". Me and Jerry were fuming at him. We had to go before the D wing Commander who informed us that as we only had about a month to serve now, we would finish our sentence in his wing. We were the first three soldiers to come out of D wing in uniform on our release.

'In October I was called in to see the D wing Commander. I knew exactly why. I had told my wife that when she was admitted into hospital to have our baby she was to ask her mother to send a telegram saying she had been admitted into hospital, but not the reason why. I was so naive that I thought I would get parole to go see my wife in Leeds. My mother-in-law duly sent the telegram which read, "Eileen admitted to hospital". The Commander asked if I knew why my wife was in hospital. I said "no", to which he replied, "We will get in touch with the police in Leeds to find out". Meanwhile I was to be locked in the wing. I think they feared I would try to escape. The police told the MCTC that my wife was pregnant and had got a water infection. I was kept locked up for three days. Two weeks later I was again called in to

126

the Commander's office who simply said: "I have a telegram from your mother this time and it reads, "Baby son born midnight. Both doing well." His next words were "lock him up" and there I was, back in the wing. My wife sent me a photo of our new son and the Staff asked me which of the three photos I had already would I give up in exchange for this one. Very kind eh!

'All incoming and outgoing mail was read by staff within the prison, so you couldn't write anything derogatory about the place or your letter wasn't sent. I can still see the one page sheet of paper that had the following at the top:

My name is............ my Number is........... and the EPDR (Earliest Possible Date of Release) .

'I still have some of the mail that I sent home. I actually managed to get a letter smuggled out by one of the lads who was having a visit from his wife which was very risky for both of us. But it was worth it to be able to write what I wanted.

'I didn't want my wife to travel from Leeds to Colchester to visit me because I saw the effect visits had on the other lads; they would be very morbid for a day or so after the visit, so I thought I would forgo that pain. I sent a letter saying she couldn't visit me on the Sunday because I was working in the Officers' Mess. I was then called into the Commander's office and reprimanded for saying we were working that day. He tore up the letter and I had to rewrite another one in front of him, saying the real reason why I didn't want my wife to come and see me.

'It was a tradition that on the morning of your release you stuck your head between the window and the bars and shouted "Good Morning Freedom" which was a well-known pop song of the time, but the staff would be watching for you doing it. It was also tradition to give your breakfast away on your last day, but hey, what a day that was, 21 December 1970. I will always remember it.

'We had to report to our depot in Strensall, York. We were given a travel warrant and after an interview with the wing Commander we were driven to Colchester Railway Station to catch a train to London where we would then get a train to York. In London we changed some Cypriot money for English pounds, shillings and pence. We had about £7 between us and bought cans of beer, After four and a half months without a drink, after two cans I was anybody's! We finally arrived at Strensall at about 12.30pm and went to the guardroom where the Guard Commander informed us that there was no bedding storeman available so he couldn't give us a room to sleep in. He told us we would have to sleep in the guardroom cells for the night. I won't tell you what we told him to do and where to go!'

In 1971 those in D wing were still not allowed any money. In an attempt to rectify this Lieutenant Colonel Gabb, the current Commandant, requested that the men be paid for the work they did in the same way that civil prisoners were paid. Nothing happened and the report died a death. Applications to join the Corps continued to flood in and in 1971 eighty-nine NCOs applied. Of these, forty-four were rejected before interview, fourteen failed the interview and nine withdrew their applications. This left twenty-two.

Night duties often caused problems for the staff. George Henderson:

'There were two night staff on duty in B wing due to the more volatile nature of the SUS there. The night duty staff officer would base himself there and the three would often play cards. They were the more senior members of the MCTC and had a spare set of keys so they would not have to leave the card school to use the marker key positioned in the wing. One night this went very wrong.

'When the morning staff came on duty and the roll was checked it was found to be two short. A check of the hut found that bricks had been removed from the corner toilet and a hole made enabling the two men to escape. Unfortunately for the night staff this was where the marker key had been and of course when the pegging clock was checked it showed the back of the toilet had been checked every fifteen minutes during the night!'

George Henderson also found himself carrying out some strange tasks:

'Near the Essex coast was a large marsh where returning Allied bombers ditched their bombs on their return from raids over Germany. Colchester Garrison had a wild fowl gun club and members used the marsh to shoot ducks and other fowl but the live bombs made it dangerous to go too far in. It was decided to open up the marsh and a party of Royal Engineers were tasked to clear paths through it and mark it with white tape. Jock and I and a party of SUS were to fence it off with six-foot steel picquets and barbed wire.

'We got the stores and our party and set off for the marshes. The six-foot stakes and wire were divided up and we went down the cleared paths. We worked our way well into the marsh and came to a clearing. Jock called a halt and issued out packed lunches. He then told me that we were going to return to the transport and go to the local pub for a drink and something to eat. I pointed to the seated men and asked, "What about them?" Jock said, "Leave it to me". He then went over to the party and told them how dangerous it was because of the unexploded bombs and that they were to stay there while we went to find a safe way out. I had my doubts, but in the end it all went well and the men were still where we had left them!'

A Staff Major from Division would visit the MCTC every Friday morning to ensure the SUS were being treated properly and to listen to complaints. At least that was the theory. George Henderson remembers that, in practice, it went more like this: 'The soldiers lined up on the parade ground in two ranks with members of staff standing close behind. The RSM would call the parade to attention and scream "The Army Visiting Officer is on parade. Any man with any complaints take one step forward now!" If a man showed any sign of movement a long arm would stretch out and catch him by the back of his collar accompanied by the whisper "Steady lad!"'

George only recalls carrying out a few duties in E wing. 'Very few SUS ended up there. One was a Royal Artillery Gunner who refused to tuck the tail of his shirt in. He spent so long in solitary that when he went outside for exercise and fresh air he spent the time on his hands and knees talking to the ants.'

By 1972 Lieutenant Colonel Gabb began replacing the barbed wire round the camp with a chain link fence. He also introduced a new system which allowed men on Stage 1 to have fourteen cigarettes or 10oz of sweets, and those on Stage 2 to have twenty-one cigarettes or 14oz of sweets. By 1973, pay was finally introduced and ranged from 10p to 28p a day. It was also arranged that detainees serving longer sentences could do more than one course. This allowed some to complete all four courses before leaving.

Former Guardsman David Thomas gives an insight into how the ordinary soldier viewed 'Colly':

'I was in the Grenadier Guards and the training regime in 1972 must have resembled what most people perceive men went through before joining the French Foreign Legion when they were based in Sidi Bel Abbcs. When the Grenadiers went to barracks where other corps or infantry regiments were stationed, the residents got the shock of their lives!

'The attitude towards discipline within the Guards may have mitigated the risk of someone from one of these regiments thinking this was the end for them on their arrival at Colchester, but the thought of the place still had a place of fear in the mind of the most hardened Guardsman.

'Many of our number served with the Parachute Regiment through the Guards (No 1) Independent Parachute Company, aka the Guards Paras, but this was still normal soldiering for those Guardsmen who joined, and as real soldiers (not just toy soldiers outside sentry boxes) they enjoyed it tremendously! G (Guards) 22 Squadron SAS also recruited from our number. A friend of mine was one such person, and thoroughly enjoyed it.

'A sinister feeling existed about Colchester though. Although never an inmate (I did have a friend who was), I did escort details for the soldiers under sentence.

'I had seen similar places before though; the Guards detention areas had glass floors in the guardroom and the cells at the back were spartan, to say the least. The toilets had no doors, the beds were made into bedding blocks (an hour before Reveille) and all the plumbing was copper or brass. Guess who cleaned this, keeping it gleaming all the time?

'The rifting was always a sign of the soldiers under sentence, and as escorts, we had to do the same! It was as if being an escort was something of a punishment in itself, especially as we had to bull our boots to the point where you could shave in them, get razor sharp creases in our No 2 suits, Meltonian our belts and clean our brasses and forage caps. The prisoners even got out of this because they wore no headgear!

'When we got wind of another poor soul being transhipped to Colchester, we would do our damnedest to make sure we were not around when they came looking for "volunteers"!'

'The Colchester of old may not exist today, and neither does the old Guards depot as current human rights legislation would not allow such things, but the memory will live on in anyone who did go to Colchester, in whatever capacity they attended.'

Jim Robinson returned to A wing MCTC in 1972 as Company Officer. Major Charles Goode of the RMP was the Wing Commander:

'The wing, which contained Stage 1 only, was made up of men who were returning to their units at the end of their sentence and included men from the Army, RAF and Royal Marines. My particular duties were to cover appeals, petitions, SUS mail, wing stores, daily inspections of the detainees and their accommodation, interviews of all admissions and complaints.

'There were six kitchens, one each to the Officers' and Sergeants' Messes, one for the junior ranks and one each for A, B and D wings.

Except for the Officers' Mess they were all ramshackle Nissen huts built out of corrugated iron which were rusting at the bottom edges and were continually running with condensation. They were plagued with rats and birds which would fly round the kitchen and dining rooms. The birds would leave their droppings everywhere. It was a nightmare trying to keep it clean and even the paint would peel off the walls because of the condensation. The unit tried all sorts of ways to sort the problem out. We had extractor fans fitted at the end of the kitchens and hoods over the stoves. We used a lot of self-help to fix the problems by building walls and screens, but nothing helped. The rats used the drains in the camp like an underground road system and would travel between the pig farm and the kitchen depending on the season.'

In 1973 Lieutenant Colonel Henry Tregear RA became Commandant. One of his innovations was to introduce independent monitoring which led to The Independent Board of Visitors. In 1973 too, several more Nissen huts were demolished as the camp slowly continued to disintegrate. Dan Cowley recalls the rubble was used in the construction of part of the NI training area buildings at Fingringhoe.

The maintenance bill for the camp that year was a staggering £87,865 and this despite the self-help provided by the trade instructors and others.

Chapter 14

'The Motor Cycle Training Centre' 1973 – 1976

Dennis Gus Hales:

'I had to escort a guy to MCTC on 31 December 1973. We flew from Dusseldorf to Luton and got taken to Colchester by car. When we arrived at the MCTC, me and another escort got a right rollocking. I'm not sure what for but I think all escorts got the same. Things like, "If this SUS has any contraband on him then you will be in the next cell." As we were in No 2 Dress we got inspected as well as the guy going into MCTC. When we were dismissed we were taken to Colchester station to get the train home. I was travelling to Yorkshire so I got changed into civilian clothes in the toilet. When I got my connecting train to Yorkshire there was a work to rule on the railways and the train stopped every few miles so the guard would carry out his safety checks. I eventually got home at 2415 so missed seeing in the New Year with my family. It wasn't a very good start to my New Year leave but at least the flight was counted as a duty flight and not one of my three free flights we got each year.'

After six months on A wing, Jim Robinson was posted to D wing which by then had been established for about five years:

'Being the Messing Officer, I never had the chance to become bored. One of the more interesting projects carried out in the kitchens was conducted by what was then called an APRE Team. This was a team of RAMC (Royal Army Medical Corps) Technicians who were there because the MCTC was the only unit in the British Army which existed solely on Army rations and supplied four meals a day, including weekends. The detainees had no NAAFI canteen to use and couldn't go

Education Wing Staff. Third from left is Major Robert Boyes, author of In Glasshouses.

out and buy fish and chips as most soldiers could do in the evenings or weekends.

'The team came and weighed every scrap of food that went into the kitchens and every scrap that came out, whether it went into the swill bin or back into the larder. As a result, we were informed that the inmates were being fed at just below the correct level of nutrition. The team reported that most of the men would come to no harm, but that long-term prisoners could suffer. It recommended that all prisoners should be given an extra cup of tea and a bun or a couple of biscuits at mid-morning, which would be sufficient to cover this deficiency. As a result of this report the unit put up a case for extra rations to be issued too. At that time they were on a normal ration scale plus the Arduous Duty Menu. Royal Navy Supplies, who covered rations, turned this down saying their men had survived on it for years and the Army men could too. It was then put to the ADMS who gave out a few swear words and said he would authorize it under his own powers, which he did.

'In 1973, drug offenders started to make an appearance. Invariably they ended up in D Wing. One was there for nine months. One day he came in front of me to complain about the food saying there was too much carbohydrate in it, too many potatoes and not enough carrots. He wanted more vitamins and protein. As Wing Commander I told him that the food was the best he could get under the circumstances, considering they were fed solely on Army rations. He was not satisfied and demanded an interview with the Messing Officer. The Sergeant Major was instructed to march him out. I then told him to march back in again.

I then introduced myself as the Messing Officer, produced a booklet giving a breakdown of all the protein and carbohydrates etc. in the food and dismissed all his complaints. He never complained again.'

Tom McGreevy spent some time in Colchester in 1974:

'Your bed pack had to be perfectly square each morning for inspection. I signed out a chess set for recreation, handed back the chess pieces, but ripped the board up and put it inside my bed pack. I got away with a perfect pack for a few days. Then they said it was too perfect and threw it out the window. Out came the pieces of chess board and I got charged with destroying Army property. I lost five days remission!

'You had the choice to go to church parade every Sunday morning, but I said I didn't want to go. I ended up painting the huts all day whilst the other lads in my spider hut lay about on their beds. I went to church every Sunday after that! I loved my time in there and I came out much fitter and a much better soldier. I went on to do another ten years service, before I left in 1984.'

The Maunsell Committee of 1974 set out the ethos of the Corps which is summed up in Robert Boyse's *In Glasshouses*:

'The punitive function is fulfilled by the SUS losing his liberty, his pay, his association with his friends. His training is to be exacting and constructive. He will be improved only by a staff able to understand him, lead him and show by example.'

The staff were now very well trained and seemingly up to the challenge. They would need to be, as they were now to be responsible for four main establishments in Northern Ireland: Long Kesh, Crumlin Road, McGilligan Camp and prison ship HMS *Maidstone*. The first MPSC Group left for Northern Ireland in August 1971 and the last group left in April 1980.

Dennis Carr, a member of the MPSC from 1975 to1983, thoroughly enjoyed being in the MPSC:

'I did an eight-week Probationers Course in 1975 which I found really interesting and was then sent to A wing in charge of a twenty-eight day platoon. There were forty-nine men in my platoon and as discipline NCO it was my job to take them from place to place.

'One of the worst jobs was sieving the coke in the morning after the night fires. We kept the ash and sieved it as we had to retain any bits of coke that were big enough to re-burn. Detainees were marched to the Diets Hall where the hatches were opened four inches and a plate of food put in front of them. There was no choice; you ate what you were given. On one occasion the Duty Sergeant asked if there were any complaints about the food. There was silence for a few seconds then a small, rather timid voice from a young RAF man piped up. "Excuse me Sir, but there's a caterpillar in my lettuce". The Sergeant looked at him, turned to me and said loudly: "Sergeant, put him on a charge for stealing meat!"

'I then went to work on D wing which was totally different. One of the OCs would start the morning by yelling "Right Sergeant Major, march the guilty bastards in."

'At short notice I was ordered to the MCTC pig farm which was now a very profitable enterprise making a net profit of £28,000 a year. There were over 1,000 young pigs bred by the MCTC. After only eight weeks training I found myself in charge and was informed that a General would be visiting.

'After cleaning everything up I marched the four detainees back for their lunch and left the Special, who ran the farrowing house, behind. The General and his staff duly arrived and began their inspection. They had only just started when the Special ran out and said: "Staff we've got a breech birth". I turned my back on the General and rushed off with the Special.

'As I was lying in the straw, naked to the waist with my arm up the pig trying to turn the piglet, I was suddenly aware that I was surrounded by shiny boots. The General and his entourage were standing watching. The General was very impressed when the piglets began arriving, especially when I explained that the lads were taught how to do this.

'Eventually, the RSM, who was now frustrated that the General's inspection was running late, whispered to the Adjutant who in turn spoke to the General and gently reminded him the soldiers were ready for inspection on the sporting field. The General turned back and remarked loudly that he was a General and could watch soldiers playing anytime. It was not every day that he could witness life being born.'

Another soldier recalls acting as escort to a young man going to Colchester:

'One SUS had been a boy soldier but when he went up to the adult Army he didn't like it and went AWOL three times. He'd got as far as Newcastle before being brought back and taken to Colchester. They took him in a room and threw his kit on the floor and told him if there

Colchester c1978 LS&GC presentation by Sir Rollo Pain.

were any discrepancies he would have to pay for it. He was made to stand facing the wall while they checked it. I was told I was not needed so left. On the way out I saw people doubling everywhere and one SUS in the guardhouse standing to attention in his best kit. I remember that the young lad was later discharged and that people who were sent to Colchester never went back – once was enough.

'My brother, who was a Sergeant, escorted a soldier back from Germany in handcuffs. Once back in England he removed the handcuffs and took the soldier for a pint in a pub as it would be a while before he would be able to drink alcohol again. He did tell the SUS that if he tried to escape though he would kill him! There were no problems and he delivered him as charged.'

Corporal Phil Lawson was one of the last soldiers to serve at Colchester Military Hospital. 'SUS regularly came into the hospital with stomach pains caused by the usual habit of eating soap which gave them a couple of days out of MCTC. I also remember letters arriving addressed to "The Motor Cycle Training Centre."'

It wasn't all work as sport played quite a large part in the life of the staff. Dan Cowley remembers the start of tug of war competitions:

'It all started during a breakfast lock-up. David Hood walked into the Staff Rest Room with the "rope" over his shoulder. He had been to breakfast in the WOs' and Sergeants' Mess. "How do you all fancy starting a tug of war team for the 1975 Eastern District Sports meeting this summer?" The looks and the stunned silence gave the initial answer, but after the men tested the thickness of the rope with both hands and realized it was difficult to touch the fingers with the thumbs the idea gained some interest. Me, John Julliff, Paddy Blair, Peter Jennings and others decided to give it a try. We were joined by some of the training team and were able to field a full team for practice – at times pulling David's car on the end of the rope and, at other times, the cricket square roller.

'An invitation was given to the Green Jackets over the road in Roman Barracks to come and train with us and test the "opposition". It was accepted and they duly arrived clad in regimental badged track suits, led by a huge Fijian Sergeant. We won two out of three pulls and this gave us some confidence. But our rubber-soled DMS boots meant we lost most of the pulls at the District Sports Meeting. We lost miserably against the Green Jackets; we had learnt the art of bluffing and to let them win until it counts! At least we had tried and had filled a meeting's programme with another MCTC Team. The only thing won out of that meeting was a severe reprimand for David our trainer.

'We packed up our rope and left for home a little tired but a lot more educated in the art of bluffing and letting them think they were better until it meant something. Although we did not realize it, the small seeds we had sown were to spring forward to something to be reckoned with. Over the next few months the seed began to sprout; two Royal Artillery NCOs, D. Annand and P. Ellis, were to transfer to the MCTC. Since Victorian times the RA had been the experts in using ropes to get guns into place. WO I Peter Andrews was to be commissioned to follow into the ranks of the MCTC, so too were T. Fryer, S. Browning, D. Carr and others.

'Over the next few years this team was to prove an inspiration to us and showed what can be achieved. The interesting addition of ammunition boots with ground-steel heel-plates, and the practice of the "Bucket" holding-stance helped create a team of great potential and achievements for nearly ten years. It was to include Army and RAF personnel, both junior and senior ranks. We won the Army Indoor Championship, Inter-Services Challenge Trophy, Eastern District Championship, Services Event at the Braemar Gathering, Royal Tournament and County Championships.'

Paul Masterton, 50th Missile Regiment Menden, Germany, was a detainee twice, in October 1974 and in 1975. After going AWOL for six months he was given nine months in Colchester:

'After being escorted from Germany I was put in a Nissen hut which held ten SUS. It was just like a concentration camp. The toilet had a flush-pull with string at the top right of the hut. In the middle of the hut was a cast iron fire which burned coal and provided the only heat.

'After being woken up each prisoner had a job to do: clean the floor, ablutions etc. My job was the fire. I had to empty the ashes. then polish it with boot polish till it shone, even if the polish was sizzling with the heat.

'Every morning there was a kit inspection. You got points for everything because you were in competition with other huts. Every month the winning hut got to move to a different level. The third level was the crème de la crème with a TV and pool table and no locked doors, so it was very important for everyone to work together. For the first few weeks we all slept on the floor so we would not crease our beds or bed packs. Every Saturday meant a compulsory haircut and every Sunday was church parade. Our weekly wage was £2.50. You could buy cigarettes or sweets. I didn't smoke but I bought cigs because they were like gold dust when the other detainees ran out. I used to get my boots polished and extra puddings!

'The showers and sinks were in another hut opposite. You only had a shower three times a week and were timed. You were also timed when shaving and washing. One RAF lad complained we were not getting enough showers. So for a week we had to shower every two hours with only a minute to strip shower, dress and get back on parade.

'Everything was at the double until a detainee died at the Shepton Mallet centre. After that everything was still timed, with two minutes for a wash and shave, but doubling was cut to a fast walk. The other detainees were mixed Army, Navy and RAF. There were some real characters. One lad used to walk every step with his right arm trailing behind him. He was pretending to walk his dog, his imaginary dog, on a lead. He was only doing it to get chucked out of the Army.

'The daily routine after inspection was weapon training or gardening, painting or loads of exercise. I was there in autumn and the leaves were falling. We had to stand under the trees and catch them. The officer said it was to save the brushes from wear and tear. Hah! I also had to paint the inside of a fire bucket full of water. The officer said: "We cannot take any chances. There could be a fire at any time so the water will have to stay in!"'

Despite this, Paul found himself wanting to remain in the Army, at least until he left Colchester. However his resolution did not last long and as soon as he left he went AWOL again. This time he was absent for a year. Dan Cowley:

Entrance to A Wing looking toward A Wing kitchen and Ration.

'One day during the summer of the mid 1970s I was on the gate of D Wing at 12.30hrs. The wing's inmates had been paraded, counted, agreed and dispatched to the only cookhouse and dining rooms then in use in the A wing area.

'The morning had been punctuated by short, but heavy rain outbursts. The staff and SUS were dressed in Shirt Sleeve Order. The staff had departed in rubberized khaki, cotton coat A1 and the detainees in groundsheets. The only other resident in the wing lines was the wing Commander and as he left his office the heavens opened up. I had ensured I re-locked the wing gate as the Commander insisted on this even when the wing was empty. He was clad in his officer's trench coat and strode determinately towards me and the gate. I looked at the rain and the distance he had to cover and thought I would just have enough time to rush out and undo it as he reached it and then re-lock it without putting my A1 on and be able to return to the gate lodge.

'The wing Commander had other ideas. He stopped just in the gate opening so I could not shut it, looked up at the rain and asked: "Now you are in the wing by yourself what have you to do?" I explained my expected duties for the forty minutes I would be alone. My shirt was by now very, very wet. The questions still came. The last one gave me some leeway for a reply. "I have better things to do than stand in the rain talking to you, Sir". He turned on his heels, the smile left his face and he headed for the officers' coffee room. I met him in Northern Ireland a few months later as he had moved on. I wondered if he remembered the rain as I did; there was a lot more of it out there.'

Ron Allen left the Army in 1993 after twenty-two years' service. In 1974 he escorted a prisoner from Germany to Colchester:

'As a Lance Bombardier, Royal Artillery, I had, as usual, booked my flight with our Movements Clerk to go on leave from Germany back home to England. In those days no one referred to it as going back to the UK.

'A few days before going on leave I was called up to see the clerk. This usually means one of two things, either the flights are booked and you can collect your tickets or the clerk couldn't get the flight days you wanted. Unfortunately there was a third thing I hadn't thought of, but had heard lots of horror stories about from those that know and that is, "You have to escort a prisoner all the way to Colly." I thought "Bloody Hell" as this is the most inconvenient thing that can happen when one is trying to get on leave.

'Once arriving at RAF Gutersloh, Germany (in those days all flights were from RAF Gutersloh) you were given your instructions to pick up

WO1 Mike Russell presenting a leaving gift to a civilian member of staff.

your prisoner and met the other escorts and the full screw (someone with two tapes) or Bombardier in charge of the escort party. I hoped that the prisoner wasn't there but the bloody nuisance was, and so I checked in. It was easy to find the escort party as everyone had to wear full No 2 Dress, "Hats Ridiculous" (No 2 Dress Hat) and bulled boots; all this bother just to go on leave. There is then lots of signing paperwork and prisoner handovers.

'Once all was well we boarded the plane and were given our seats just like you see on the American films when they are escorting prisoners on flights. We hoped ours didn't have a hidden knife or a gun. Some way into the flight, food was served so we had a quick vote as to whether the prisoner could have some as well. I said "no" but was out-voted. Then the prisoner asked if he could buy some duty-free cigarettes which started the next discussion. I again said he couldn't but the senior escort said he could as he would need them to barter with in prison. I think he was talking from experience but I'm not too sure now. He might have watched the same American film as me.

'After one and a quarter hours we landed at Luton Airport and were met by a mini bus to take us to Colchester Prison, a long way from London where I was heading. By the time we arrived it was getting late in the day. Hectic orders were barked and shouted by the prison staff and more paperwork was exchanged. Eventually we rushed to get changed out of uniform and into civvies and to get the next train to London. At least we had got rid of the prisoner who was left there for the next two years of his life, hopefully breaking rocks.

'As expected we arrived in London to find that all the last trains for the night had left and some of the guys still had a long way to go. One of the guys was from a guards regiment and suggested going to Hounslow barracks for the night, so we had a whip round and came up with £5 pounds for a taxi there. It was okay for me as I just phoned my dad to come and pick me up, but the other lads must have spent the night on the guardroom floor, all thanks to prisoner escort duty.'

David Thomas remembers escorting a prisoner to Colchester:

'Despite being a streetwise kid myself, having been brought up on a 1950s sink estate, I still had some trepidation when I was detailed to escort a soldier under sentence going to Colchester. I am told that some regiments asked for volunteers for this duty, but it was orders and obedience which made the Guards the most disciplined soldiers in the world; not allowing thought and decision-making amongst the grunts.

Winners Eastern DIstrict Minor Units League MCTC football team.

'The hapless soldier was rifted out of the guardroom by an unsympathetic Guards regimental policeman and was continuously rifted for a good few minutes (they had to have their last bit of enjoyment before the SUS departed for his Colly Holly) before being "helped" into the waiting Land Rover, hot and sweating, where I was seated in the rear longitudinal seats.

'The NCO who completed the escort glared at the SUS and told him to sit bolt upright and stare at the opposite side of the Land Rover for the whole journey from Victoria Barracks, Windsor, to Essex. I was ordered to ensure that the SUS obeyed this instruction, which I felt was tantamount to punishing me too!

'And my punishment didn't end there. On our arrival at Colchester, both escort (the NCO and I), and the prisoner, were vigorously drilled by a typical (what you might expect) military policeman and generally treated like accomplices. After a while, I did wonder whether the MP had thought that the driver (from our MT section back in Windsor) had delivered three Soldiers Under Sentence on his own!

'Eventually though, we did separate, and the SUS was shown to what would be his lodgings for the next eight weeks. We received a sort of apology for the treatment, but I was glad to have made the drop, and be back in the Land Rover heading back to Windsor, a free man.

'There was much more chat on the way back and the NCO (who seemed a different man to the one I went there with) explained that Colchester was not dissimilar to the Guards depot, in that it would take the prisoner back to basics and rebuild him as a different man, fit to rejoin the ranks from where he came. He laughed as he told me: "Of course, Colchester is nowhere near as bad as the Guards depot." I laughed too, thinking of it only as a humorous quip designed to break up an otherwise monotonous journey. I thought no more of it at the time. The NCO went on to explain that the welcome is designed to shock (it certainly worked for me), again a psychological means of putting the fear of God into the new prisoner and to help make him dread what he would face during his sentence.

'I knew the SUS from previous, social encounters in the NAAFI and pubs around town, and even conversed with him at scoff and the like. He was from Nottingham and had a tendency to go AWOL, and as a repeat offender, he was given the stiff sentence at Colchester. I bumped

Information Room c1977–78 Colchester.

into him some time later in a local tavern, where we recalled his time there. That night I learned something which came as a surprise to me. He told me that the shorter sentences served in the guardroom were far more severe in terms of discipline and harsher in terms of punishment (clearly demonstrated immediately prior to my leaving for Colchester on escort duties), debunking the myths put about by those senior soldiers milking their own self-perceived importance some months before. I then recalled the "joke" the NCO had told me and wondered if Colchester was all it was cracked up to be. Many years after my departure from the Army Conservative MP Michael Howard suggested that what young offenders needed was a "short, sharp shock". He probably saw Colchester Glasshouse with its scary reputation as the model.'

Chapter 15

'Let's break the door down'
1976 – 1980

By 1976 Paul Masterton was married with a son and his wife persuaded him to give himself up so he could get on with the rest of his life. So in February that year Paul arrived back in Colchester, but this time as a soldier who had been discharged:

'I remember it was a lot easier. The Provo Sergeants knew you weren't worth bothering with or worth training back as a soldier. You were still in a strict regime. I was frog marched as were all prisoners daily. I painted, swept, cleaned and washed everything that didn't move. But when other prisoners had a lesson in weapon training I and the others were kept separate. To be honest they were not sure what to do with us. Their job was to train, not to nurse or even care about prisoners going home at the end of their sentence, which I don't blame them.'

Bill Coleman (ACC) spent just under a year in the MCTC. Rather miffed at his sentence and treatment Bill was rather uncooperative and subsequently spent ten months in A Company:

'It was a shock to the system, very tough, and the staff had you running everywhere. The Diets Hall at this time had holes in the roof, broken windows and birds flying round it inside and I can remember bird droppings on the table. At the weekends there were card games and the "best barracks" competition with the prize being the privilege of having the radio for the weekend and the Sunday paper.

'I remember a party of five Royal Marines, which included a Corporal, arriving one morning. They arrived in the hut and we offered them cigarettes to make them feel welcome. They refused, huddled together and then the Corporal banged on the door. When a member of staff arrived they told him they wanted a meeting with the Commandant immediately or they would march right out of the camp. Much to my amazement they were granted an interview and by the afternoon they had all left. For weeks afterwards, whenever anyone was caught laughing or smirking, they would say they were just thinking about becoming Royal Marine Commandos!

'The regime made people so fit that several left and joined selection courses for the Commandos or SAS. Money was tight; we were given just enough money to buy half an ounce of Old Holborn tobacco and some soap powder. Any pennies we had left over we pooled together with the other men in their hut to buy something extra. Visits were only one a month and, if the visit order did not arrive, you were not allowed in, however far you had travelled.'

By 1977 visits by The Board of Independent Visitors began. The Board consisted of local notables including an MP from each party and they were able to visit without warning. The visits usually happened twice a year and continued until the MCTC came under the auspices of Her Majesty's Inspectors of Prisons (HMIP) in June 2004. Tony Moore:

'My friend Donnie did a six-month stint. He was the only Corporal in the British Army who managed to scramble the whole of RAF Bruggen by phone when he was drunk and saying there was a bomb outside one of the hangers. This was during the troubles in Ireland. He went in at 16st and came out at 10st and said he didn't enjoy it.'

Jim Robinson had once again returned to Colchester after some years in Hong Kong:

'As QM I became directly involved in plans to rebuild the camp. This was a subject that had been raised several times before, ever since the early 1950s. No one believed it would happen. However, my first order was to rewrite the Q Brief for the rebuild. In other words write down literally everything that would be required in the new camp, including shelving in stores and electric power points. A study had already been carried out on the feasibility of moving the MCTC to another area and to make use of an existing camp. Canterbury Barracks and RAF Tangmere were just two places considered as serious options. In the end, mainly because of the public relations aspect, it was decided that MCTC should remain in Colchester where the population had already accepted the idea of a military detention camp in their area.

Staff and SUS from D Wing, Colchester, during the 1977 firemen's strike.

'It was now necessary to make sure we had the rebuild. I put my thinking cap on and realized it all came down to money. How much did it cost to maintain the camp? It obviously did not cost enough and I realized that many of the repairs and maintenance had been done on a self-help basis, with materials begged, borrowed or stolen. It was essential to stop all self-help and pass all repairs to PSA. The maintenance costs rocketed and I think it was finally noticed.'

Although most detainees were compliant with the rules there were always those who caused problems. Dan Cowley:

'The C block cells housed "difficult" SUS and the staff were drawn from A and D wings. In the late 1970s one of the inmates barricaded his door with his body. He did this by placing his back against his wooden bed supported by his pillow and then placing both feet against the door (the doors opened inwards). After much discussion and requests the inmate still refused to move. The discussion then moved to the gate lodge.

"Let's break the door down" was the only suggestion. But how? SSGT Leslie Greenwood, our only Olympian in shot-put, discus throwing and welly-wanging, stepped forward and offered his right shoulder. This provoked much scepticism and medical thought but that

147

was dismissed and it was decided to give it a try. The shoulder was applied after a three-and-a-half-foot run across the corridor. To the surprise of all, the body barrier held. To the shock and the merriment of all including the SUS, the door frame and the door collapsed inwards taking with it the wooden dowels and screws from the surrounding walls with the SUS underneath. He was in hysterics, but this was soon to be brought to an end by his reality check and new cell. The cell door was subsequently replaced with an all-metal barred gate.'

Patrick Lally:

'I joined the Irish Guards in October 1979, which is something that was expected of me being that I came from a long line of Irish guardsmen. In 1985 while serving in Munster, West Germany, I got involved with the wrong type of friend and ended up court-martialled and sentenced to 9 months detention and dismissed from the service (the saddest day of my life). I arrived at the MCTC Colchester at the beginning of April to begin my sentence. It was late at night and very stormy when we

Independant Board of Visitors c1980. Lt Col Leon Paul, Mr P.C. Benham, MBE TD, Mr P. Holmes, ACIS, Dr R. Axon, MB Bs, Brigadier M.E.M. MacWilliams, CBE DSO MC TD.

Painting presentation to WOs' & Sgts' Mess 1980 Brig J.F. Thomas, CBE, Cpt Peter Goddard, Maj Sidney Harris and Lt Gen Sir Rollo Pain, KCB, MC, c1980 ..... Corps weekend.

drove through the gates, which along with the stories that young soldiers hear about the place made it seem even scarier! Within the hour we were processed and allotted to our huts. They were the original Nissen huts from the time the camp was used for Italian prisoners of war.

'The next day was spent doing the milk run, which was all the running around getting all the paperwork done, medical checks etc.

'The staff mostly seemed to be older men doing extended service, and indeed there were a couple of them who had originally been Irish Guardsmen. The staff were very decent and rarely raised their voices. Although I was in D wing, which was soldiers being discharged after their sentence, the men in A wing were basically being re-trained and returned to their units, and had a much harder time.

'D wing was pretty well relaxed, and we were supposed to do courses to prepare us for civilian life, but I never met anyone who had actually been on one. We were paid about £2.60 a week I think, which mostly went on essentials and a small pack of tobacco, and of course mars bars, which for some reason had become the currency inside.

'The food was awful, and was always very small portions, there were a couple of almost riots while I was there because of the food. For example, Sunday was nearly always a slice of spam in batter, two roast potatoes and two carrots, sugar was never allowed, so puddings and tea were always a bit of a let-down. We went on a run one morning and about four guys dropped out because they just didn't have the energy! I

149

always tried to get on a work party at the officers mess, where we would get a decent meal during the day.

'I think we were allowed visitors once a fortnight, my Mother came to see me once, which I wasn't expecting, and truth be told I really didn't want her to see me there, what with the shame I felt I had brought on the family. Visitors would bring food in for whoever they were visiting, and you could eat and smoke as much as you wanted to for those two hours.

'Once I had settled in it wasn't too bad. I tried to get on as many work details as I could, just to keep busy. The new block was almost finished by that stage, so there was a lot of stuff they had us doing there. The men there were from every regiment, there were a couple of RAF guys too, and one sailor. None of them seemed the imagined bad types; I guess young men just get into trouble sometimes.

'I had a great deal of respect for the staff, they were very fair and not in the least bit intimidating. My time there went very quickly and in my last couple of weeks we were all moved to the new blocks, which although modern and comfortable weren't as comfy as the Nissen huts! I was released on 15 July 1985 at 11.00 am and I was distraught at being a civilian again. I was given £4.00 and a ticket to Birmingham, which was my home town. I often think about my time there and the people I met, and mostly they are good memories. The only problem

LS&GC presentation by Lt Col Leon Paul c1979.

150

with a court martial and a sentence at MCTC is that it does follow you around for the rest of your life.'

The tell-tale clock was still in operation up until the late 1970s. Dan Cowley:

'In 1979, WO I (RSM), "Tug" Wilson did the best thing for the staff and the Corps when he organized the scrapping of tell-tale clocks and got rid of them with the help of the Quartermaster who back-loaded them, never to return. The RSM then replaced them with a fifteen-minute check log book. This demonstrated a form of trust in the integrity of the staff and was a much appreciated change in the night watch duties and in the attitudes of the administration.

'We did not "fiddle" to gain sleep or to remain in the gate lodge at night, but to see if we could beat the system and a lot of us did, though many failed by going too far too often. Expecting to get away with placing the clock in a bucket of water, not once, but twice, deserved all the problems they got and demonstrates how silly some of the staff could be.

'In the small hours of one of my last "In Charge of Night Watch" duties I entered D wing and found the single night watch Sergeant asleep. I checked the wing and signed the log leaving the correct amount of spaces for the night watch. I checked the wing later and he was still asleep. I again checked the wing "residents", signed the book in the correct place leaving the correct places for the Sergeant's times, moved to another location and telephoned D wing and hung up before it was answered.

'I retired and went to work for English Electric as a security supervisor and more than eighteen years later one of the contract female patrol staff asked me if I knew David Chenier, one of my colleagues. I told her I did but that I had lost contact with him over the years. She then related the above incident and added: "David said at that time you had held his career in your hand". David went on to become a WO II in the Corps. I had completely forgotten this incident but we had many discussions about it from then on, and he still owes me a beer. As I said, the attitudes to other staff had taken a drastic change, I think for the better.'

A soldier from the 1st Battalion, The Cheshire Regiment, was given eight-six days' "Soldier On":

'I arrived at MCTC during the autumn of 1979. We were transported from the train station to the unit in the early hours of the morning. Once

151

Officers' Mess Boundstead Road c1980.

*WOs' & Sgts' Mess
MCTC Colchester c1980.
The new fireplace.*

inside the main gate we were doubled up to reception by a member of the staff who were all NCOs. After a strip search we were taken to a hut to await an escort to our accommodation in the new entries wing. There were five bed spaces on each side with a black pot-bellied stove in the middle of the room. The stove was out but the room was filled with smoke that hung in the air and it was absolutely freezing cold. In the haze I could just make out shapes huddled under grey army blankets. Then a voice asked, "Got any fags mate?" to which I replied, "Yeah". We were allowed to take twenty fags into the unit and the start of your

LS&GC presentation by Brig R.C. Middleton OBE to Sgt Harry Doherty.

Tow the Commandant Out – Lt Col Leon Paul OBE 1980 having handed over command.

sentence. The inmate showed me how to make my bed and where to put items into my soldiers' box in the expected order. I didn't sleep that first night as I waited to meet my jailers in the morning.

'"Outside for diets" came the command. We were doubled up to the cookhouse, another Nissen hut, to be served a breakfast of scrambled egg, a piece of bacon or a sausage, a tablespoon of beans or tomatoes, a mug of tea and a doorstep of bread and jam. Then we were doubled back to our wing to start our day's work.

'The NCO in charge of my wing was known as "Two Tone" because he would pick up your boots on kit inspections and scream in your face "These boots are two tone" if they weren't highly polished or bulled off all over. He would then proceed to throw them to the bottom of the hut. I would smile to myself and think "You have a nice day too!" The discipline regime at MCTC didn't bother me at all and I thrived on the challenge. Near the end of my time I was granted the grand title of trustee and allowed to escort Red Badges, so-called because they had to wear red badges to identify them as escapees.

'There wasn't any television in our wing and you only got to listen to the radio once in every nine days which was something to look forward to. We were only paid about 20p a week and we were allowed to spend it in the shop to buy razor blades and stamps, that sort of stuff.

'It was while I was queuing up at the shop that I recognized a face of one of the staff. Five years previously we had both been on the same course in Aldershot. He recognized me straight away, pulled me to one side, shook my hand and asked, "Bloody Hell, what are you doing here?" I replied, "I could ask you the same question!" His first name is Peter and he served in the Kings Regiment before transferring to the MCTC Staff. If you read this Peter, all the best to you!

'I was so desperate for a smoke one night I shaved the hair from my blanket, rolled it in a fly paper, lit it, took one drag and burnt my lips and nose. Next morning I reported sick with my burnt nose and lips. Two Tone said to me with a smile, "Ran out of baccy then?"

'On release from MCTC I was given a warrant, told to report back to my battalion in Germany and was informed that I was on twenty-four hours probation. If I committed the slightest offence I would be rearrested and made to serve the rest of my sentence. You are also searched when you leave to make sure you are not carrying someone's mail which had not been read for censorship.

'I have no regrets or hard feelings against MCTC. On returning back to my unit we were posted to Tidworth. It was the time of the National Prisoner Officers strike and several prisons were set up in old army

D Wing Nissen huts c1981.

camps. Our company was tasked to guard these civilian prisoners. The camp we were in was staffed by members of staff from MCTC. By this time I had been promoted to Corporal and was in charge of my own men. Imagine the faces of the MCTC staff when they saw me posting my men to guard duty.'

Lieutenant Colonel Leon Paul OBE, Royal Anglian, left in 1980. He had been Commandant since July 1977.

Chapter 16

The Rebuild
1980 – 1984

Lieutenant Colonel Tim Illingworth took over from Lieutenant Paul as Commandant in November 1980 and in *In Glasshouses* recalls: 'He wrote to me in glowing terms about "The Corps" and what a marvellous unit I was to command. His introduction when I arrived was brief and to the point. "Never worry, whatever goes wrong the Corps will look after you!" The words were to ring true throughout my term as Commandant, at no time was I left without sound advice and never without support.' Padre Smith:

> 'I was delighted to be given my own personal pigeon hole at the MCTC.
> I must have "arrived". Such are the euphoric delights of a new padre at

A plaque at the farm showing its opening in 1982.

this honourable establishment. To say that I enjoy my work at the MCTC is an understatement and this is much to do with the way the staff and SUS alike have made me feel so much at home and very welcome. My main periods of activity centre around Sunday morning worship and a regular visit each Wednesday. Most Sunday mornings at about 0930 St George's echoes to the sound of well-known hymns, not always to the taste of the musical purist, but certainly just the cup of tea for the enthusiast at heart. Holy Communion follows the main act of worship and the attendance varies between five and twenty-five. On Wednesday mornings I visit as many people involved in the day to day administration of the MCTC as possible.

'Wednesday afternoon is "Padre's Hour" when a film is shown or there is a period of instruction and discussion. At the end of these periods there has often been lively debate. I always try to end the day with a game of football with the SUS. The treatment I receive is often relevant to the sermon I preached on the previous Sunday morning. If I mauled them over the compliments are returned in full measure.

'Personal interviews with the SUS are a vital and important part of my ministry at the MCTC. I dare to believe that in an atmosphere of confidence, concern and prayer, decisions are taken and problems resolved that affect a man's whole future life for the good.'[21]

Michael Nottingham was Assistant Commandant from 1981 to 1985:

'One of my duties was to run the MCTC pig farm. The aim was to teach agricultural and farming skills to those SUS who were being discharged from the service on completion of their sentences. It not only involved the cleaning and feeding of livestock in their accommodation, but also keeping an eye on pregnant sows when they went into labour, which seem to happen all too frequently! The MCTC had a contract with Eastern Counties Farmers based in Ipswich to which we sold our mature livestock. This enabled the MCTC to buy fresh stock and breeding sows.

'During my time there a problem arose over one of the sheds which the pigs slept in. It was about 60ft long and had to be moved from its present site which was wanted for SUS accommodation.

'To get round the problem, SUS from D wing paraded one morning around the shed and on the command "Lift" they got the shed shoulder high and were marched to its new location. It was quite a sight but passed off without a hitch.'

Meanwhile the plans for the rebuild continued. Jim Robinson:

'Meetings were held every month to go over the requirements for the rebuild and it was necessary to justify to the Treasury every inch of brickwork needed. One of the things I wanted was to have the toilets and ablutions built into the SUS rooms, that way they could have a shower and a shave before unlock in the mornings and would be able to clean their own ablutions before parading.

'But the biggest arguments were over the church, the Officers' Mess and the gymnasium. The treasury felt the SUS should use local churches until it was explained that this would mean moving a possible 200 SUS through the local council estate and that local churches could not accommodate that many people. The Treasury finally agreed, provided that the main church had a dual purpose. So we agreed to let the C of E church be used as the unit cinema during the week, with screens to seal off the sanctuary.

'Chessington could not accept that the MCTC carried out more PT than any other unit and wanted us to have the minimum size PT Hall. In the end they decided to come to Colchester themselves and have a meeting with the current Commandant Lieutenant Colonel Leon Paul, architects and engineers.'

Although Jim argued his case he eventually had to settle for less than he wanted. 'A reasonable gym, but not as good as might have had! Later, just as all the drawings were being finalized, we had a visit from the Director of Army Quartering, General Lord Lane. He came equipped with a big axe.'

After looking over the plans the Director reduced the number of rooms in the Sergeants' Mess, the number of classrooms in the Education Centre and the SUS accommodation. Three years later they had no option but to reapply for extra accommodation for both SUS and staff.

Meanwhile plans for the rebuild could now begin and it was decided to carry it out in two stages. The first stage was to rebuild the SUS accommodation including kitchen and dining rooms, offices and ration stores. Once complete, the old accommodation would be demolished and the new camp built round the existing one. In 1983 the foundations were finally laid and on 6 July 1984 the Colonel Commandant, Sir Norman Arthur, performed the topping out ceremony. A silver trowel was placed in the Officers' Mess, a symbol that the long-awaited rebuild would finally go ahead. Dan Cowley:

'During the rebuild of the MCTC the C block cells were dismantled and some graffiti was found on the underside of one of the wooden sleeping

Annual Brightingsea raft race 1981.

platforms. Over the years a pencil had been used by many SUS to inscribe the underside of the platform and the pencil then re-hidden. One of these platforms was retained for display.

'The cell blocks faced north and south and their small high windows provided the only natural light access. The only ones to get direct sun were the west-facing cells after 1400hrs. At certain times in the afternoon the sun fell on the inside of the metal-skinned cell doors. With the door at the correct angle one could make out the shadows of past scratches. It was possible to see intricate designs of German helmet plates and badges, together with gothic scratched names and dates. These had been painted over many times but the depressions were still visible. One I recall was a nine-inch high double-headed eagle and text scroll of Austrian or German origin with mottoes on the scroll.'

The Corps Journal from 1982 points to another find. 'What imagination the mind can conjure up at some object coming to light after an unknown period of years. Staff Sergeant Carr, NCO i/c piggery, was recently demolishing an old hut when he found the rusting remains of an old bayonet hidden down between the two layers of roofing and brought it into the RHQ for the museum.'

John Hopkins of Royal Corps of Signals was detained at the MCTC between January and April 1984 for six months detention and then soldier on:

'On arrival at the gate even my escort was worried. He was shouted at by the guard and double marched to a small hut. He was then dismissed and me and the other three SUS were marched into a long Nissen hut with white walls and small tables along the sides. We were told to lay out our kit, and then sit down on chairs which faced the wall. That is how we sat awaiting our turn to have our kit checked. Mine had been checked before leaving Germany to make sure that everything issued to me was there.

'After our kit was checked we were told to pack it. Our civilian clothes, which were in a suitcase and labelled, were placed at the end of the hall. I had tried to beat the system by ramming 4oz of tobacco into my baccy pouch as I had been told that you could take one pouch in with you. But to no avail. I was allowed 1oz of tobacco, one pack of Rizzlas and a box of matches (no lighters). The rest was put in my suitcase.

'We were then doubled to the main compound of A wing, my home for the next four months at least. We were met by the staff who lined us up and told us where we were to be "residing". We put our kit by our beds, then marched to the bedding store to pick up our sheets and blankets. We were given half an hour to make up our bed pack and lay our kit out as per the instruction sheet on the wall. We were then doubled to a small hall where we met the wing Commander and he explained the regime, what he expected and what would happen if this did not happen.

'We were marched back to our Nissen hut with a wood burning stove in the middle and the door was locked. There were two of us "new boys" and after introductions the others explained what the routine was: 0700 reveille, 0730 wash, 0800 breakfast, 0830 first inspection, 0900 education/training, 1230 lunch, 1330 second inspection, 1400 education/training, 1700 dinner, 2200 lights out.

'Beds could not be made up till after dinner, and bed packs had to be made before breakfast. Mondays meant wing Commander's inspection when the radio would be awarded to the best room of Stage 1. This was a very sought after reward as it provided some entertainment between the hours of 2000 and 2200 every night.

'All other inspections were carried out by wing staff. It was during these you were looking for a recommendation. Three recommendations in Stage 1 in one week would get you moved to Stage 2. In Stage 2 you needed five recommendations to move to Stage 3. All of these meant more freedom around the compound and Stage 3 meant moving out of the main compound.

'I was woken by the night staff shouting at either window or doors (doors remained locked until the day staff took over at 0730). I got up and sorted out my washing stuff. We stood by the door waiting for the staff to unlock and then doubled to the ablution block. We had to be quick as there were a lot of bodies to get washed in a short period of time with a limited number of sinks. Then we doubled back to the hut to get dressed, make bed pack, and again stand by door with KFS and mug in hand waiting for breakfast. We would then be paraded by the main wing gate and marched to the kitchen which was also an old Nissen hut.

'Breakfast was always the same, so too was the ration – one rasher of bacon, one sausage, one egg, beans or tomatoes, and a mug of tea. My tea-drinking was slightly different from the others. Since the age of fourteen I had not taken milk in my tea. I explained to the duty staff that I could not drink milk and after some discussion I was allowed to have a black tea made for me instead of using the urn. This did mean that throughout my time at MCTC I never had cereal as it would have shown that it was a preference not a dietary thing.

'After breakfast we were marched back to the compound. I noticed that two groups of people were different. One group always arrived and paraded in the front of us, no matter which hut was let out first, and the other group would be outside waiting. The mystery was solved when I spoke to another SUS. He told me that the first group were Stage 2 guys who lived in a separate part of the compound and were not locked in at night and so made their own way to join us. The others were stage 3 and they lived outside the compound and had much more freedom. The above procedure was carried out for every meal.

'Morning and afternoon inspections never changed. Staff came in and threw your kit everywhere if it was not as the diagram on the wall instructed. It took you at least a month to get your first recommend, and you had to really stick to the rules to get that.

'Education and training took us back to the basics and you had to be at a particular level before you could be moved up a stage. My upward movement was hampered as I suffered from chest pains. They were not sure what they were and even after medical exams at local hospitals it could not be decided if it was angina or a pulled chest muscle. This alienated me slightly as I was excused a lot of physical stuff such as the log run which did not go down well with the others.

'Being quite bright (I went to grammar school and the Army Apprentice College at Harrogate) I quickly moved up the system. Military training was also quite easy for me. I enjoyed it as we were taught how to use almost every weapon that an infantryman would use, including the GPMG, 88mm. As well as the normal weapons, I was trained in LMG, pistol, SLR.

'During Stage 1 you were paid £2.50 a week and this was to cover all your expenses such as boot polish, Brasso, soap, razor and luxuries like sweets and tobacco. I found out that we were paid in coins to stop people having notes smuggled in.

'Visits were fortnightly as there was only one visiting hall – the same hall as the reception hall – and it was shared between A wing and D wing. I was lucky and my wife made every visit. She had been moved out of our quarters in Germany and was lodged in a hovel for wives who had been dumped or left in the lurch by hubby going to jail. She got help with transport costs as we had two children. Her life was also rough as the place she was staying in was like a prison. No visitors were allowed and her rooms were either side of a corridor through which other residents had to pass. After my release I had to get special permission to stay with her before returning to my regiment.

'During my stay I found a way of supplementing my income. My wife would bring in 50p coins and pass them to me. While I was playing with the children I would poke them down my socks. As long as they were put right you could march properly back into the compound with them. Visitors were not allowed to take anything with them at visiting time, no money or fags, but they could take in magazines and papers. When you returned to the compound these were thoroughly searched, but no one ever checked inside your socks.

'Staff always asked for volunteers to clean the wing offices. SUS jumped at this chance, as if you were careful you could get your hands on the dog ends in the ash trays. This was dangerous as if you were caught you lost remission and recommendations for that week and this put you back a long way.

'I lost remission early on in my sentence. I was really fed up with the way we were treated, but as letters were censored you could not say so. But a young chef in my hut was due to be released and I asked if he would sneak a letter out for me. He agreed and so I wrote to my wife giving full details of how nasty certain staff were. The chef walked out in the morning and I thought nothing of it and went as usual to training and education.

'Mid-morning I was called out and marched back to the compound and straight into the wing SSM's office. He asked me if I had asked X to take a letter out for me. I told him I had – there was no point in denying it. He said I was going to be charged with an offence against whatever rules it was. I was marched out to my hut and the staff told me to get my best kit on ready for "Orders".

'Within about ten minutes I was marched to the wing Commander's office. The offence was read out. I pleaded guilty and got three days loss of remission. When I got back to my hut I was told my new earliest possible date of release. But in the long term it had not really changed as my new release date was a Sunday and as MCTC do not release over weekends it meant that I would go on the Friday so I only actually lost one day.

'Day to day stuff was a routine. At weekends the staff would organize something for us to do during the day and we were never allowed to get bored. One time we had a volley ball match, hut against hut.

'Sundays were the busiest times. Everyone went to church in the morning and the evening was cleaning time. No matter what the weather the stove in the middle of the hut was never lit on a Sunday.

Ball Room being renovated c1982.

Lt Col Tim Illingworth and Phil Calloway being presented the LS and GC.

Come the evening we would chip in a bit of boot polish each and give the stove a good brush. Some people managed to acquire some chalk from the classrooms and the stove was made to look quite impressive. The radio was the ultimate goal. If we had any leftover wood, coal or paper, it would be neatly piled, clean and tidy in the hearth. Then, on the Monday, we would wait after the inspection for our hut Sergeant to come back and say the magic words "the radio is yours". But as well as a reward it was the carrot. If anyone messed up in any way they could just as easy take it away. During my time in Stage 1 our hut won the radio three times out of eight inspections – not bad as there were six other huts.

'It was a revelation when I got moved to Stage 2. Not only were we not locked up at night, we had access to a bath, instead of a quick shower a couple of times a week. We also marched ourselves to the breakfast line. We still had to join the others and march with them for education and training but we got an extra 50p a week.

'We had one bad experience when someone upset a staff member and he took it out on all of us by not only throwing our kit around, but the furniture as well. He knocked over wardrobes and all sorts and gave us just an hour to sort stuff out "or you are all back to Stage 1".

'Once during education one time the geography teacher took us out of camp to give us a test. This was great as we were allowed to take our smokes. During the journey he asked questions to test our map-reading skills and we stopped a few times for a fag.

'At first, training was the most boring bit as they took us back to the basic stand at ease position and we had to call out the time as we did when we were raw recruits. But overall it was very useful as it helped us to get rid of bad routines we had fallen into. It actually helped some to start back up the ranks when they rejoined their units.

'I made Stage 3 with two weeks left of my sentence. Most SUS if they toed the line made Stage 3. This enabled you to live outside the compound. I was allowed to retrieve the tobacco that had been put away when I first arrived. It was three months old and had not been stored in an air tight container. But it was tobacco and it saved me a lot of money in my last couple of weeks. When you made Stage 3 you could apply to go down town. Not many did as you had to wear full 2 Dress which made it a bit obvious where you were from.

'We did get to see a lot of the surrounding countryside as the log run and other fun activities took place outside of the compounds.

MCTC Half built 1984.

MCTC RAF Course 1984; the first full course.

'On release I was told that I had to travel in full 2 Dress until I had reported to my unit - 11 Sigs at Catterick – and that I was still under sentence until I had arrived and reported in. If caught doing anything wrong or not properly dressed I would be brought back to finish my sentence in full.

'There was only one really bad down point. During my sentence my granddad died. My dad wrote to me and of course the letter was stopped for censorship. I was called to the wing office and asked if my granddad was close to me. I said that yes, of course, he was and that he had been so proud when I joined up. They then informed me of his death and also added that as he was not a close relative I would not be allowed to go to his funeral. This really gutted me and in a way I blamed myself for his death. I thought that the shock of him finding out I was at MCTC killed him. On the day of the funeral I was excused work for the morning and allowed to go to the chapel. The Chaplain was a great guy and allowed me time on my own, before we prayed together.

'After rejoining the Corps I was posted to the School of Signals in Blandford. I only had less than a year to serve to finish my twelve years. I was made a Regimental policeman which was an interesting job.'

Chapter 17

'Where the f*** are your boot laces?' 1984 – 1990

In July 1984 the MCTC won the Army Tug of War Championship at Aldershot. It also welcomed a new Commandant, Lieutenant Colonel Andrew Parsons from the Scots Guards.

Whatever detainees thought about Colchester it was still probably better than the Royal Navy Detention Quarters in Portsmouth where Nick had the dubious pleasure of being detained for forty-eight days in 1985:

'I was seventeen and had only been in the Royal Navy a year when I had a drunken night in Plymouth and fell out with a naval patrol.

Demolition of Junior Ranks Club MCTC 1987.

Demolition of old huts c1987.

'It was an eighteenth-century Victorian prison and a world apart from the twentieth century. There were no visits, no outside working and the grounds were very small. You started off with a third remission and any misdemeanour meant it would start going back up. If you weren't out of bed on time or your bedding was folded wrong you lost a day.

'We would be taken to the Naval PT School where we had to swim within a certain time. If you didn't better your lap time each day you lost remission and could even have days added. We were woken at 0500 every morning. There was no pay and only two hours of telly each week, *Top of the Pops* and *Porridge* – the only time we ever laughed.

Demolition of WOs' & Sgts' Mess 1987, Junior Ranks Club in the background.

'We were detained in individual cells with an iron bed and wire-based locker, a sink and a bucket. The cells were so small we could touch the walls. There were three landings. You started on the bottom landing and after thirty days moved to the second floor and then to the top landing. After twenty-one days you could watch TV on an extra two nights a week and buy biscuits. The library was very basic and the newspaper was usually a week old.

'However, the food was very good. In fact it was the best food I ever had in the Navy. It was cooked at the centre, was piping hot and there was plenty of it.

'Our time was spent mainly in cleaning the cells, landings, wings, bathrooms and ourselves, and in physical exercise. We also cleaned pans and peeled spuds. The cigarette ration was only two a day and we could only smoke outside or when watching telly. I was only seventeen and didn't smoke so I had half a dozen boiled sweets a day instead which I saved until the evening. We were allowed to write a letter every other day and there was no limit to those allowed in.

'The best job was cleaning the Officers' Mess as the officers would leave cigarette butts which we used to trade. There was no nastiness as we were all volunteers and there was nothing to gain by causing trouble. We were more concerned about losing our remission. I only lost two days remission.'

Sgt's Mess Games Night c1981.

Andrew Stevens was an electrician on HMS *Cambletown* in 1985:

'We had just come back from the Falklands and the ship was full of nutters. We were drinking heavily and were caught playing games which led to headlines about "Devil Worshippers" in all the newspapers. Not having read the papers I had rather a rude awakening when I arrived at Colly. Because of the headlines the screws hated me. They shouted "Think you're a hard man?" at me when I arrived and the first six weeks were dreadful with staff threatening to kill me. But after that it got much better. By twelve weeks I was Stage 3.

'Detainees earned merits each week to progress to Stage 2 and after that the regime was nothing like as harsh. I was only the second Navy person to go there and I went there because the naval prisons had all closed down. The staff had no idea if my uniform was right which made inspections hard and I had no idea about speed walking. When they started running off I just stood there watching as I had no idea why the guard had run off! I got eyeballed and shouted at for that.

'I was in D Company as I had been discharged. It was not the nicest of places, but better than A Company where they got grief from the moment they arrived until they left.'

But the regime in the MCTC had changed considerably. Once detainees reached Stage 3 they were able to go into Colchester every second weekend. However, they weren't allowed to go in any pubs or post offices or anywhere they could get money.

Visits were also strictly monitored. Detainees had to sit to attention. They weren't allowed to lean on tables or allowed tea and biscuits, although their visitors could have these. Andrew's first visit from his wife was particularly poignant. She had been pregnant when he'd first arrived so when she came to see him it was the first time he'd seen his daughter. However, rules at the time stated he couldn't hold her. But the staff turned a blind eye and he was able to hold her for a short time:

'Food was disgusting. We had chicken supreme every Friday night. Nobody ate it and I haven't touched it since. I can't even think about it now! We didn't get Christmas dinner because there was a food fight in the Diets Hall!

'I worked on the farm with the pigs. There were four boars and when they had babies they would be like puppies, running up and trying to get us to play with them. But it wasn't all fun. If a sow went into labour in the middle of the night I was woken up and had to run up to the farm to

Armoury Pioneer Shop and C Block prior to demolition.

pull the babies out of the way as soon as they were born in case the sow rolled over on top of them, which could happen if she was tired. I would then clip their ears with the date they were born and file their teeth down because they were sharp and would make the sow bleed otherwise.

'I was also in charge of building chicken coops when a TV crew arrived and was mortified when I was filmed in my wellies which had "left" and "right" written on them! I also had a tame chicken called "Yellow Legs" and when I called she would come and sit on my shoulder. There were also two large greenhouses full of vegetables and I spent much of the time going round camp with a large trolley selling sausages (from our pigs), eggs and vegetables. I gradually got to know which eggs were likely to have double yolks and sold these to the staff I liked.

Armoury, Pioneer Shop and C Block after demolition in 1986.

'There were considerable problems with foxes so after humanely killing chickens that suffered prolapses we filled the carcasses with poison and put them on the fire. The foxes would often eat the remains and that would help keep the numbers down. I really enjoyed working on the farm as I was left on my own most of the time. By the time I left my relationship with the staff was so good I received Christmas cards from them in the following years. Staff explained to me that it was their job to terrify newcomers. They would be chatting away to me and a new guy would come in and they would change completely. I've seen 15st guys shaking with fear from the threats, swearing and gobbing off, but it's just to reinstill discipline and training.'

In 1986 the SUS finally moved into their new accommodation and the decaying Nissen huts, so long a feature, began to vanish as the brick buildings took over. It was not only the SUS who were pleased to be moved. The staff too, were delighted to be working in buildings with hot and cold running water and central heating. There was also a new Commandant as Lieutenant Colonel Parsons had moved to pastures new in Zimbabwe. The new Commandant was Lieutenant Colonel Simon Fordham of the Welsh Guards. Major (Retd) Donald Young replaced Major (Retd) Cox in the Welfare Department. Retiring after ten years, Major Cox wrote of his time at MCTC in the MPSC Journal: 'On leaving

QMs' Department MCTC – Capt Mike Russell 1987.

172

Training Wing Nissen huts just before demolition.

the Military Corrective Training Centre on retirement today I wish to put on record my regard for your Corps. Before my posting in I had but scant knowledge of its work and composition, but after ten years I am filled with admiration at the fine manner in which all its tasks and actions are carried out. Truly professional.'

By 1986 it had become established practice for the new Mayor of Colchester to visit early on in his year of office. The MCTC also welcomed Councillor Bob Russell and his wife to lunch in the Officers' Mess on 27 May. The Board of Visitors were also shown round the new build.

Steve Alex from the RAF Regiment spent eighty-four days in MCTC in 1986 for fighting. 'I was housed in the new buildings and I can remember the highly polished floors. It was very strict and you were not allowed to speak while you were waiting for food. You had to stand to attention with your utensils in your hand.'

Outside activities continued and in May 1987 the projects team took the SUS to the Higham Horse Show where they helped out in the arena. In June they were in Thetford Forest Stamford Training Area erecting pheasant runs. They returned to Thetford in October to dig trenches for the installation of projector moving targets, only to wake on the Friday morning to find the hurricane had flattened the forest. Several trees had been felled by the storm at Colchester and the SUS spent the next couple of weeks clearing them.

Dom Prest was sentenced to six months for AWOL:

'In February 1988 I was taken by Land Rover to MCTC from my base at Windsor. I remember the driver "Jack" Frost but cannot remember the

173

other names of the escorts. I was dressed in my No 2 uniform but without laces in case I tried to hang myself in front of two escorting guards!

'When we got to Colchester the driver could not find the camp, so we stopped at the Argyll & Southerland Highlanders camp for some lunch in the guardroom. They brought me a meal of spag bol (funny how things stick in your mind). I also remember how well the RP staff spoke to me. I had a lot of respect for them after that short visit.

'After lunch and directions, we went on our way (200 metres to MCTC!) My first memory of the place was a bit of a building site because the old Nissen huts were being replaced by the new blocks. We arrived at the guardroom to be met by one of the camp staff. He bellowed at me to stand on the coloured spot, then paused and asked, "Where the f*** are your boot laces?" I replied they had been removed as per orders from escort staff. He then let rip at them about what they thought I was going to do with my laces "with you two there!" I thought that if I was going to be beasted every hour God sends for the next six months, then their ears wouldn't stop ringing for the best part of that!

'After my escort staff had gone I was booked in and taken to an old Nissen hut. Our bags were removed to storage as we only kept certain

Main road from main entrance into camp, MCTC 1985, Summer.

Main road from main entrance into camp, MCTC 1986 Winter.

equipment. I remember being with three other lads when we had a medical, were stripped to our underwear and inspected for whatever. Everything was explained about what was happening which was a bit of a surprise really. It wasn't the hammering an SUS would get back at camp.

'After being processed I was very pleased to be told that I would get a third of my sentence knocked off for good behaviour. We were then marched to our respective blocks. I remember D block was for those getting discharged and F Block was for females. I was put in to a temporary room with two other people until we were allocated to a dorm. I recall that weekend being a very long one ...

'My dorm housed seven other lads. It had a bathroom linked to it with two sinks, a toilet and a shower. There were also spy holes so staff could view from outside. Each bed had a locker above it where your equipment was folded away in regimental order. At the side was a plastic chair and a small shelf where your tooth brush and shaving kit had to be laid out I think each bed was made up with your No 2 hat on top. There was a hanger by the door, where all No 2 uniforms were hung.

'I was given a card to lay at the foot of my bed which had the information: **24710132 SUS Prest; Awarded 116 days detention; EPDR 02 June 1988**. This was recited during inspection every

175

morning. One of the first things I was advised to do by my fellow inmates was to make a "chuff chart" recording the number of days left to release in the back of a note pad. It was good psychological exercise every Sunday evening to cross off a week's worth of dates.

'The main lights went on at 0600 every morning. (The night lights were on in the room all night and towards the end how I wished to sleep with the lights off.) Everyone got up for a wash and shave and to get ready for breakfast. The whole block paraded to be taken over to the dining block about 20ft away. I was told each meal contained enough calories to get you through to the next meal.

'Every person started off with the basic weeks "1, 2, 3" which was all marching and running. Drill was no issue for me after being through the Guards Depot at Pirbright and I didn't mind doing it. But after drill came PT and I was in for a shock. After being AWOL for ten months and not involved in any PT at my camp prior to going to MCTC, I was carrying a bit of weight. To top it all the Staff in charge was a tug of war freak and insisted we all carried a half-filled sandbag in each hand everywhere we went. I have never felt pain like that since, although, to be fair, the staff carried them also.

'At the end of the third week of basic we had a pass out parade in front of the camp Commander. On successful completion of this we

St George's Church, MCTC Colchester, 1988.

Major General Sir Norman Arthur CBE topping out at MCTC, 1986.

went on to the advanced weeks one to eleven which consisted of weapons, NBC, first aid etc. These were all taught to a higher level than a soldier would normally get and the class sizes were quite small, so more tuition to each individual was available. This was when I started to understand what one Staff had said in my first week. "You as a soldier have broken down, that's why you have come to me. I intend to put you back through the sausage machine to break you down and rebuild you in to a better trained soldier than most in your regiments. This will give you the skills and confidence to push on." A test at the end of each week ensured you progressed to the next stage. If you did not pass you had to redo the week. I started to mix with more and more guys from different regiments and corps and two lads from 45 Commando helped me greatly not only with my fitness but also with weapons. These two lads helped me achieve what a lot of people can't and won't do – push through the pain barrier. I can say hand on my heart that this does exist and to go through it during a run and feel like you are only on a stroll is amazing.

'During my stay there was a prison officer strike. This meant that most of the staff went to cover the civilian prisons and instructors were brought in from the training camps. Our new instructor was from the Coldstream Guards. He smoked like nobody I've ever met, but was also a very fair person and didn't judge any of us, I remember once he took

177

us to the firing ranges and stopped off at a shop and bought us all a can of Coke. How nice that tasted! He also used the site to our advantage during NBC training with the old buildings that had been reduced to rubble used as a back drop to what a nuclear attack may look like.

'Routine in the block was boring. After we had our lunch, the staff went for theirs. That meant we were locked up in our rooms sat on those horrible plastic chairs doing our kit as sitting on beds was not allowed until sleep time. The same happened again at dinner time. After dinner and the doors were unlocked, you had the chance to do your ironing for the following day. There was only one iron so blokes queued to try to get everything done in a two-hour window.

'We won the radio a couple of times for having the best room. We used to listen to Radio Caroline before it sunk! Every evening before the rooms were locked, the tea trolley would come round with a mug of tea and a nice slab of cake. You never got this kind of room service back at camp.

'The staff were a mixed bunch. The head Staff was a right dick and seemed to get off on winding the lads up. I just wish he had worn his hat in a more professional manner as it really wound me up. There was a Marine Commando, a big Scottish fella, firm but fair, and a very nice man who didn't judge at all. There was also a little Scottish bastard they

Sanitation party MCTC Colchester c1988.

called "Shergar". I believe he was from the Black Watch Regiment where he was also despised. I remember coming back from the cookhouse one day to find our end of the block in uproar. Someone had trashed the rooms, all the polished floors were scuffed and marked, and this prat had a smug look on his face. I thought at one point a guy from one of the Scottish Regiments was going to kill him. Shergar was removed from the block and worked at the guardroom for the rest of my time there.

'We were given a small allowance each week; I think it was £2.20. I was amazed at what you could get for that, one pack of ten fags ("tailor-mades" we called them, only to be smoked one per day), one pack of rolling tobacco, one pack of rolling papers, one Mars bar and a couple of stamps. You were not allowed to carry more than ten per cent of your allowance over to the following week.'

In January 1988 F Wing opened to accommodate the WRAC and wives of SUS. The women followed the same regime as their male counterparts. D block, previously known as C block, opened on 6 April 1988 and in the next six months received more SUS than C block had in ten years. Jack Sharp recalls: 'I served six years at the MCTC from 1987 to 1995) working on D wing. They were the best years of my life!'

On 9 April 1988 it was time for the official dedication service of the new church which had been named the Church of St Michael. The Chaplain General, The Venerable Archdeacon J. Harkness OBE QHC, the Deputy Chaplain General the Reverend Tom Robinson QHC and the Principle Roman Catholic Chaplain to the Forces, J.N. Williams VG, conducted the service which included the handing over the keys by the architects and builders, the blessing of the altar and the blessing of the bell. The bell came from the original church of St Michael and All Angels which stood near the entrance of the camp. Because it suffered from vandalism the vicar asked the MCTC to take the bell down and make use of it.

Dom Prest was still at the MCTC:

'The FA cup final between Liverpool and Wimbledon was taking place and we asked if we could watch it even though I wasn't that much in to football at the time. The whole block was told that if they wanted to see the game then *everyone* had to take *all* of the weapons from the armoury and take them on an eight-mile CFT (combat fitness test) in the allotted time of, I think, one hour and forty minutes. If one person didn't want to do it then no one got to watch the football. Everyone got their kit together and got every piece of hardware from that armoury. The lads

The copse on the Training Area MCTC Colchester after the hurricane in 1987.

who weren't as fit carried the easier weapon and the really fit lads from the Commandos and Airborne went way beyond with some of the gear they carried. Respect lads! The run was completed, the weapons put back in the armoury and the match was watched in the afternoon. Not everyone watched it but they still went through the pain of the run. This camaraderie at its best I think.

'I was once told to help clear away some kit in the camp across the road. My mates the Argyll & Southerland Highlanders had had a sports day or something. I was working with another guy from MCTC and we were carrying a large crash mat to the stores when we decided to take a short cut across the drill square. There was no one around so we thought we would be OK. But three-quarters of the way across a Scottish voice boomed out. "Oi, what are youse doing?" We both froze, dropped the crash mat and smartly came to attention. A bloke in a skirt (kilt) came steaming over to us. We said we were from MCTC and were taking the crash mat to the stores. He promptly told us, "There is only one person allowed on his drill square without permission and that is God! And he's only allowed on there because I can't f*****g see him. Otherwise he'd get a bollocking!" This was classic. Only a drill pig could come up with something like that.

'Every Sunday we had a parade when we were all asked if anybody had any complaints. It was mooted throughout that if you did have a complaint and the visiting officer thought it was frivolous, then you

A signed portrait of the Queen presented to the WO and Sgts' Mess.

Sgt Chris Coslett taking reporters over the assault course, Roman Barracks, c1983.

were in for the high jump. I heard loads of mutterings within the ranks but nobody ever stepped forward. But one Sunday a guy *did* step forward to say that the showers had no anti slip mats. He was promptly marched away to speak further, I assumed, about his "issue". We later saw him being marched at 200mph around camp. I guess the visiting officer thought it was a frivolous complaint.

'During my last week I was not able to sleep and not just because of the night lights. On release day we were told to get in to our No 2 uniform, wished the rest of the lads "Good luck" and then went to collect the rest of our kit which had been put in storage at what seemed a life time ago. We were all given £5, a talking to from the camp Commandant and were then marched to the guardroom and told to stand on one spot. When called we had to move one step forward on to the next spot to be spoken to by the guardroom staff (the spots are about 5ft apart and you need to be about 11ft tall to do it!). If your step forward is not good enough you are threatened with being turned round to complete your stay with them. How they must laugh when you have gone! At the guardroom I was told that I was still a soldier under sentence, an SUS until midnight that night, and could be called back and locked up at any time. I was to report to my camp guardroom with the paperwork. I was then ordered on to the transport with my kitbags, paperwork and travel warrant. We were taken to the train station and offloaded and told not to darken their door step again or else. I was free at last! I remember buying a newspaper and thinking, "I don't have to share this with eight other lads. Great."

'I returned to my unit in Windsor, allocated to C Squadron, and then spent time in Cyprus, Germany, Canada and Gulf War 1. I left in 1992.

'My experience with MCTC was not as bad as I had expected. I think when the word "Colchester" is mentioned within the services, an image of the stockade is brought to the fore but it is not like this at all. The documentary *The Glasshouse* made some years ago has most of the characters I have mentioned in here, although it is a watered down version of what it is actually like.'

The new camp was officially opened on 15 July 1988 by The Secretary of State, George Younger MP. He was met at the gate by the Commandant, Lieutenant Colonel Simon Fordham, the Provost Marshal, Brigadier N. C. Allen OBE ADC and the 2i/c and inspected the Quarter Guard, consisting of SUS, MPSC officers and NCOs. The Secretary made a speech and unveiled the commemorative stone which is made of Stonecutters granite. The Corps flag was unfurled and the parade marched off accompanied by the Regimental Band of the Argyll and Sutherland Highlanders.

Chapter 18

Changes
1989 – 1994

In 1989, thirteen former POWS from the 120 who undertook training for the Roman Catholic Church while POWs during the Second World War, visited MCTC. They were accompanied by relatives, fifteen priests and Father John Harvey of the Church of St James the Less in Priory Street, Colchester. Some of his congregation who were hosting the ex-POWs on their stay in Colchester also attended. The men bought several items of memorabilia from their time in Camp 186. These included a guitar made from "surplus" POW bed frames and a ring made from two florins (two-shilling coins) which they presented to the MCTC.

Although little remained of the old camp, with only one hut retained for posterity after the rebuild, they were able to use the old plans and aerial photos

Ex POWs visit MCTC.

MCTC RAF Course 1984, the first full course.

of the camp to orientate themselves. In the 1922 Corps Journal several of the visitors recalled their 'initial horror' at arriving from 'other, gentler camps, such as that at Market Drayton to find a barbed wire cage and for many months, tough, angry Polish guards.'

That same year Lieutenant Colonel Fordham left and the new Commandant, Lieutenant Colonel Nick Emson MC of the Coldstream Guards arrived. The new education wing was now well established and had acquired six computer/word processor/monitor systems to teach computer skills to the SUS of both A and D wings. One detainee who served a six-month sentence in 1989:

'I received a "Dear John" letter which led me to plan an escape. It sounds very dramatic thinking back, but at the time it seemed very serious. I did escape whilst being escorted for treatment to Queen Elizabeth Military Hospital (QEMH) at Woolwich. I then subsequently handed myself in after a day at a local police station and had to return to MCTC. I got two weeks added to my sentence and had three days solitary confinement with the loss of mattress and bedding. I believe two of the escorting Military Provost staff lost their long service good conduct medals over the incident. Looking back it is not something I am proud of.'

Danny Mills:

'I was really glad to get there in 1989 as I had already spent five days at the Royal Scots detention centre in Werl. As I was classed as an outsider (a Corps and not Regiment) they pretty much went to town on me. Anything after that was going to be an easier option! When I arrived at the guardroom, having been escorted from Germany by people I had never met before, my eyes were opened. The escorts got ragged all over the place. In my eyes they had not done anything wrong and it was more of a show of power from MCTC staff. I suppose it was a way of putting the frighteners on anybody that witnessed it and spreading the word that you never wanted to be in there.

'All the detainees who arrived at the same time were taken into a small annex of the guardroom and told to drop their trousers. Everyone was then "inspected" by a medic to make sure no one was bringing in any uninvited guests!

'MCTC was split into three parts. I was placed in A Wing which was for all soldiers who were "soldiering on" after their sentence was completed. Soldiers in D wing were being discharged on completion. I remember there were a lot of attitudes in that side and they were mainly kept separate from A wing. The D wing detainees did most of the manual chores on a daily basis such as kitchen duties.

'The other wing was known internally as "solitary". I never saw the place but was made aware that one person was in there, a WO2 called Joe. He was a pay WO2 who had been embezzling small amounts from soldiers' MMA claims over a few years. Regardless of the crime committed by all detainees, the crime of stealing off other soldiers was deemed the lowest. I heard on the grapevine that WO2 Joe had completed twenty-one years' service when he was caught. He was discharged from the Forces on completion of his six months and lost his entire pension.

'There was the option to be promoted (internally) during your time there. Every week you had an assessment based on drill, fitness, main instructors' reports etc. If you started soldiering and getting on with it you would get promoted each week. Those on short terms, such as myself, wore a yellow tag on our shoulders to show we weren't there for very long. Long termers, there for between four and six months, normally wore a red tag.

'The funnies I remember were things like trying to have the best room. Everyone was in competition with each other for the radio. I thought it was compulsory (and I suppose it was for fear of a beating

Pioneer Dave Wilkinson and George Younger MP during the opening ceremony, c1988.

from your roommates) to scrape the paint off everything metallic you owned such as polish tins and toothpaste tubes and shining it. We never won the radio whilst I was there!

'I look back and grin at the stupidity of some things such as never being allowed to have an empty tube of toothpaste. Every time you used it you had to blow back into the tube to make it look full again. Other amusements were pulling the laces out of your boots and tying one to the last hole and swinging it out of the window to the next room. This was our way of trading cigarette papers, matches (sliced into three with a razor blade to make them last longer) and tobacco. There were no bars as such, just very thin windows.

'One final little bit I recall is that every Friday an MP would turn up for a parade and ask if anyone had any complaints. Everyone was briefed beforehand that they would be in the shit if anyone ever said anything. On one occasion a Scots Guard decided he was going to make a formal complaint during this parade. I was never really sure what happened to him, but I suspect that he wasn't given an extra guard duty!'

(*I was a little confused about the toothpaste so I asked Danny whether the tubes had to be full to look tidier*). He said: 'The toothpaste ... yes, everything had to be immaculate. We had to break open razors to scrape the paint off everything and shine it up.' Danny also recalls the Scots Guard attempting to escape, getting on the roof and trying to pee on the staff below! He further remembers: 'Whenever we went for a run, which was at least once daily, we had to stop at the guardroom to check out the "Red Star parcels". These were detainees classed as a flight risk. It was really annoying to the staff as they had to provide two extra staff as security on each run.'

On Friday, 17 November 1989, the Secretary of Defence, the Right Honourable Tom J. King, visited MCTC. After a short briefing from the Commandant about the unit's role and structure, Mr King was shown round the accommodation blocks, training wing and the farm.

In 1990, in response to the collapse of the Soviet Union and the end of the Cold War, the government of the day began the restructuring of HM Forces. The MPSC was subsumed under the auspices of the Adjutant General's Corps which was formed on 6 April 1992. The AGC also encompassed the Royal Army Pay Corps, the Corps of Royal Military Police, the Royal Army Educational Corps, the Army Legal Corps and the Staff Clerks from the Royal Army Ordnance Corps.

The Women's Royal Army Corps was disbanded and its members were transferred to other corps of the Army, including the Adjutant General's Corps. The new Corps consisted of four branches: Staff and Personnel Support (SPS), Provost (Royal Military Police (RMP), Military Provost Staff (MPS), Educational and Training Services (ETS) and the Army Legal Services (ALS).

Mortuary MCTC.

On 5 April 1993, the clerks from the Royal Corps of Transport, The Royal Pioneer Corps and the Army Catering Corps were also transferred to the AGC on formation of the Royal Logistics Corps. Three months later, on 1 July 1993, the clerks from all other Arms and Services were subsumed into SPS Branch. The Military Provost Guard Service (MPGS) was formed in 1997 and is part of the Provost Branch. Jim Robinson:

'This was not a happy mix! Although the two Provost Units lost their Corps status and were joined into one branch of the AGC, the Provost Branch, luckily they retained their individual hat badges. It must be admitted that the formation of the AGC was a big mess. Nothing was organized properly and there had been no coordinated planning. One example of this was just before the actual start of the AGC. A Colonel in the RAPC told me of the changes and talked about the funds of the Association. He understood that the Adjutant General would take over your funds and that the Charity Commission had said he could do so. He was very much taken aback when I told him that the funds were nothing to do with the Adjutant General, and that neither he nor the Charity Commission could do anything unless the Trustees said so.

Richard Simpson remembers visiting Colchester. 'I was doing my warrant officers course at Woolwich in 91. I couldn't believe how smart the place looked. All the squaddies looked happy, especially the soldier on guys. Before I visited I had pre-conceived ideas of everyone running about, but it was far from that. The staff actually cared about the soldiers under their care and the pride they took in returning soldiers back to their units as reformed characters was obvious.'

Lance Corporal Webster ACC joined the Catering Platoon in April 1991. Writing in the 1991 Corps Journal, he said: 'The catering Corps currently consists of nine chefs and a master chef. We are divided between the SUS main kitchen, Corporals' Mess and the combined Officers' and Sergeants' Mess Kitchen. We cater for between 180 to 200 SUS daily on four hours' notice. The chefs in the main kitchen work very hard as there are only three working split shifts. Credit must also go to any SUS cooks who help with the daily workload.'

The year 1991 also saw the arrival of a new Commandant, Lieutenant Colonel Patrick Gascoigne MBE, and the departure of Father John McGrath after five years as the MCTC padre.

Squadron Leader Paul S. Brennan RAF (Retd) remembers Colchester for a slightly different reason:

'In 1992 I was the Flight Commander for the last entry of apprentices at RAF Cosford. A whole batch of them had been doing some creative accounting with their travel claims and were treated to stays of various lengths in a number of different regional detention centres. The two with the greatest number of claims were sent to Colchester for sixty days! One of them was the "mastermind" while the other was simply a young and gullible lad who had no idea of the seriousness of what he was doing. Towards the end of their time, I was required to visit and inform them of their fate. The main culprit was to be discharged on completion of sentence and the other was to be "recovered" back into training with the expectation of graduating with his peers as planned the following year.

'Although I was an officer in uniform I felt guilty! I am not sure why but I just felt this sense of foreboding and almost walked straight back out again. I was greeted by a fellow RAF officer, whom I assumed, by the look of his rather expansive waist line, had not served with his own regiment for some time. He informed me that he had actually been forgotten by the RAF and not had any form of annual appraisal for a number of years. He said he hadn't drawn attention to himself as it suited him to stay at Colchester for a number of personal reasons. He said that as long as he still got paid every month, it was his intention to keep his head down and say nothing!

'As the Flight Commander I made a conscious decision not to differentiate between the apprentices who "went away" (ten of them) and those who didn't get caught! At the end of the course I had to recommend three apprentices for a competition to win enough free flying hours to gain a private pilot's licence. A day after the forms went in, I realized that my second choice was a young man with sixty days in Colchester on his CV! I called my boss to let him know in case there were any repercussions. He said not to worry as it clearly demonstrated that we had successfully rehabilitated him back into the mainstream RAF!'

Neil Howard (651Sq, 1 Regiment Army Air Corps) was nineteen when he was sentenced to sixty days for possession of cannabis in1992:

'I was sentenced with a friend of mine and we were placed in the Regimental cells in Hildesheim, just outside Hanover, in preparation for Colchester. It was continuously drilled into us that we were not to let the Regiment down anymore. It certainly had the effect of making me wonder what on earth I had got myself into. The myth of the Glasshouse was in full flow. The anticipation was horrible and very nerve wracking. The day came and I was escorted on the flight from

A detainee room from the 1990s. You can see how bare it is compared to the later picture.

Hanover to Luton and then Luton to Colchester by two NCOs going home on leave. They were not amused. Another myth of Colchester was that if your escorts lose you they have to serve your sentence!

'Upon arrival at the big metal gates I was told to stand on the green circle, my escorts on the red. A barrage of abuse was screamed at me and I was welcomed in. The escorts weren't, and remained on the other side to witness my humiliation. I definitely remember the Staff screaming at me as I stood there clutching my kitbag. The last thing my escorts saw of me was as I disappeared quickly whilst struggling with my kit at a ridiculous pace. It was then into a room where my kit was literally tipped out onto the floor and sifted through.

'One thing that does stick out is one of the staff asking me if I smoked. I did back then. He immediately dug all the polish out of my tin and tipped it on the floor! He went onto to explain that I should scrape all the paint off the tin and then using a spoon push it out from the inside on both the lid and the base. I had to twist it off at the dip which opened the tin so that a boot lace could be threaded through. A knot is then tied to prevent it going all the way through and the lace is doubled back over the ridge as the opening device. This metal shiny circular ball was where I used to keep my tobacco, papers and matches with strike.

'I was asked if I'd got all that and then told to clear up my mess! I was on A wing and was given a green band to wear to show I was on the basic first rung of detainee status. The cell was an eight-man dorm and my arrival was seen as extra work for those already into the routine because of the standard expected of your locker and kit. Your shirts had to be squared off; the height of the top pocket flap and the width of the top pocket buttons. There were little tricks to minimize disturbance of your locker. As both your socks had to be identically squared off and stacked up, I used to soak all my socks, except one pair, in shaving foam and water. I used dominoes to shape and create a flat front, by placing the domino inside the sock, folding it over and then placing them all down the back of the radiator to dry. This set the socks in a uniform shape. The remaining pair was worn during the day and hand washed in the sink each evening, thus not disturbing my now perfect locker. Best room equalled the radio, but it was only for a couple of hours each night.

'It was constant mental pressure and physical training. I've never been particularly religious but I went to church each Sunday for a sit down and to relax – as much you can in the Glasshouse. But even that was a drilled event and we were marched there by the standard 147 paces a minute.

'Mealtime was another drilled event as we had to be lined up in three ranks wearing lightweights and trainers and with plastic knife, fork and spoon in our blue plastic cups. Your cup is held behind your back with your thumb holding your cutlery in place. We were then marched off to collect our trays. This all had to be done in silence and if we were caught talking it meant twenty press ups. But there were unique ways like thumb touching or finger tip touching. I definitely remember these!

'It was constant go, go, go with no let up during the day. It was either physical training or drill out on the square. One lad got an extra two days on his sentence because he was found with a cigarette in his boot after a visit.

'It was a long sixty days and I was extremely relieved when it was finally over.'

Paul Mills is a Master at Arms in the Royal Navy Police. He joined the service in September 1989 and continues to serve:

'In 1993 I was a Radio Operator (General) First Class RO1(G). I was attached to the Naval Provost Marshal Portsmouth as a Travelling Escort Driver, escorting naval prisoners from HMS *Nelson* in Portsmouth to MCTC. I also picked up convicted prisoners around the country to convey to MCTC.

'On one occasion I picked up a prisoner from Plymouth who was a stoker (Marine Engineering Mechanic) who had been given a lengthy sentence for assault. Me and Able Seaman Missleman AB(M) Jan T*****, took him from the recess facility in HMS *Nelson*, up the A3 in Hampshire and then stopped at a Shell garage to refuel. When I got back to the vehicle I said to AB T*****: "Right we are off then." He grunted and said: "Just waiting for ***** then". Jan had let him out of the vehicle, lent him some money and told him to go for a wee and to get him twenty Bensons! After much panic, I found him in the queue, two from the front, with some crisps and an ice cream!

'The journey to MCTC was very stony as you can imagine. When we got there we had to do the usual thing of standing on the spot outside the guardroom; red spot, green spot. One of the corporals was possibly confused because we were in civilian clothing. An RN prisoner transfer officer came out and said that if we wanted a cup of coffee we should just go down the lane where the back door to the mess was open. We drove down and had just parked up when one of the stewards came out and invited us to sit down. He gave us a starter, a main meal and coffee and generally looked after us for an hour or so. As we left, I asked where we paid and the steward said, "No problem. Sign with your mess number". As two ABs (in effect privates) we had just spent an hour and a half in the WO and Sergeants' Mess! The steward went a funny shade of purple, uttered a few choice verbs and asked us (not so politely) to get out. As the senior service you can get away with murder with the Army!'

Tony Yarwood, Parachute Regiment:

'I was in the MPS from 1993 and left the Army in 2003. Coming from the Parachute Regiment I loved my fitness and this was first on the agenda when I took over as RSM. If a soldier was not fighting fit in my eyes then he or she is a risk. I believed this essential element of soldiering was the key to a successful career. I made a point of accompanying troops, be it detainees or staff, on their fitness tests. I could feel my ears burning when I approached the troops who were just about to go on a run or tab. They probably said to themselves: "Oh no, the RSM coming with us. S**t". I also made a point of visiting the classrooms where the detainees were being taught weapon training, first aid, NBC or fieldcraft.'

Martin 'Jock' Laird was given 112 days in 1993. 'It was crap to be honest. I met some good blokes and had some laughs with an RAF REG bloke E**** and some other guy (150 SUS L****) who used to do the "Monty Python knights that say nicht" routine. Great stuff really but the food was rubbish.'

On Thursday, 4 November 1993, Her Royal Highness the Duchess of Kent GCVO visited MCTC in her capacity as Deputy Colonel in Chief of the Adjutant General's Corps (AGC). She was greeted by the Lord Lieutenant for the County of Essex, The Lord Braybrook JP, the Deputy Colonel Commandant AGC (RMP/MPS), Major General CBQ Wallace OBE, the Inspector of Military Prisons and the Commandant of MCTC, Lieutenant Colonel P.E.C. Gascoigne MBE SG. She planted an oak tree in front of MCTC HQ to commemorate her visit before being briefed on the role of the centre by Gascoigne and Brigadier Cameron.

After coffee with the staff and their wives the Duchess began a tour of the establishment. In A Company there were several displays including signals classes, NBC warfare drills, bayonet fighting, anti-tank simulator work and some gymnasium-based fitness exercises. From there she toured the education wing where the Senior Education Officer described the vocational and resettlement training given to those being discharged from the Services. The tour finished with the accommodation for female detainees, followed by a visit to the farm.

The last remaining Nissen hut from the war time POW camp – circa 1990s. No longer there now.

In 1994 there were several more changes. A new Commandant, Lieutenant Colonel Glen Grant, Royal Artillery, arrived. The MPS now had their first female members of staff. Investigations were made into the feasibility of outside contractors running the unit and the MCTC had to prepare its own bid to run the establishment.

A fifteen per cent cut in the budget necessitated a major reorganization which led to several posts being civilianized. Despite the cuts, work continued on the building of more accommodation for the female wing, the Sergeants' Mess and extra room for the SUS. This was necessary because of the extra tasks taken on by the MCTC such as the detention of female SUS, the safe custody of officers and the transfer of all Royal Navy SUS after the closure of the Royal Navy Detention Quarters (RNDQs) at Portsmouth.

Also in 1994, a television crew visited Colchester and made the film *Glasshouse* for the Channel 4 series 'Cutting Edge'. Staff who watched the programme later that year were disappointed as it appeared extremely biased, concentrating as it did on two men from D wing. Jim Robinson remarked: 'They missed out on all the positive aspects of the unit such as the welfare work, counselling, education, and the men from A wing.'

Chapter 19

Marching Towards Better Citizenship 1995 – 2000

Despite the misgivings of the staff, there was a huge response to the programme. It resulted in over sixty ministerial questions in Parliament and a rise in the number of visitors, especially from the Home Office and Prisons Department. It was undoubtedly instrumental in the setting up of the Her Majesty's Youth Offender Institute (HMYOI) Colchester. Max Aitken:

'I went to MCTC to undertake the "Probs Course" on 7 February 1994. The course was twelve weeks long as it was the second last course within the "old methods". I had come from serving with the now defunct 5 Airborne Brigade to MCTC. I had Rod Douglas (Scots Guards), Gary Speirs (Royal Irish), Chris MacDonald (Royal Irish), Adi Brock (RLC), Lex lambert (Coldstream Guards), Keith Shorty Green (Royal Signals), Julie Greenwood (WRAC I think), Diane Wright (ACC), and Axel Foley on my course. We were there when they were filming the Channel 4 documentary.

'I did my wing training on A wing under the guidance of Sergeants "Skiff" Skiffington and Bob Shaw and Carl Davies (WO2), but ended up on D wing under Baz Ainsworth – who puffed away on a pipe and relied on a timesheet held in his hat before he made any decisions regarding the SUS. Life under him was never fast-paced. I lasted six months in the wing before being moved to the training wing/gymnasium under Graham Giddy (WO2).

'It was the CO there at that time who instigated changes for the better. He was Royal Artillery, a Commonwealth athlete I believe, and he went through MCTC like a whirlwind, upsetting all those "dinosaurs" who could not or would not accept change. It was

Presentation to Lt Gen Sir Rollo Pain by RSM C Gingell.

predominately the best thing that happened to the place in my opinion. I wrote a paper for the CO requesting that he implement changes to their antiquated escape procedure, and after speaking with SUS from both wings, I knew they would not follow what we then had. The CO changed it accordingly and I think it was WO2 Steph Powers who was told to undertake this. 'I was there from February 1994 until October 1995, when I went to AGC Worthy Down as MPS Platoon Sergeant.'

Clive Rowland went to Colchester in 1996:

'Having spent eight and a half years in the RAF as a Police Dog Handler, a serious error of judgement ended my career after a prolonged investigation and a District Court Martial.

'I was sentenced to 112 days at MCTC for two thefts and arrived there with a great deal of nervous expectations but mature enough to face my errors and get on with it. D Company would be my new home for a while where I would learn to make bed packs again and stand to complete attention when members of staff were present.

'I was escorted to the guardroom, met by a very large MPSC and processed but once inside it wasn't that bad. In fact it was quite relaxed really provided you jumped when asked, and overall the discipline not what I thought. For the three months I was there I enjoyed most of my time embracing the regime. It helped me reflect on what I had become.

I met some very nice people including the staff, who in most part were honest and caring and, although I looked forward to my release date but not so much my future, I felt very strange leaving having been so used to a uniformed structure.

'MCTC shaped me. It made me face my fears and even now when I go anywhere I am not comfortable with I think, "Well it can't be worse than MCTC".

'It's fifteen years since I left MCTC. Life has been a struggle but I have worked hard to gain a career working with troubled young people and helping to guide them in life away from similar misfortunes that I experienced. I'd like to say that it helped me and I hope that it continues to do that for others who may be in similar situations to me.'

In 1996 the staff and detainees of the MCTC decided to pool their energy and once again raise money for Children in Need. They were determined to better their previous total of some £1,700 raised in 1995.

The detainees of the confinement block suggested a Land's End to John O' Groats cycle and row event, some 1478km to be completed in twenty-four hours in the gymnasium. By 0500 on 24 October the challenge was complete but with seven hours still to go they decided to carry on. By midday they had completed a total of 2011km and raised £1,043.57.

Youth Offender Sign side by side with the MCTC sign during the experiment in the 1990s – picture courtesy of Lt Col J E M Crowe.

The main fund-raising event took place on 15 November when the detainees pulled an open decker bus decorated by children from local schools, around the local married quarters. There was also a car boot sale and bouncy castle at the Musket Club and in the evening a disco and prize draw. The whole event raised £3,702.70p.

New Commandant, Lieutenant Colonel Julian Crowe, from the Scots Guards arrived in 1997. He began preparing for the Young Offenders intake:

'In April 1995 Home Secretary Michael Howard visited MCTC. He was particularly impressed by the quality of training offered to the SUS and by the quality and enthusiasm of the Military Provost Staff. He also noted that MCTC had spare capacity and that part of it could be used for Young Offenders under his control. He wrote to the Secretary of State for Defence, Malcolm Rifkind, and proposed a trial to compare the MCTC regime with a High Intensity Training (HIT) regime being established at Thorn Cross Young Offenders' Institution in Lancashire.

'The strategic aim of the project was to establish, in a year-long trial, a YOI to provide selected offenders with a regime which follows, as closely as possible, that provided in D Company MCTC, with a view to reducing recidivism in the YO population, and to train prison staff in the Army's approach to managing detainees. D Company comprises those SUS sentenced to detention and dismissal from HM Forces and their regime prepares them for civilian life by providing trade and rehabilitation training.

'The operational objectives laid down for the YOI by the Prison Service are: "… To teach self-respect for individuals, authority, property and society, to instil self-discipline, to give individuals self-confidence and esteem, to impart moral values, to be physically demanding, to teach life skills and to provide rehabilitation training."

'The Mission Statement outlined the aims of the project. This was to develop a model establishment, the aim of which is to turn young offenders into better citizens and prevent their return to crime. This is to be achieved through a demanding regime of training, rehabilitation and care intended to promote self-discipline, self-confidence, self-esteem, self-motivation and self-pride.

'The ethos behind the project was to treat, train and encourage YOs, so that they realize what is worthwhile in life and seek it; to foster the habit of discipline of the right sort – imposed discipline leading to self-discipline – and to encourage personal responsibility in its application to life and communal responsibility. Young offenders are to be made to feel that whatever their background, they are never free from their moral responsibility and that it is in their own personal power to say yes or no. They must know that to live in any type of society there are rules by which all must abide, that they should face life as it is, and not as they might wish it to be, and to put their past, whatever it was like, behind them and build for the future.

'There were three phases to the HMYOI Colchester trial, the first of which was to select suitable candidates aged eighteen and twenty-one with between four to eight months to serve. They had to be suitable for open conditions and not be a danger to the public as well as mentally and physically able to cope with the regime. It was also important to pick those who were likely to benefit from it. The Deputy Governor and MCTC Senior Education Officer would be responsible for the training regime and the evaluation would be conducted by Professor David Farrington, Dr Kate Painter and colleagues from the Institute of Criminology, Cambridge University. They would study the behaviour of the YOs during their time at the YOI, and then again after a suitable interval to assess the impact on recidivism.

'The staging system that was already in place in MCTC provided rewards for good behaviour and was considered a vital element of the regime. Offenders should arrive every six weeks after the first intake and the ratio should be one member of staff to every two YOs.

'The YO regime is to be based on firmness, tempered with understanding and the avoidance of harsh treatment. Young offenders will be required to drill to the laid down standards and to march about the establishment at all times. They are to refer to all members of HMYOI Colchester and the MCTC as "Sir" or "Staff" and are to request permission from staff to speak or carry out any action. Staff are to treat YOs correctly at all times and are to issue "SMART" orders – Specific, Measurable, Attainable, Realistic and Timely.'

The scheme started in February 1997 and ran for thirteen months but Lieutenant Colonel Crowe had his problems. 'There is without doubt much ill-informed opposition to the YOI Colchester project among the staff of certain YOIs. This has become particularly obvious from YOs' comments during the interview process, although in some cases the regimes themselves also have a marked effect on their attitudes.'

The reception programme was designed to run over four days to allow the YOs time to settle in. They arrived by Prison Service transport on a Thursday morning. Lieutenant Colonel Crowe:

'On arrival they are documented, issued with basic clothing, measured for uniform and given a meal. They receive an opening address from the Commandant on their first evening. The following day uniform is issued, hair is cut and medical assessments are carried out. Over the next three days they are introduced to the regime of the YOI so that on the Monday morning they are at an acceptable standard to take their place alongside the SUS of MCTC. They receive lectures from the Chaplain, the Samaritans and the Board of Visitors. Mandatory drug testing is also administered.

'Some YOs have been apprehensive about what was awaiting them, but this has very quickly been dispelled through a calm and efficient reception procedure, and by the positive attitude shown by staff to all new arrivals. The standard of kit and area cleanliness achieved in a short period of time has been remarkable, with great enthusiasm and pride being displayed at a very early stage.'

Brig Mike Matthews present to WO & Sgts' Mess a picture of stone cutters, RSM Bill Wilson.

Despite opposition from local MP Bob Russell, the Labour Government and the Prison Governors Association, it appeared to be a great success. Jim Robinson remembers comments from some of the YOs. 'One said "This is the first time I have not had to watch my back", another that "This is the first time I have been treated like a man".' The NCOs certainly enjoyed working with the YOs and the prison officers who were attached, enjoyed working in the military environment here.

Feedback at the time also seemed to show the scheme was successful as Lieutenant Colonel Crowe states:

'The YOs' attitude towards the regime is reassuringly positive. Once fully integrated into the regime they rapidly become smart, polite, self-confident and enthusiastic. They comply willingly with the regime and display pride, self-discipline and respect. They appear to have a positive attitude against re-offending and towards obtaining worthwhile qualifications and employment on release.

'It would be easy to say that this is only natural because YOI Colchester receives "model prisoners", but they are from a broad spectrum of backgrounds, and it is felt that equal success could be achieved with YOs charged with more serious offences. The offenders respond to being kept busy on worthwhile activities, and to being treated in a fair, humane and adult manner. They all indicate that they are very happy with the standard of catering, even though only one choice of menu is offered. They also respond to a clean environment and look after their accommodation; there is no graffiti in evidence. The use of the Samaritan line has not yet been requested.

'It is not just the military staff who felt the trial was successful. The reaction of families during visits is most reassuring. All comment on how smart and well their boys look and how positive, self-confident and happy they seem. They are also impressed by the interest shown by staff in their well-being. All seem thoroughly in favour of the regime and the perceived good effect it was having. A greater concern is the perception of the remainder of the prison population, encouraged by some members of staff and the national media, that HMYOI Colchester is being run as a "Boot Camp", with harsh treatment and "in your face" discipline. It is hoped, where possible, to overcome this adverse impression by taking Stage 2 YOs along during the interview process for new intakes.

'As expected, discipline has not been a major problem. To date, there have been only minor breaches of discipline, including three fights. Soon after arrival offenders are encouraged to come up with their own "contract" regarding behaviour. It is also worth noting that most of the YOs responsible for the disciplinary incidents have apologised to staff afterwards. The most remarkable, but not unexpected, aspect of the regime has been the lack of bullying. The offenders say they feel safe in the Colchester environment.'

HMYOI Colchester opened on 20 February 1997 and closed on 31 March 1998. During the time that it was in operation, sixty-seven young offenders were admitted. Reported Lieutenant Colonel Crowe: 'Of these, five were removed to other establishments for disciplinary reasons and forty-eight were released on completion of sentence. The final tranche of young offenders, whose sentences had not expired, were transferred during the week of 23 – 27 March 1998 to establishments of their choice. Ten chose to remain together in the Carlford Unit, an enhanced YOI regime at HMYOI Hollesley Bay near Colchester. To date, it is believed that six of those released have re-offended, including one who committed his offences having absconded whilst on a community visit, but one of these cases is as yet not fully confirmed. Our Senior Research Officer has predicted a recidivism figure of twenty-six per cent over the two-year period of the evaluation, but this figure has yet to be substantiated. The previous best re-offending rate for any other prison regime is believed to be forty-six per cent.'

On Wednesday, 8 April 1998, at a Special Council Meeting held at Colchester Town Hall, the borough conferred the rare honour of the Freedom of Colchester on 156 Provost Royal Military Police and Military Corrective Training Centre. The Freedom of the Borough had only been granted three times since 1968 and was the highest civic honour a local authority can convey.

On Friday, 3 July 1998, the Duchess of Gloucester visited the MCTC for the first time since becoming the Deputy Colonel in Chief to the Adjutant Generals Corps, and on 4 July 156 Provost Company and MCTC exercised its privilege of marching through the streets of Colchester with bayonets fixed. The Band of the Scots Guards led the twenty-minute procession followed by the MCTC Commandant Lieutenant Colonel Crowe SG on horseback. Major R. W. Silk MBE RMP, Officer Commanding RMP, rode in a Royal Military Police Land Rover which also contained the Freedom Scrolls.

In April 1997, Staff Sergeant Tony Yarwood was made SNCO of projects and has since overseen more than fifty at MCTC. Various outside projects continued in 1998 at St Helena Hospice and The Winged Fellowship. There was also the replacement of sinks and toilets at Kingsford Junior School and work at Alderman Blaxill School to provide access to a medical centre. The detainees helped raise money outside Sainsbury's at Stanway for the Army Benevolent Fund and helped erect and dismantle equipment for the Colchester History Fayre.

Tony Yarwood went on to win the first – and only – Wilkinson Sword of Peace in MPSC/MPS history, was RSM during the MPS Centenary and re-wrote the Regimental Police Course criteria. He also represented the unit at cross country, squash and football and made thousands of pounds for charity while IC Projects:

'I had the pleasure of serving under Major Alan Licence. He was the OC and I was the CSM of A Company. He was probably the best officer and OC that I have served under in Para Regiment and the MPS.

'Do I have any regrets about serving at the Glasshouse? I enjoyed what I achieved, but left slightly disillusioned at the lack of support for staff in such a small and unique place. My loyalties were always with the Parachute Regiment and still are today and maybe that did not help. Needless to say it is a unique organization and each and every member of staff should be very proud at what they do there for those soldiers who require pointing in the right direction.'

By 1999 female detainees were no longer kept in F Wing. They were now segregated in the male Company lines. The new Commandant, Lieutenant Colonel S. A. Jasper RTR, arrived and Lieutenant Colonel Crowe left for pastures new after receiving an OBE in the New Year's Honours List. 'I viewed this primarily as an award for all the members of staff at the MCTC, both military and civilian, for their combined efforts during my time as Commandant. Without their constant support, it would have been impossible to realize the many achievements of the past three years.'

Chapter 20

HMIP Comes to MCTC
2000 – 2004

The previous ten years had brought massive changes to the MCTC. By 2002 all SUS rooms had radios, there was a choice of three menus, the food was ordered in advance and cooked to order, and the SUS were allowed to talk during mealtimes. In addition, they were allowed one free ten-minute phone call per week. Weekend visits from family and friends were increased to both mornings and afternoons, and the detainees were given the opportunity to participate in adventure training and outward-bound activities such as hill walking, canoeing and sailing. A video library had been introduced and all SUS were allowed to watch videos at the weekend at the discretion of the staff. Those in Stage 3 could also watch them during the week.

There was new suicide awareness and self-harm policy which included in-depth interviewing of SUS on admission and the creation of the BS (Blue Star) category for those deemed at great or immediate risk. It was also possible, at the Commandant's discretion, for SUS to go on temporary release for compassionate reasons such as a funeral or the birth of their offspring. Citizen Advice Bureau and drug and alcohol counsellors visited to assist those who needed help. Detainees in A Company could attend maths and English classes in the Education Centre, something which had previously only been available for those in D Company. A computer terminal was installed in E and C blocks for use under supervision, and swimming was introduced as part of the physical training programme. In 1999 Garsia Platoon was formed to provide a more vigorous structured twenty-eight day short-term training programme for those with sentences of less than forty-two days.

Stage 3 SUS were now allowed to attend outside college courses and the SUS in D Company were allowed to rest on their beds during weekend patrol period. There was compulsory structured PT during weekday evenings and remedial PT for those who were injured. IT Skills became part of the vocational skills programme for those being discharged, and homeless charity Shelter held weekly housing surgeries for those being discharged.

A slightly less positive change was that all cooking was now done by civilians, thus removing the possibility of training SUS in that area.

Craig 'Pat' Patterson started at the MCTC in 2000:

'I think I started my MCTC chapter as another one was about to close. During my Probationers' Course everyone was issued with a SD hat except me as they didn't have my size. These were worn constantly and some members of staff looked as they had

This is the MPSC badge on the wall by the gate – picture courtesy of WO2 Craig Patterson.

been screwed on when they removed them! Dark blue berets were now the norm. The marching was conducted at a more normal pace and the corridors which used to resonate with screams from staff with high blood pressure now appeared slightly surprised whenever voices were elevated to that kind of unnecessary level.

'Detainees could now speak to each other at the dining table and beds in D blocks made with woolly blankets had slipped away almost unnoticed. Thankfully detainees could light their cigarette from the match of another without someone mentioning "trafficking".

'I have seen some very difficult-to-manage detainees over my tenure. Out of fear they would probably never conform to any real degree and will probably struggle in most environments because there is always a boss and there are always rules. But I have seen many, many more rise from the ashes of a troubled childhood or an unsustainable career to become members of the Special Forces or take up the job opportunities earned while training under sentence. Every corner I turn in the MCTC brings a memory back, from the supervising of detainees leaf-clearing to briefing Provost Marshals.'

In 2001 a new Commandant arrived, Lieutenant Colonel Matthew van Grutten, from the Queens Dragoon Guards. One of those to pass the latest Probationers' Course was Brian Chenier, 'following in my father's footsteps' [22]. Brian was in the AGC (MPS) from 2001 to 2011 and FTRS (HC) from 2011 to 2013:

'My first real memory or knowledge of MCTC goes back to when I was aged ten in 1979. My father was serving in the Military Police and was away on a course at Colchester. I had no real understanding of what this was but knew that if he passed it I would be moving back to the town where I was born in 1969. At the time the family were in Northern Ireland and when the call came through that my father had passed his course we set about packing and cleaning at a rapid pace.

'I have fond memories of Sunday lunches at the MCTC Warrant and Sergeants' Mess, Corps weekend summer fetes and the obligatory children's Christmas party and disco. I was always struck by the calmness of the setting at Berechurch Hall Camp which was only a short but pleasant walk from our house. This was a walk my father and I shared on many occasions when we visited the Mess to play snooker (an excuse for my dad to have a few pints and whinge with the other staff). As I grew older I formulated my plan to join up and settled on the idea of becoming a military policeman but there was always something about MCTC and the idea of working with the SUS that appealed to me.

'On the many trips to the Mess as a child to play snooker I heard some of the stories shared between the staff. I recall one about a sailor who had been absent for a number of years after jumping ship in the Far East. He had become a Buddhist monk and was hidden away in the Tibetan mountains enjoying peace and contemplation when a letter informing him of his father's serious illness eventually found him. A ticket was purchased and wearing sandals and saffron robes he travelled back to the UK, sadly arriving too late. The authorities were alerted on his arrival that he was AWOL and he was arrested, held at MCTC and eventually detained. Out of respect for his beliefs and circumstances, he was allowed to maintain the trappings of Buddhist life and spent his time at MCTC wearing his robes and following his own religious disciplines. After his relatively short sentence he was discharged from service and provided with a ticket back to Tibet. One has to assume that is where he remained.

'In 1985 I joined up as a Junior Leader training out of Bovington and attended my first Remembrance Day service in uniform at MCTC.

'Many years later in 2001, I returned to MCTC, this time as a Sergeant in the RMP to start my Probationers' Course. I had been posted to 156 Pro Company RMP six months before and had enjoyed patrolling my old stomping ground and had visited MCTC a number of times in an official capacity. Long gone were the Nissen huts I remembered from my father's day. Also gone was the ropes course in the trees that lined Stonecutters Avenue. But the water obstacle on the assault course where I had spent hours hunting newts was exactly as I remembered.

'At my interview on the pre-course assessment week the Deputy

Commandant asked why I wanted to transfer and what I knew about the job. This was of course a no brainer, but I am aware how glib my answer must have sounded. Luckily (I think) he knew my father and therefore was able to brief the others that I was probably being truthful.

'Shortly after my transfer to the MPS from the RMP, six members of 156 Provost Company Royal Military Police were killed in Iraq. I personally knew three of them very well. In fact two of them, Corporal Si Miller and Corporal Paul Long, were on my team immediately prior to my transfer. I attended the funerals of all three, the first one being for Si in Washington, Tyne & Wear. It was very well attended with Red Caps everywhere and a large number of civilian police colleagues, some of whom were ex-RMP. I was there wearing the No 2 Dress uniform of a Sergeant in the MPS. Also present was a young soldier from the Light Infantry.

'About six months later I was inducting a new detainee in my role as the Company Clerk for A Company and asked him why he had gone AWOL. He explained that his best mate had been killed in Iraq but his unit had refused to let him attend the funeral as he was LI and the funeral was for a "Monkey". So he went absent and was AWOL at the funeral, which he found slightly amusing as he was surrounded by RMP, Civilian Police and "a screw from Colly". I explained that I was that screw and that in light of his circumstances I would be happy to arrange to take him to the memorial garden at 156 Provost Company so that he could have some time there. I also arranged for the parents of Si Miller to visit him when they next attended Colchester. The detainee had grown up with Si and the attitude of his unit was deplorable, but the irony of the situation was not lost on any of us. I later found out that some very senior members of the RMP present that day were aware of the AWOL status of one of the mourners but compassionately chose to turn a temporary blind eye.

'Between 2001 and my end of service in Feb 2011, I was witness to many changes, some small but many quite monumental in the big scheme of things. MCTC went from being relatively insular and a bit of a mystery to the outside world to being opened up to scrutiny from HMIP.

'The subsequent changes are too many to mention but in my opinion they focussed on fulfilling the recommendations made by HMIP and on the whole were for the better. New positions were established, postings increased, operational deployment to Iraq and later Afghanistan were numerous, and the resultant increase in commitments led to a hugely significant change – the establishment of a TA company. Number 1 Company MPS (V) was set up and I had the honour of being appointed the first permanent Staff Instructor. This was a huge challenge and one I enjoyed. Working with a great team of non-regular, TA and civilian colleagues was a highlight of my whole career. During my time at MCTC I met some truly inspirational people, not all of them staff. Working in such an environment you get to see some of the best – and worst – in people, but when you have played a part in bringing out the best in some of the worst it is hugely satisfying.'

Major (Retd) Paul Ludbrook became Welfare Officer in January 2001 and began making a number of changes, including bringing in many outside groups to provide advice and help to struggling detainees:

'At the turn of the millennium work had already been undertaken to improve the welfare services available to MCTC detainees in the form of drug and alcohol counselling (this service has now been extended to include anger management). The topic of the day was the disproportionate number of ex-Service personnel who were homeless and living rough on the streets of London. It was wrongly perceived that detainees released from MCTC and discharged from the Service were a major contributor to London's homeless population. Although this was not true, it did provoke sufficient interest to develop a number of new initiatives including the full-time post of Housing Officer.

'Outside MCTC, Tri-Service Resettlement were developing a package for Early Service Leavers with less than four years service that would be available to all Service personnel, including those in detention. Almost simultaneously, the Department for Work and Pensions (DWP) in conjunction with the Home Office, developed a scheme called "Freshstart" whereby Jobcentre Plus provided a bespoke service for HM Prisons. Unfortunately, MCTC was not included as part of this initiative and separate negotiations between MCTC and Jobcentre Plus had to take place. Fortunately, the outcome of those negotiations was positive and detainees now discharged from MCTC and the Service enjoy the benefits of employment advice and assistance from Jobcentre Plus on a similar basis to those released from HMP.'

In 2002 the MPS Corps celebrated their centenary. Over 350 past Commandants, members of staff, widows and others, attended one or more of the events; an informal dinner on Friday, Beating Retreat and a formal dinner on Saturday and a church service on the Sunday.

In 2003 the Education Centre added four new qualification-earning courses in the Garage Skills workshop: tyre fitting, wheel alignment, shock absorbers and exhaust fitting as well as a Fork Lift Truck Basic Operator course. These were in addition to those already offered in brickwork, plumbing and painting and decorating.

It was also the year the Military Provost Staff (Volunteers) reappeared, having been axed in 1968 by Harold Wilson's government. It was reformed in response to a gap in the British Army's capability of Prisoner of War handling in the Gulf. The only qualified experts in this field were those at MCTC, but any deployment had an immediate impact on the operational capability of the centre. In response to Operation Telic (the codename for the UK's military operations in Iraq) the unit had recruited, selected, trained and mobilized the new unit in a little over four months; a remarkable achievement.

In 2004 a new Commandant arrived. Lieutenant Colonel Mike Nicholls of the King's Regiment and the Education Centre celebrated having 253 SUS gain nationally recognized qualifications. It was also the year HMIP came to call. Major (Retd) Paul Ludbrook:

'In 2003, Her Majesty's Inspectorate of Prisons was invited by Headquarters Provost Marshal (Army) to include MCTC as part of its inspection programme. The first HMIP inspection of MCTC took place in June 2004. During the interim period the Commandant appointed the Welfare Officer as the Child Protection Coordinator (CPC) with responsibilities to develop a Child Protection and Safeguarding Policy and to establish a training regime to deliver child protection and safeguarding training for all new members of MCTC staff. Thereafter, there would be refresher training on an annual basis .'

Despite misgivings, the initial HMIP report in 2004 was far from as critical as many were expecting. It stated that as an establishment it was essentially safe, well maintained and well supervised. Facilities for personal hygiene, outdoor exercise and accommodation were well provided. Although many detainees were anxious before arrival, once here this anxiety dropped and eighty-one per cent said they felt safe on the first night. Over eighty per cent said they had never felt unsafe or been bullied by either staff or other detainees.

However they were concerned that those deemed at risk of suicide were routinely placed in C block which had a very limited regime as it mainly housed those under investigation. Although the staff were well trained and had detailed knowledge of those in their care, this was undermined by the detainees being placed in strip clothing which, although intended for safety, was likely to heighten risk of depression. They also raised concerns that, as in all service settings, detainees under eighteen years old shared accommodation with adults. They felt that locked accommodation presented risks. They were also concerned that there was no efficient confidential complaints procedure and that equality and diversity procedures were incapable of dealing with discrimination.

Resettlement in A Company was considered good, but in D Company where literacy and numeracy levels were as low as those in other custodial establishments, basic skills training was inadequate and insufficient to meet the need. Employment training was also inadequate and the small welfare department was struggling without a cohesive corporate strategy to provide all the help that was needed. There were also concerns that there was an attitude within HM Forces that the 'bad' soldier should not receive more in the way of resettlement than the 'good' soldier. This, they felt, was a mistake and would add to the likelihood of detainees reoffending in civilian life. But overall the report found a safe, well-ordered environment with a level of concern for the welfare of detainees, especially for those returning to active service.

Iain Finch:

'I was OC D Company and C block for most of my time at MCTC (June 2003 - Dec 2005). Until August 2003 I also at times had Command of A Company. I worked principally with Major Mick Biegel the former SEO, who was awarded an OBE in the 2004 New Year Honours List (when Sergeant Mark Watts (later RSM) was awarded an MBE). That was really the beginning of "HARDFACTS" (Health, Accommodation, Relocation, Drugs and alcohol, Finance, Attitudes, Children and families, Training and Support) process in which he and Major Ludbrook have, I'm sure, had a major part. Part of my message to my D Company SUS was the "fire triangle of life", a simple and frank message that pieced together accommodation, relationships and employment into a format that could be understood by guys who had all had basic fire fighting training. They could understand that if you took one of these elements away then the fire in the middle – "life" – which promoted stability, stimulated desire to do well and enhanced success, would go out.

'I was also the Suicide and Self Harm Prevention Officer (SPATO) and worked closely with the Eastern Region Prison Service SPAT to focus our efforts on these very very serious issues. This included painting C block pink! I understand it was then shut down after I left due to lack of trade and staff able to man it 24/7.

'I am still in occasional contact with Major Biegel who comes to MCTC to audit the Learning Centre from time to time. The "highly commended" award that sits just inside the Education Centre was awarded just weeks after he left. Major Corcoran and Major Neil Lewis (former SEO) accepted it on a National Awards night of the

Learning and Skills Council (I think) on behalf of the centre Command. The Education Centre had progressed so much it eventually produced 900 or so nationally recognized qualifications in a calendar year. I can't honestly remember the statistics but in 2002 I believe it was about nine, in 2003 it was 450 and by 2004 up to just over 900; all through Mick's works in conjunction with D Company. HMCIP had many things to say about our programmes and in late 2005, just as I was leaving, HARDFACTS was born under a different title.'

Chapter 21

'Awesome'
2005 – 2010

Robbie served thirty-two days in D Company in 2005:

'I still remember my number from there. My first impressions on arrival were somewhat mixed to be honest. Before meeting any of the staff I was absolutely terrified. I'd heard horror stories of what the place was like and how horrible the staff were to any servicemen unfortunate enough to be sent there. The first member of staff I spoke to managed to calm me down somewhat though. He was a Sergeant in the Army and was fairly laid back, and explained to me calmly that the staff weren't there to make my time difficult, just to do a job. I was searched to make sure I didn't take anything that I shouldn't, then issued with the kit that I would require for day to day life, like PT kit, full 95 uniform etc.

'Because I smoked I was placed in a room with other smokers (nowadays I suppose we'd be described as social lepers). There were nine or ten in the room. I can still remember some of the names, but others have been lost in the fog of memory. There were some absolutely hilarious moments and, truth be told, I soon worked out that if I kept my head down and got on with what the staff asked of us, then the days were fairly easy.

'The most similar experience to compare it to I suppose is basic training in the Army. The same goes for the food, none of it was what you would call Cordon Bleu, but it was good enough, and I've definitely eaten a lot worse.

'My daily routine was fairly simple; wake up, shower, shave, get kit ready for inspection, go for breakfast and get inspected afterwards. Then we had to parade in front of the company offices where people would be sent to do various details or go on whatever educational courses they had signed up for. I was doing a security and conflict

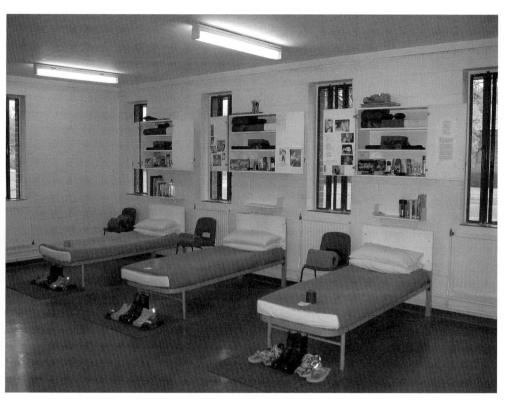

A detainee room circa 2010 – picture courtesy of WO2 Craig Patterson.

management course while I was there, although, to be fair, I've never used it.

'We'd break for lunch and march back to the scoff hall before returning afterwards for afternoon lessons. After dinner we could either stay in the room listening to the radio, reading and chatting among ourselves, or we could go to the gym. I spent most of my time hitting the gym in honesty.

'All in all, I found my time there fairly relaxed, easy wouldn't be the right word but it wasn't difficult either.'

(I deliver a housing brief each to all new detainees. The padre normally comes with me and once Padre Stevenson (2010 – 2012) asked them what they thought about MTCT. One detainee replied 'Awesome!')

Stacey Everett's former boyfriend was in Colchester in 2003. 'He wrote home and told me to be careful what I wrote to him as letters were read before he got them. He said it was what he'd heard a real prison was like but with loads of extra fitness as they did two PE lessons a day. There was also the marching up and down the parade square. He said his room had been good so they were given the radio but they had to behave to get the batteries the next day. When he came out, his experience meant that all he did was go to the gym.'

213

Stacey, who today works for Glasgow's Helping Heroes, also escorted a prisoner there in 2006. 'When we got there a scary looking Army Sergeant came over and in a high voice told the lad to grab both his bags and get to other end of the parade square in double time and within five minutes. I'm not sure if he got there in time, but I was definitely glad to get out of there.' Jane Oliveira-Da-Silva:

'My first impressions of MCTC came in 2006 when I joined the Welfare Department as a drug and alcohol counsellor and anger management therapist under contract through my employer, Open Road, a local D&A recovery and support agency.

'It was immediately apparent to me that a sense of quiet order and safe boundaries underpinned the day to day routine. The team members, under Welfare Manager Major (Retd) Paul Ludbrook, were all dedicated and caring individuals. Their professionalism and innate understanding of the complex identity of individuals within a Forces correctional training environment meant that all DUS were received and listened to with respect not only in relation to their roles and experiences within the Forces, but also as valued individuals. This ethos has never changed despite the natural changes of key staff over the years I have been privileged to work there.

'I feel it is a haven of integrity, professionalism, humour, warmth and respect for the individual. This has been a hugely enlightening and valuable experience for me and a privilege to work with both the team, and the 500 or so men and women I have counselled in this time.'

In January 2007, HMIP carried out an unannounced inspection. Again the report was broadly positive and found considerable improvement had been made in managing those deemed at risk of significant harm or bullying. C block was now closed and vulnerable detainees were managed on Company Lines. But HMIP still raised concerns about those under eighteen years old. There had been progress in dealing with equality and diversity, although the report found that the civilian company running the kitchens appeared to lack an understanding or commitment to this. The complaints system had improved, but healthcare was less satisfactory, with a particular concern about mental health and counselling.

Training had improved in both companies and the inspectors were particularly impressed with the Gordon Platoon citizenship course. They still felt there was too little literacy and numeracy training for those returning to their units and not enough careers advice for those leaving the services. Detainees now had full access to pre-release and anger management as well as housing, debt and employment advice, but those awaiting sentence still had little to do.

Arrangements for visitors had improved and although there was still no visitors' centre funding had now been approved. But overall the inspectors were impressed by the improvements which provided the staff with a basis to continue to develop best practice.

In a move to introduce more robust training for the SUS, in 2007 week-long Battle Camps were introduced. Virtually all A Company moved to Stanford Training Area near Bury St Edmunds for five days. This vast area of land allowed them to practice a variety of different attack combinations that they could not do within the confines of the MCTC or Friday Woods. It was so successful that it became a permanent feature in the sixteen-week training cycle.

At the same time, the Projects Department was also busy. In addition to their on-going commitments to raise money for SSAFA and the ABF, in the spring the staff and SUS went to Ipswich to brighten up the streets, paint fences, cut gardens, generally tidy up and to lay concrete paving at Orwell's sheltered housing unit. They also went to Wellington Children's Centre in Ipswich to decorate and transform five rooms. The centre is a place young parents can go to meet other families and relax. In July they were busy helping St Helena Hospice's Summer Fair in Colchester by setting up the marquee and gazebos, collecting donations from visitors and taking everything down and tidying up at the end. The same summer they built a wildlife pond at St Michael's School at Leigh-on-Sea with the help of local companies Kent Blaxhill and Waterwise.

In August they took part in the Mersea Island Festival in Essex and helped children with mental and physical disabilities participate in activities such as climbing, zip wire, archery, paintball, team sports and games. They were also involved in helping the NSPCC with their fundraising book fairs, sorting and carrying thousands of books, and with local businessman Mike Daniels's West Mersea Free Church's Harvest for the Hungry, collecting and delivery parcels of clothes, food and other goods from businesses and taking them to Chelmsford.

Lieutenant Colonel David G. Steele ('Scud') arrived at MCTC on 6 May 2008 and was Commandant until 5 May 2011. It was during this time that some of the biggest changes took place:

'I arrived in early May 2008. I had visited briefly in mid-March 2008 when the previous Commandant was still in post. I had been well briefed but still had tens of questions and uncertainties. In the next few weeks I settled in and started to learn.

'The first big issue was an announced inspection by HM Inspectorate of Prisons in early November 2008. An "action plan" was

The MCTC farm was briefly renamed Steel's Farm after Lt Col David Steel in 2010. It has since reverted to Fresh Start Farm – picture courtesy of WO2 Craig Patterson.

in place, designed to answer the observations and criticisms of the previous (unannounced) inspection in late 2007. This, I was assured, was well in hand. But I had nagging doubts: the trouble was that HMIP's terminology was unfamiliar and, to be honest, many of its observations were not exactly pointed. Its comments seemed less than direct. I re-read the 2004 and 2007 reports and began to see similarities which indicated that some 2004 recommendations were probably still unanswered in 2007. The question was, were those issues now fixed?

'In the meantime, I learned the arcane language unique to the place: "diets" instead of meals, "office party" instead of Commandant's Interviews, "i/c Sides" instead of Platoon Commanders, "bells" instead of alarms – the list just went on. I got to know the people. I walked around the lines, talked to detainees, visited training and watched the staff at work. I visited prisons, HM Chief Inspector of Prisons, the Judge Advocate General, the local Brigade Commander and many, many others of the great and good of my new circle of professional friends. I went on a two-week HMPS incident command course but learned much less than I had from Prison Service colleagues about running the country's custodial establishments. I attended the monthly East of England

Regional Custodial Manager's meetings and gradually learned another set of new terminology, jargon, practices and policies. As HMIP's November inspection approached, I started to understand just what had been deftly written between the lines of the previous two reports.

'With only a week to go, and many careful scrapes through the action plan accompanied by the sage advice and thoughts of the Deputy Commandant, I had a moment of revelation. HMIP had been trying, all too gently, to point out that we had no informative doctrine, that told us what MCTC was really there for and how its core business was meant to be carried out. Yes, we instinctively knew what we were there for, that we had Imprisonment and Detention Rules, lots of corporate memory, an excellent reputation within the MOD for doing a great job of turning wayward service personnel around and giving them new impetus in life, but we had no well-thought-through doctrine recording and informing us of how we should actually go about this "turning around" of those wayward souls – or why we should be doing it in the first place. Oh dear.

'The inspection process was fascinating; revealing for us as well as for the Inspectorate and very thorough. Our verbal debrief at the end of the week was not as bad as feared but neither was it as positive as we would have wanted it to be. Early drafts confirmed that we still lacked that fundamental doctrine and thus the logical path to everything else that we were, or should be, doing. This also meant that without clearly stated targets to achieve, we would find it difficult to measure our success or failure and we would find it difficult to argue coherently for necessary resources to deliver against agreed aims.

'The staff were a little crestfallen (actually, very crestfallen) that the report maintained old criticisms. We did not wait for the final written report five months later. There was much communal head-scratching, navel-gazing, agonising about structural changes and worry about how to really move forward and decisively answer those criticisms. What was apparent from the outset, and hugely positive, was the strong desire of virtually every member of staff, military and civilian, to tackle the challenges and get it right; "Belief" as the Deputy Commandant repeatedly called it. But the scale of what we had to do was undoubtedly daunting.

'Step one: Introduce the concept of an Offender Management Unit (OMU) and staff it with the right people. All prisons and youth offender institutes (YOIs) in England and Wales already had an OMU. The OMU centralises the assessment of offenders and the subsequent planning of interventions to successfully address offending behaviour and offenders resettlement needs. In MCTC's case, our OMU was certainly to do that – eventually – but, initially, it was to act as the hub for change; a "brains-trust" in other words. Step forward Captain Jason Hutchinson and Staff Sergeant John Wharton as the main men. Researching, sketching out ideas, visiting prisons and YOIs, making friends, networking, ruthlessly borrowing and tailoring external advice, the OMU hit upon some core principles early on.

'First, adopt the principle of offender management – that one size does not fit all and each and every detainee thus needs to be individually assessed and have a sentence plan tailored to meet their needs. Then adopt "ASPIRE" as the process for offender management: Assess, Sentence Plan, Implement, Review, Evaluate. Then we needed a template against which to carry it all out. The key here was to borrow the National Offender Management Service's "pathways to reducing reoffending" and to rework these pathways to our own purposes. Thus arose "HARDFACTS" - Health, Accommodation, Relocation, Drugs and alcohol, Finance, benefit and debt, Attitudes, thinking and behaviour, Children and families, Training, education and employment and finally Support (from external agencies).

'Now we had the bones of our doctrine. But it needed to be written down in a usable document. And we needed a practical guide explaining every bit of it. Who would actually write these? Where did the expertise and understanding to be able to do this writing reside? It became apparent that the only place to look was internally: we were just too dissimilar from HMPS and the Probation Service to be able to call upon any expertise there. So the Commandant went away to Scotland for a climbing holiday in his caravan, accompanied by a laptop and copious quantities of decent red wine. Three weeks later, we had a draft "Resettlement Strategy", our first expression of formal military offender management doctrine. The OMU set about improving it and drawing up an Offender Management Manual to provide the practical guide.

'Throughout the period of thinking and planning, the rest of the staff were beavering away making detailed changes to the regime, starting up new courses for detainees, improving noticeboard content, reviewing detailed training programmes, writing *A Guide to MCTC* for new detainees, sorting out the "easy wins" from the inspection report and improving the decor and living arrangements for the detainees. Meanwhile, they were being trained in all the changes taking place and for more changes yet to come, writing and adopting new Unit Standing Orders and much, much more. MCTC had a real buzz about it!

'Let us not forget that throughout this time, we continued to support contingent operations in Iraq and Afghanistan, providing fully trained custodians to each theatre and managing the very significant UK strategic risk of holding, in fair and decent conditions, the many security and criminal detainees captured by UK forces during those operations. We also supported the Operational Training Advisory Group in training UK forces for deployment, through HQ PM(A)'s Custodial Branch, continued inspections of, and licensing regimes for, all UK unit custody facilities, answered all the weird and wonderful questions (from MOD staffs, Members of Parliament, Freedom of Information Inquiries, units and more) that flow into MCTC day by day and, unsurprisingly, continued to admit, detain, train and rehabilitate the one thousand or so UK Armed Service detainees entrusted to our care every year. And the brand new Armed Forces Act 2006 (AFA 06) was due for implementation on 31 October 2009. This last issue created an immense amount of work to ensure that we were both ready and competent in time. It was indeed a busy year!

'Late one evening in early 2009, the Commandant and Deputy Commandant could be found in the Commandant's office, scratching their heads and staring intently at hand-drawn flip-charts showing facts and calculations. The issue at hand? Earned Remission, a new feature to the custodial regime introduced by AFA 06. Just how would MCTC operate a system that appeared to be simple, almost trivial, yet in its detail was fiendishly complicated?

'Defeated, they left later that evening for consolatory red wine and, in at least one case, irritating dreams of streams of calculations and numbers in a grid! A day or two later, the Deputy Commandant received a message from the Commandant. "I've got it. I think I know how this can work." Patience and persistence does pay off. A method was born, a process for doing those wretched calculations was introduced and "shadow running" of a few current detainees' cases was started in order to see if it really would fit the bill. Many months later, after we had introduced Earned Remission, the RSM, Mark Watts, suggested to the Commandant that the process and calculations required just a little too much agility and detail than most were prepared or able to put in. "Can't we come up with some sort of automatic calculator, Sir?" Blast the man! Many months after that and thirteen versions later, we finally had an automatic calculator that passed muster – and still does.

'Within a year of the November 2008 inspection, MCTC had changed beyond most people's recognition. Yes, it was in the same place. Yes, detainees still arrived at all hours of the day and night and yes, shifts came on duty and off, but the thought, the processes, the courses, the regime and so much more had changed fundamentally. Not everything was done, though. Full Sentence Planning for all detainees only came to fruition in the latter half of 2010, some courses, certainly needed and long planned, only started in early 2011 and the Offender Management Manual was only published around Easter 2011. But the majority of issues had been tackled head on and answered to our own satisfaction by early 2010.

'Whizz forward now to a Monday morning in early June 2010. Commandant's "Haul-Up" (Steel's name for Office Party) had just finished. All was right in the world and the day had dawned clear. The telephone rang. "Yes, Commandant." "Sir, it's the main gate. There's a bunch of people here who claim to be HM Inspectorate of Prisons." Oh boy, an unannounced inspection.

'Thursday, the verbal debrief. Our marks had gone up in every area which was almost unheard of! A clean bill of health was given. The sigh of relief could be heard in Upavon! HMIP appeared confident that we had finally worked out what to do, how to do it and had actually done it. Some things obviously still needed work; some recommendations had not been fully answered and a very few recommendations had been effectively refused. But we had got over the worst, fixed the really difficult things and so impressed the Inspectorate that they actually smiled. Happy days! Champagne that night, for sure. The Deputy Commandant's smile would have lit up the night sky. In the following days, the staff were walking around with their backs extra straight. The Provost Marshal seemed particularly happy. Even the detainees worked out that something was right in the world.

'MCTC exists to carry out legal punishment, to reform and rehabilitate, to deter and to turn out, the three Armed Services and our civil society; detainees who are, after sentence are happier, more confident, more self-disciplined, self-reliant people and less likely to reoffend. I never once doubted that we did that. But now we have an external inspectorate that says we do it, and do it well. We should be self-confident and happy that we do this, for we do it for good reason and we set and maintain very high standards. Long may it continue to be so.'

Chapter 22

'There are no priorities'
2011 – 2012

As the one and only Military Detention Centre the MCTC receives its fair share of visitors - 'a bit like a ******* zoo' as one member of staff was heard to remark. These vary from politicians and senior Service Personnel to visitors from various civilian organisations, all eager to be shown round. Those who arrive with prior expectations often leave pleasantly surprised at just how mistaken they were. This also applies to the detainees, many of whom still have no idea what to expect and fear the worst.

So what do the visitors and detainees see when they arrive? Craig 'Pat' Patterson:

'Everyone arrives at the main gate lodge – most units would call it the "guardroom". It's where all visitors to the camp report. Units should notify Receptions that a detainee is coming but that isn't always the case, and although they have already been approved by receptions the detainee's paperwork is briefly checked at the main gate lodge before they are escorted round to the Receptions building. It is kept locked when detainees are in there and it's here they sort out their kit, deciding what kit will stay with them and what, if anything will be sent back to their unit. Once that's done they are assessed by the Reception Staff and then see the doctor for a brief health check. The Reception area is a large room with rows of chairs facing a large TV. Detainees sit and wait to access medical services or welfare appointments and can watch DVDs about military training, drink and drug awareness and other issues.

'All detainees see a Welfare Officer during the induction process and those in D Company see them again before they are released. St Michael's Church is the MCTC church. Weddings have taken place there, although I've never attended one. There are also Services of

Remembrance for members of staff as well as funerals. Staff and detainees also attend carol services at Christmas and we always have a large Remembrance Sunday Service there, as you would expect. Outside the church there is a flagpole with a small plaque indicating when the centre opened. Directly ahead is HQ which houses the Commandant, RSM and various other personnel including the administrative staff and the paymaster.

'We have several civilian staff who teach forklift, plumbing, car mechanics, welding and various other skills. In the education block detainees are able to access computers, apply for jobs, use the library and attend classes on basic skills, literacy, numeracy, other NVQs and whatever other exams they need to pass the courses they take in here. They can also achieve Level 2 qualifications in the Safe Use of Veterinary Medicines, Basic Stockmanship and Welfare.

'C block is the only building that resembles a prison. Its rooms have barred doors, unbreakable glass and metal mirrors. There is also an unfurnished cell. But it's not routinely used and hasn't been for several years although the facilities are still in place if needed.

'There are two accommodation blocks. They are mirror images of each other so if you can find your way round one you can find your way round the other. D Company is for those leaving and A Company is for those going back to their units. The stage system is the same. When the detainees first come in they are Stage 1 and are put into eight-man rooms. After twenty-eight days they can be promoted to Stage 2. They then receive a red tag and move into the smaller six-man rooms. After a further six weeks they can attain Stage 3 status. They then come out of this building and go round to the back. Here they are not routinely locked in at all and are pretty much left to their own devices, with minimal supervision.

'They don't come under the Company number checks as once they've reached Stage 3 they are afforded considerable status and respect and several privileges. For instance they can have their own watch and keep their mobile phone in the main gate lodge so they can use it while on parole every Wednesday or Saturday afternoon. When on parole they can leave the camp, go into town and even have a meal with their relatives, but they are not allowed to have any alcohol. There is also a big difference in the amount of money they are reimbursed. Stage 1 detainees are only allowed £6 per week but Stage 3 have £30 per week. They are also entitled to four days' reintegration leave to try to find work and to get to know their families again.

'Between A Company and D Company are the two dining halls;

again they are the exact mirror image of the other and they also serve the purpose of keeping the companies separate.

'At the end of D Company is SCP, the custodial wing which houses four categories of prisoners; those waiting for court martial, those awaiting transport to HMP and those on Rule 90 – solitary confinement although I can't remember when it was last used. Rule 90 means no contact with other detainees or phone calls. They see the Padre and Commandant briefly each day, take their food in their room and the only book they are allowed is the Bible. It's a pretty harsh sanction, but as I said I can't remember when it was last used. It's used as a cooling off place for when detainees get heated.'

'The other block is F Block (now used as Custodial AAUCSC – All Armed Unity Custody Staff Course – STA Training Wing and is home to No 1 Company MPS (V). It was built for female detainees but it's not a very well-constructed custodial block. There are too many corners and it's hard to check rooms so it's only really used for training and conferences now. It hasn't been used as a custodial building for almost ten years. Any females are now housed within either A or D Company blocks. This is also the home of the TA arm of MPSC who are based here.

'There's a drill square for the detainees which is also used by staff in the pacesticking competition that normally takes place around March/April time.

'The gymnasium is for both staff and detainees and there's a weights room and main gymnasium. This building is the training wing. It's mainly used by A Company to enhance military skills such as map reading, weapon drills and fieldcraft but all detainees attend an Induction course here which includes Parenting Skills. We also have a DCCT (Dismounted Close Combat Trainer) and of course, like all military bases, an armoury.

'There is not much more to say really except that it's a 100-acre site built to house a population of about 270 maximum. [23] We can house 316 at a pinch although if we have 200 here it feels like it's bursting at the seams. Up the far end outside the inside wire is the WO and Sergeants' Mess, the Officers' Mess and a small club called The Jubilee Club which provides accommodation for junior NCOS. It's normally only used by medics as all the staff are of SNCO level. The Regimental home and museum of the MPSC is also up that end as is the farm where the detainees work.'

Lieutenant Colonel Rupert Shaw believed that every aspect of service provided by staff in MCTC was of equal importance and that there are 'no priorities'.

This pretty much sums up the ethos of the MCTC.

In May 2011 Lieutenant Colonel Rupert Shaw took over as Commandant. With D Company now providing an excellent resettlement service he set out to increase A Company activities and to utilize some of the skills of the detainees held there. The two-fold effect was to provide even more efficient service personnel and increase the variety of training available. The farm was also enlarged and began to grow vegetables. Major (Retd) Paul Ludbrook:

'During the last decade there has been considerable development by the Welfare Department in educating detainees about the support available to them both in Service and ex-Service. As part of the induction process into MCTC, detainees attend a welfare interview, receive presentations on housing, drug and alcohol misuse and the services available to them from the Citizens Advice Bureau whilst in MCTC and beyond. At quarterly intervals the Royal British Legion speak about the services they provide to both in-Service and ex-Service personnel and the Veterans Welfare Service give a talk to those detainees being discharged. A protocol has been established with the Naval Personnel and Family Service and RAF Personal Welfare Support to visit detainees from their respective Service at MCTC at monthly intervals. The Army Welfare Service located in Colchester is on hand to assist Army detainees when required.

'Detainees are permitted one two-hour visit each week from families and friends. These visits have been adjusted to take place at the weekend and there are now no visits from Monday to Friday. The original three visit periods per week, one on a Wednesday and two on a Saturday, have been extended to four on Saturday and Sunday morning and afternoon.

'The importance of detainees maintaining contact with their family, particularly children, has been recognized. So the visits programme now has a Child's Play Day one a month on a Saturday which lasts for five hours with lunch provided. Facilities available to visitors now include toys, vending machines. Creation of a dedicated waiting room and children's play area is underway. Family and Parenting courses are conducted and with the support of a local charity, detainees are made aware of the services available nationally through the Sure Start Children Centres.

'Detainees are inducted into MCTC and their exit from detention is equally managed. Those discharged from the Service attend a final welfare interview and are provided with a welfare information pack. This last interview usually occurs within ten and twenty days of a detainee's date of release and any support plan, if required, is formalised. It may suggest the detainee (with their agreement) is referred to the Veterans Welfare Service as a Vulnerable Service Leaver and help with the provision of temporary accommodation. With a returning detainee's permission, a report will be forwarded to the Service unit indicating any outstanding welfare related matters.'

The big event was the long-awaited inspection by HMIP in January 2012. Thanks to the hard work of the staff and previous Commandant, Lieutenant Colonel David Steele, the HMIP Inspection team, led by Nick Hardwick HM, Chief Inspector of Prisons, gave an extremely good report, which was published in March 2012. Each successive report had noted improvements and this was no exception. It stated that the centre was a very safe and positive place with very good relationships, plenty of activity and constructive preparation for the future. In fact the MCTC was now a very impressive establishment with a 'good' rating against all of the healthy custody tests, something that very rarely happened. There was very little bullying and, because of the good support and monitoring of vulnerable detainees, very few instances of self-harm. Any historic child protection issues were dealt with well, security was proportionate and the rules applied fairly which meant force and segregation were rarely used.

The positive culture previously only found in A Company, was now apparent in D Company and, although there were no female detainees at the time, sensible arrangements were put in place to ensure they were not isolated. Equality and Diversity issues had improved as had health services.

Detainees were kept busy; education and vocational training for those leaving the services were good, and numeracy and literacy provision was outstanding. Detainees had very good help with debt and finding work and accommodation on discharge. Some detainees had even found work placements. Overall the report was one of the best ever given by HMIP and coverage of the MCTC in the local media was very positive.

Chapter 23

'I saw two very tall men in long grey coats just standing watching me'

Given the nature of the buildings and its previous history it is unsurprising that stories of strange happenings have persisted. Dan Cowley:

'I was detailed for night watch in B wing in November 1971 under the charge of night watch Staff Sergeant "Dicky" Drakes MPSC. It was around 0130 hours on a damp and misty Sunday morning. I looked down the central walkway of the wing towards the dividing gate and fence leading to the basketball court and shed area and saw the i/c nights walk from left to right at the fence line. I thought Dicky was walking round the back and would drop in to see me after visiting D Wing. I then realized that because of the mist I could not see the rear fence beyond the dividing gate and fence and wondered how he had entered the wing without me seeing.

'I grabbed the clock and walked to the right-hand side of the wing to start an early round in the direction of a Stage II. It was the direction I had seen the i/c nights walk and I thought I would catch him at his own game. I completed my search and patrol in a "sneaky-beaky" mode hoping to surprise him. I found no one. Getting rather concerned I toured the line again and finished off with a complete count of the wing residents including the Stage II rooms to ensure they were all accounted for. Stage II and Stage I were intact. I made another thorough check of the wing lines including the TV room but did not discover the i/c night watch. I again checked that I could not see beyond the fence and gate. I telephoned D Wing and was assured that Dicky was not there and hadn't been for a number of hours. The main gate was the next port of call where I was told Dicky had left for A wing fifteen minutes earlier.

On the right hand side of the photo there is an outline of a woman with a high collar and long dress – it appears to be late Elizabethan or early 17th Century dress. Courtesy of SSgt Lorraine Bennett.

This is a close up of the above. Courtesy of SSgt Lorraine Bennett.

Rather bemused I contacted A wing and asked to speak him. To my confusion he was there and said, "I am on my way". We then checked all our residents could be accounted for. Neither of us could not explain what I had seen or why I was so convinced it was him. I have often wondered if he thought I was one of the staff that did not like being on my own at night …

'I have not heard of any other unexplained occurrences in the MCTC, although it was said that behind the 18-ft wriggly tin fence of the old C block could be a foreboding place. I never felt this. However, there are numerous ghost stories related to various areas in the camp. F Block, in particular, is said to be haunted, something that may or may not be related to a suicide in cell 3 back in the 1990s. Lights can be seen coming on and off at night even though the building is unoccupied.'

Sandie Clark:

'I had heard a few stories about F Block being haunted but didn't really give them much thought. I've worked there on and off for nearly five years and on a permanent basis since October 2012. Although it's quite creepy at times, I'd never had any issues until January 2013.

'I had been in the kitchen by cell 3 and was heading back up the corridor when a man clearly said to me, "Wy aye Sergeant Major". When I turned round there was nobody there. It didn't scare me at all and as my work colleague came round the corner I just stood there looking puzzled.

I've since had another experience in the same corridor. I was vacuuming one of the offices when I heard someone place some keys on the desk. I looked up to see who it was but again there was nobody there and no keys either.

'One member of staff reports feeling a tap on the shoulder, but when he turned round no one was there, while another was making himself a cup of coffee in the kitchen and the spoon on the work surface began moving. There are numerous accounts of the building being locked and in darkness at night but the lights being on when the staff went to unlock it in the morning. Other stories recount lights going on and off in the building even though there is no one in there. Most staff will not go in there after dark.'

Brian Chenier:

'For many years I had heard of strange happenings in F Block, which was built to house the YOI "Boot Camp" pilot. I was working there uncharacteristically late one evening as the PSI for No1 Company MPS (V). I finished at about 2000hrs and was closing everything down when I heard a tune of some kind being whistled. I wasn't aware of anyone else in the building but checked anyway as I didn't want to lock anyone in. I thought maybe it was a DUS Prowler or night watch Staff Sergeant. But the building was empty and as I was about to lock the final door before leaving I heard the whistling again, this time as if it were almost next to me. I locked the door and left. Concerned that it must have been somebody else in the building I went back in and checked again, it was empty.'

Sergeant Lorraine Vickers-Bennet has another eerie tale:

'F block is notoriously haunted. When I first joined up I was interviewed in there and went to use the toilet. This meant walking down a corridor and past three single cells and the "dojo" (where we conduct C&R training). As I walked down the corridor I heard footsteps marching right behind me. I swung round to see who it was but no one was there! After relating this I was told that two people had previously taken their own lives in F block, one in the dojo.

'Reports of lights turning themselves back on after being turned off are rife even to this day. I/c nights are all too aware of this and not many of them will venture into F block on their own. They send the DUS Prowler instead.

'Another member of staff, Staff Sergeant Robert O'Reilly, a hardcore MPS soldier who does not believe in the paranormal, ventured into F Block doing his checks while on night watch. He told me that as he walked down the corridor and neared the dojo he felt a hand slap him on the back right between his shoulder blades. The hand then stayed on his back and moved down his spine. He swung around and said "Come on then, show yourself". Suffice to say the spirit had achieved his aim to get noticed and didn't respond further.'

Other buildings also have their ghosts. A figure in white was regularly seen walking through closed double doors in the Medical Centre. The author:

'I sometimes get into work just after 0700 so I am on my own in the Welfare Department. One morning I heard a voice calling "Hello". Thinking it was the cleaner I replied, "Morning, how are you?" There was silence. Slightly confused I went into the corridor and walked towards where I had heard the voice. There was no one there, the corridor was completely empty and the main reception area was still in darkness. A few moments later the cleaner came in through the outside door at the church end of the corridor.

'I have also heard what sounded like a conversation between several people coming from the Reception end of the corridor, near the kitchen. Thinking other members of the Welfare Department had arrived I went to greet them only to find dead silence and the place completely empty.

'Another morning I heard footsteps walking through from the church. They continued past my office to the reception area. I assumed it was a member of staff as boots make an easily identifiable noise on the floor. However, it was unusual for no one to speak or put their head in my door and say hello. Although I was typing on my keyboard at the time I did not see any shadow as they walked past my room. I then heard the reception door banging closed. Curious I rushed out to see who it was, but there was no one in either the Welfare Department or the reception area, which again was in complete darkness.

'I was standing talking to the cleaner one morning and leaning on the door frame of the entrance to the kitchen. All of a sudden there was a crash. A large plate had "fallen" from the shelf and smashed on the floor. It had been securely stacked, flat on the shelf. There was no way it could have fallen off on its own. This was the only time something was broken though. After that it was only spoons that "flew" through the air! In fact, spoons falling off the shelf became a common occurrence. There was never anyone near the kitchen when it happened although there were people in the Welfare Department.'

Other colleagues in the Welfare Department have also witnessed strange events. Lauren Wilson:

'There have been a couple of incidents within MCTC that have led me to doubt in my over-imaginative imagination and believe in the possibility of the supernatural. The first occurred when I was sat working at my desk. The shadow of a man entered the office, paused, and then departed. I didn't think anything of this at first as the office often has lots of traffic. However the department was completely empty, I hadn't heard any doors open or steps approach the door, so how could it be that I had just seen the shape of a man in the doorway? I kept this to myself and put it down to a trick of the light, but a later conversation with my colleague led me to believe it could be something else. It turned out that my colleague had also seen an unexplained shadow in the same doorway which they didn't think to mention at the time either, so could this figure have been one and the same?

'During the same conversation it was also unveiled that we had both seen similar forms in a different location. Once, when I was turning off the lights in the inner property cupboard, I saw a figure in the corner of the adjoining archive room. It appeared to hesitate and then move out of view. Again, I used my rationale and thought through what could have caused the shadow but in all honesty, as there was no one else in the cupboard with me, there was nothing else that could have caused the silhouette.'

Lauren was not the only person to see this:

'Re ghostly goings on. Did my glasses need cleaning? I'm don't know if this is worth mentioning because I'm not sure what I actually saw but here goes ....

'One day in the furthermost top corner of the cupboard before the property room, I thought I saw a shadow. Perhaps it was just that, a shadow. I didn't think too much of it as I was focused on getting out the property bags. That same day, I thought I fleetingly saw another shadow – again the shape was discernible – in the doorway of our Admin Office.

'I mentioned this to my colleague who coincidentally thought she'd seen something similar in the same areas that day.'

One particular area of A Company is freezing cold at night and another, between the Diets Halls of A and D Companies, feels eerily spooky when staff walk through there at night on their way to check on the detainees.
Sergeant Lorraine Vickers-Bennet:

'I have experienced unexplained knocks, bangs and footsteps while on night duties in A Company. One night while on watch alone in the Company gate I heard someone marching down the corridor. The footsteps became quieter as they got nearer, telling me that a colleague was possibly creeping up on me. I shouted out "I can hear you – don't bother creeping up on me" as I was so convinced someone was there. With that the footsteps got louder and someone marched into the area just outside the office and banged their tabs in. It was so loud I jumped up and looked outside. No one was there![24]

'Another time when I was standing outside the office in the company gate area I looked towards Stage 1 platoon bubble. I saw two very tall men in long grey coats[25] just standing watching me; they stood well over 6ft tall (I am just short of 6ft 1in so they were approx 6ft 3ins). I called my colleague Sergeant Gav Hawkins who saw nothing.

'Another colleague, Nick, who was on night watch a few weeks later, took me to one side as we had a handover from his night shift and told me that he didn't believe in ghosts, but that he had walked right through what he believed to be a man well over 6ft in a long grey coat (Nick was himself over 6ft). This confirmed what I had seen previously.

'Every time I do a night watch there is unexplained activity ranging from footsteps, shadows, knocking on doors (from empty rooms) and voices in the early hours. Although it is presumed they came from the DUS, the place where the voices come from is always empty.'

Several detainees report a feeling of being watched in their rooms even though there is no one there and one detainee saw something materialise in the toilet in his room after he repeatedly tried to stop the toilet door opening. Having received permission to take pictures inside the MCTC Lorraine went into this room. Matthew Alltree (Detainee):

'One evening me and a member of staff turned all the lights off in the room and the staff got their mobile phone out with a camera on and torch. When the torch was on we noticed a lot of orbs flying round in the room and next to my locker there was a shape of a person, a shadow-like figure.

'I've also heard that a couple of the other lads have had similar experiences with the ghosts in MCTC. One had been asleep when he felt as if somebody was pushing his head in the pillow. When he got up there was nobody in the room and the locker door started to open on its own.

'There was another person asleep in bed in the same room and he woke up screaming saying that the room wasn't right and somebody was sitting on his bed staring at him. That night the lad could not sleep there and went to the staff who put him in a single cell for the night.'

Mahmut Bilgili (Detainee):

'Having spent some time at the MCTC I was aware of the stories of paranormal activity witnessed by other detainees. However up until one night I had never experienced anything myself. I woke up and thought I saw something approaching me from the bottom of my bed. I didn't take much notice of it or put much thought into it initially as I had just woken up and still couldn't see things very clearly. Then suddenly I felt the presence of something or someone beside my bed looking over me, only to realize there was nothing there.

'I jumped out of my bed and ran five metres to my right towards a fellow detainee's bed to tell him what I had experienced. He responded by telling me that a few months ago another detainee who was sleeping in the same bed space had experienced something similar and his bed moved by itself. This didn't help my state of mind so after lying back in my bed for two minutes I decided it was time to go see the staff and explain to them what I had seen. I asked if I could spend the night in the single man room as I was really shaken up by this experience.

'Unfortunately that wasn't my only experience of unusual activity which I still cannot seem to explain or understand. Two weeks before that I was in my bed struggling to sleep when I heard a bang or what sounded like an object being dropped or thrown. Before switching the lights off I remembered seeing my roommate's boots at the bottom of his bed on the bed mat, regular routine for him. He was fast asleep and when I heard a bang, I called his name. I didn't get a reply so I got up to investigate. When I reached the centre of the room I noticed that his boot was thrown onto its side and was at least three metres away from where it was before the lights went out.'

Brian Chenier:

'On many occasions in E Block I experienced the sensation of being followed while carrying out night patrols, but on checking there would never be anyone there. I always thought this was my imagination but one night I was walking between A and D Company in the area of the company offices when I was aware of something approaching me but couldn't see anything. It was just a feeling. I instinctively stepped out of the way and immediately felt a strong wind rush past me towards A Company. It was like being on railway station platform as a high speed train rushes by. I have not experienced being followed since.'

Even HQ does not escape unscathed. A member of staff unlocked the building one morning only for the cleaner who arrived later to find it locked. Brian Chenier recalls one night in C Company:

'I experienced an event in C block that spooked me. I was on nights and had just carried out a check on cells 1 and 2 where both soldiers appeared fast asleep. Moving to cell 3 I heard a clear banging on the door of one of the other two cells. I quickly checked them both and both soldiers seemed to be in exactly the same sleeping position. I again went to check cell 3 but this time I could clearly tell that the door of cell one was being hit hard. I was right next to it so looked through the hatch and the soldier had not moved, neither had he had time to move to the door, bang on it and get back onto his bed.'

Dan Cowley was interested in the strange happenings and did some extra research:

'Camp 186 did not have living accommodation in these locations but did have ablution, urinal and association areas. All of these were notorious for violence and intimidation because they were unsupervised. POWs were permitted association with Guards and maintenance Servicemen in what is now the drill square and what was then the main gate area. This can be seen in the painting by Otto Geib.

'The only contradiction is F block/B Camp and the church and Reception Area. The first was an administration/accommodation area and the second was the close confinement cells. When the MCE first moved into Camp 186 these areas continued to be used for the same things.

'The latest map that has been found of Camp 186 indicates a loop in the perimeter road of Camp A. This could mean that C block would have been included in the association areas, both in Camp 186 and in the initial days of the MCE.

'The hand moving down the back could indicate homosexual advances which were known to take place regularly within the ablutions, theatres and construction areas of A and B Camps[26].

Members of staff have told ghost stories to lighten up the long, sometimes boring, night duties. One also recalls peering through the window of a room and seeing a group of detainees using an Ouija board after lights out. He waited for an opportune moment and banged loudly on the door, frightening the life out of them!'

Chapter 24

The Last Words

As I write in 2013, a new play area is being constructed for children when they visit their parents here at MCTC. At the same time, many of the staff are concerned about the future of the centre. Changes to custodial rules, the building and increased use of detention facilities on garrisons and the drastic reduction of HM Forces to its lowest level since Napoleonic times, has led to falling numbers of detainees. In addition, many of its regular visitors who went AWOL several times in a futile attempt to be discharged, have achieved their aim and are now civilians. For those serving in what's left of HM Forces, it's now considerably easier to get discharged as units frantically make the drastic cuts forced on them by politicians.

Despite the uncertainty, life continues as normal with detainees here benefitting from years of accumulated wisdom. Normally it continues its good work away from the glare of media attention. However, every now and again, a high profile detainee arrives and MCTC finds itself once again under the spotlight, with TV and news crews camped out on the grass opposite the entrance. The last few years have seen considerable publicity over the detention of anti-war campaigner Joe Glenton and former SAS sniper Sergeant Danny Nightingale. As their stories lose public interest the Glasshouse fades back into obscurity until others take their place.

It is worth remembering that the personal accounts in this book not only tell individual stories, they are also indicative of the ethos, morals and ways of thinking about crime, justice, punishment and rehabilitation of the nation as a whole. These have moved on considerably since 1947 and the changes in practice and behaviour in the MCTC reflect this. Thus, although in many of the earlier accounts the conditions in detention seem harsh and very severe, they should be read in context of how life was in the outside world at the time. It is also worth mentioning that the majority of the detainees throughout the decades were used to military discipline when they arrived at MCTC, so accepted it with little complaint, the exception, of course, being National Servicemen.

Finally, despite the excellent HMIP reports, the MCTC and its staff are not

The MCTC at dawn – courtesy of SSgt Lorraine Bennett.

complacent. Each day brings new challenges and they strive to meet these as and when they arrive. They have set themselves very high standards in the care and wellbeing of the detainees and the emphasis is on maintaining and improving these, as and when necessary. Thanks to their dedication and hard work many detainees go on to have long and productive careers, either in the Armed Forces or outside.

But I will leave the last words to Lieutenant Colonel Steele:

'Other memories? I have recounted much about our changes towards the end of the first decade of the twenty-first century. But there was so much more such as good friends easily made, the warm welcome which *always* came from the members of the Warrant Officers' and Sergeants' Mess and fun parties – the highlight being Burn's Night in the Combined Mess in 2009 with actors in costume. Who could forget "The Twa Dugs"? There was also the occasional smell of the pigs wafting into camp from the Fresh Start Farm, the magical cherry tree blossom throughout camp in April and smiling detainees cutting about with a sense of purpose – well, mostly so! We mustn't forget Colin Pethick's well-practised patter to multitudes of visitors about how detainees are trained in plumbing and tiling.

'Other memories are the gate lodge team, the Military Guard Service, feeding grey squirrels at the barrier and the long entrance road lined with daffodils in the spring. There was "mass sticking" of staff after the annual pace-stick competition, a few beers fairly obviously supped by one or two staff between competing and "massing", the burble of the Deputy Commandant's TVR (when it wasn't raining and when the car was actually working). And the quizzical looks on the faces of Navy and Air Force detainees (and staff) when they were trying to work out how things were done at MCTC.

'We have a quiet "Thank you, Sir....and please thank the staff for me" from a few detainees realizing that their lives have been changed for the better by the care and attention of the staff and who are big enough to say so when it matters. There was the occasional false general alarm resulting in staff sprinting from every nook and cranny of camp towards the apparent trouble, then walking slowly back to places of work when they realized that the alarm was not quite as alarming as first thought and the knowing smiles of the Countrywide grounds men as they kept the estate in good order.

'There was the simple honesty of the detainee who went absent without leave for nearly a month in order to nurse his scalded ferret back to health, Battle of Britain skies in high summer and the unmistakable Rolls-Royce sound of a Hawker Hurricane on lucky days. MCTC, what a wonderful place. I miss it already.'

Notes

1. First report of Inspector General, 1899, p41 *In Glasshouses* by Robert Boyes.
2. Dan Cowley believes there may have been three ships of which only the name of one is known.
3. *In Glasshouses* p58.
4. *In Glasshouses* p107.
5. For more details of the report see p100, *In Glasshouses.*
6. Ken Free – *Camp 186 Lost Town at Berechurch.*
7. In early 1945 large numbers of German parachutists arrived in the camp. They would loiter outside the Nissen huts where interrogations were taking place to observe the new intake. Most of these new POWs would use the Nazi salute when entering the hut as a way of ensuring those watching outside considered them to be loyal Germans.
8. The Interrogation Centre in Kensington was known as 'The London Cage' and was the most feared of all the interrogation centres.
9. Sergeant Featherstone's words from a telephone conversation in summer 2011. He was in the Bedfordshire and Hertfordshire Regiment and was demobbed in August 1947.
10. *Crime and The Services* p67 by John Spencer; Routledge Keegan and Paul Ltd.
11. Ken was an amateur boxer who qualified for the 1948 Olympics.
12. *In Glasshouses*, p276, by Robert Boyes.
13. Robert Whorley, a gunner in the RA, did two years National Service and then twelve years in the TA.
14. Malcolm Wilson, Royal Enniskillen Fusiliers, was posted to Chatham after his time in Colchester. He vowed not to ever go back to Colchester which he describes as a 'horrible camp, inhuman' and he never did. He was then sent to Berlin as a Regimental Policeman and reached WO2.
15. Bromide was issued in both Army and civilian prisons to lower sex drive. It was stopped because it could adversely affect sexual activity later in life.
16. The RSM referred to was WOI Boulter and was, in fact, MPSC.
17. The Queen's regulations and *The Queen's Regulations and Manual of Air Force Law* have since been amended to delete any offence of homosexuality.
18. Name supplied.
19. Name supplied.
20. Name supplied.
21. MPSC Journal, 1980, p16, 'Revspot'.

22. Provost Marshal's Notes, Brigadier M. Nugent, Corps Journal 2001 p2.

23 There is a working capacity of 267 bed spaces with an additional seventeen bed spaces in C block.

24. Dan Cowley says Lorraine was not hearing DMS boots as they make no sound and Ammunition boots have long gone out of service. That only leaves Jack Boots.

25. Dan Cowley: 'The long grey coat firmly puts this into the 1946-49 time frames. The location may be of no significance at all if one accepts the generally recognized requirements for a "haunting" – a traumatic, violent or happy event from which the effects are absorbed by the surrounding area. It is then "re-enacted" hours, days, months, years or even centuries later when the correct conduits are in place. The rebuild of the old Camp 186 meant all of the rubble was crushed and the reinforcing metal work removed. It was then used as ballast for the foundations of the new buildings. Obviously no parts of the old camp were put back in in the same place. So are the sightings spirits of the lost looking for their old resting places after being disturbed?'

26. Documented in *Camp 186* by Ken Free, p33.

Appendix 1
HMIP Inspections

http://www.justice.gov.uk/publications/inspectorate-reports/hmi-prisons/other-jurisdictions/military-corrective-training-centre-colchester

Appendix 2
Contributors

Dan Cowley
Sergeant Stanley Featherstone
WO1 Avery
Major BO 'Jimmy' James
Frank Bell
Ken Sparks
Ronald Thirst
John Ticker
Sid Young
Rupert Cooper
Brian Hartington
Christopher Clack
William Ravenscroft
Major Chandler
Leslie Morgan
Robert Whorley
Peter Pasola
David Biscombe
Lieutenant Colonel Jim Robinson
Douglas Corder
Corporal Alan MacDonald

Bob Johnson
Brian Sutton
Malcolm Wilson
Wally Reeve
Alan Donovan
'Nobby'
Ray
Patrick Leonard
Peter Hunt
Tony Ford
Corporal Grahame Barclay
Peter Hornsey
Gordon Davidson
Roy Rogers
John Belcher
Iain Stewart
Pete Thomas
Major (Retd) Patrick Graham
George Henderson
Major (Retd) L.W. Prescott
Roger Taylor

Peter Mallet
Jim Broadstock
Barry Sillitoe
Geoff Phillips
John Corley
Gerry White
Roger Tucker
Roger Ivermee
Mike Barry
Trevor Barlow
Neville Paddy
Captain (Retd) D. Eeles MBE
Alex Taylor
Gerry Phillips
Lynn Eldridge
Billy Mitchell
Sapper Barry Craig
Jim Watters
Martin Hoare
Stan Brown
Martin Bourke
Gareth Jaxon
Frank Bowron
Richard Bennett
'Mac'
Rod Rodway
Harry Angier
Jim Murray
Captain Rod Leonard
Reg Lamb
Bryan Morris
Richard Hamilton
Benjamin Graham
Alan Ford
Amanda Crampton
George Henderson
John E. Garner

Geoff Thewlis
Guardsman David Thomas
Dennis Gus Hales
Tom McGreevy
Dennis Carr
Corporal Phil Lawson
Paul Masterton
Ron Allen
David Thomas
Bill Coleman
Tony Moore
Patrick Lally
Michael Nottingham
John Hopkins
Andrew Stevens
Steve Alix
Dom Prest
Jack Sharp
Danny Mills
Richard Simpson
Lieutenant Corporal Webster
Squadron Leader Paul S Brennan
Neil Howard
Paul Mills
Tony Yarwood
Martin 'Jock' Laird
Max Aitken
Clive Rowland
Lieutenant Colonel Julian Crowe
Craig 'Pat' Patterson
Brian Chenier
Maj (Retd) Paul Ludbrook
Robbie
Stacey Everett
Jane Oliveira-Da-Silva
Lieutenant Colonel David G. Steele
Sergeant Lorraine Vickers-Bennet

Appendix 3
Commandants

MCE

Lt Col S.C.W.W. Rea OBE	Essex Regt	June	1947 – 1949
Lt Col A. C. Young	Beds and Herts Regt	Dec	1949 – 1952
Lt Col H.C.R. Hose DSO	Beds and Herts Regt	Sept	1952 – 1955

MCTC

Lt Col J. McDonald OBE	KOSB	Sept	1955 – 1958
Lt Col P. L. Badham-Thornhill OBE	RA	Sept	1958 – 1962
Lt Col I.N. Ryle OBE MC	RTR	Jan	1962 – 1964
Lt Col J.H.L. Parker MC	RA	May	1964 – 1966
Lt Col G.A. Coaker	RA	Oct	1966 – 1969
Lt Col R.K. Denniston OBE MC	QO Highlanders	Dec	1969 – 1971
Lt Col A.M. Gabb OBE	WFR	Dec	1971 – 1974
Lt Col H.A. Tregear MBE	RA	Apr	1974 – 1976
Major G.S. Carter	RA	Jan	1977 – 1977
Lt Col L.C.J.M. Paul OBE	Royal Anglian	July	1977 – 1980
Lt Col T.J.R. Illingworth OBE	Royal Irish	Dec	1980 – 1984
Lt Col A.P.H. Parsons OBE	Scots Guards	Feb	1984 – 1986
Lt Col S. Fordham	Welsh Guards	Aug	1986 – 1989
Lt Col N.E. Emson MC	Coldstream Guards	Feb	1989 – 1992
Lt Col P.E.L. Gasgoigne MBE	Scots Guards	Feb	1992 – 1994
Lt Col G.A.B. Grant	RA	Apr	1994 – 1996
Lt Col J.E.M. Crowe	Scots Guards	Jul	1996 – 1998
Lt Col S.A. Jasper	RTR	Oct	1998 – 2001
Lt Col M.W. van Grutten	QDG	Jul	2001 – 2004
Lt Col M. Nicholls	Kings	Jan	2004 – 2006
Lt Col R.C. Holroyd	DWR	Feb	2006 – 2008
Lt Col D.G. Steel	Scots	May	2008 – 2011
Lt Col R.H.S. Shaw MBE	Rifles	May	2011 – 2012
Lt Col I. St Logan	RGR	Sept	2012 –

Appendix 4

Inspectors of Military Establishments

Brig R.H. Maxwell CB ADC	1952
Brig R.H.L. Oulton CBE	1955
Brig P.H. Richardson DSO OBE	1958
Brig G.F. Upjohn CBE	1960
Brig C.G. Buttenshaw DSO OBE	1962
Brig R. Davenport OBE	1965
Brig L.F. Richards OBE	1968
Brig P.N. Davis CBE	1971
Brig D.B. Rendell CBE MC ADC	1974
Brig M. Matthews CBE	1977
Brig J.F. Thomas CBE	1980
Brig B. Thomas CBE	1983
Brig N.C. Allen CBE ADC	1986
Brig A.R. Bell MBE	1990
Brig I. Cameron	1992
Brig I.W. Fulton OBE	1995
Brig M. Nugent	1999
Brig C.A. Findlay MBE	2004
Brig E.O. Forster-Knight OBE	2009
Brig R.W. Warren MBE	2012

Index

Everett, Stacey 213
Essex Regiment 35, 38
Featherstone, Sgt Stanley 32
Field Punishment Centres 11, 22
Field Punishment 11, 12, 16
Fingringhoe 56, 131
Firmstone, Maj Bob 30, 52
Finch, Iain 210
Flogging 1, 2, 3, 8
Foot, Michael, MP 54
Ford, Alan 114
Ford, Tony 67
Fordham, Lt Col Simon 172, 182, 184
Fornham Hall 33
Fort Darland 23, 25, 35
France 15
Fraser, Col JA, DSO, DCM 24
Friday Woods 47, 89, 215

Gabb, Lt Col 128, 129
Garner, John E 120
Garsia, Lt Col Michael Clare 9, 28
Gascoigne, Lt Col 188
General Court 1
German, Germany ix, 23, 30, 31, 32, 41, 43, 71, 110, 120, 136, 140
German POW 28, 29, 30, 31 33, 35, 112, 183
George V, King 29
George VI, King 53
Gibraltar 14, 18
Gilbey, Maj Geofrey MC 24
Glasgow 15
Glasgow's Helping Heroes 214
Glasshouse 37, 43, 45, 57, 67, 88, 98, 144, 182, 194, 203
Gloucester, Duchess of 202
Goddard, Cpt 149
Gosport 5, 14
Graham, Benjamin 114
Graham, Maj (Rtd) Patrick 78

Grant, Lt Col Glen 194
Great War 10, 13
Greenlaw 5
Grenadier Guards 65, 129
Grones, Father 31
Guttersloh 113, 140

Hales, Dennis Gus 132
Hamilton, Richard 113
Harris, Maj Sydney 94, 149
Hartington, Brian 38
Henderson, George 78, 115, 119, 121, 126, 128, 129
Henry VII 1
Hereford 15
Her Majesty's Inspectorate of Prisons (HMIP) x, 146, 209, 211, 214, 215, 217, 220, 225, 235
HMS Maidstone 134
HMYOI (Her Majesty's Youth Offender Institute) 195, 199, 202
Hoare, Martin 101
Hohne 96
Holmes, Mr P 148
Hornsey, Peter 69, 70, 71
Hong Kong 14, 74, 146
Hopkins, John 160
Hose, Lt Col 53
Housing (Temporary Accommodation) Act 1944 32
Howard, Michael, MP 144, 198
Howard, Neil 189
HRH Duchess of Kent 193
Hull 22
Hunt, Peter 66
Hyderabad Barracks 28
Hythe 29

Illingworth, Lt Col Tim 156, 164
In Glasshouses 5, 13, 19, 23, 40, 41, 133, 134